Highly entertaining and instructive

"Written with great informality and considerable wit, and studded with anecdotes and illustrative examples, this book none the less is a serious and intelligent scrutiny of sex attitudes as publicly manifested in these United States of ours . . . Obviously this is a study of the first importance and it appears that Dr. Ellis has made a most mature approach to it."—James Farber, *King Features Syndicate*.

"This is a particularly valuable book for the unsophisticated reader because it uses source material so blatantly commonplace that no one will have trouble recognizing it. The author quite deftly makes our attitudes toward sex look ludicrous—which of course they are—and only the most blind will miss the point. But none of us need feel immune, for we are all tarred by the same culture. I'm afraid even the most sophisticated reader will find himself laughing at the many examples of sexual humor culled from the data by Dr. Ellis."—Dr. Lionel Ovesy, *The Nation*.

"*The Folklore of Sex* is vastly amusing; it is principally an indictment of the American attitude because that attitude is outwardly one thing and secretly another. Despite all codes of ethics and morals, despite laws and conventions, Dr. Ellis proves conclusively that the greatest transgression of all in these United States appears to be getting caught."—August Derleth, *Madison Capital Times*.

" . . . executed in such a way as to present important psychological truths to the general public, so simply that they may be easily understood, and so humorously that the lesson is highly entertaining as well as highly instructive."—Dr. Norman Haire in the introduction to the British edition.

"Mr. Ellis's point of view throughout is wise and enlightened."—Bertrand Russell.

The Folklore of Sex

By Albert Ellis, Ph.D

A Black Cat Book

Grove Press, Inc.   **New York**

Acknowledgments

Acknowledgment is herewith made to the following publishers and individuals for permission to quote copyrighted material:

Peter Arno, for quotations from *Sizzling Platter*.

Bennett Cerf, for quotations from *Laughter, Inc.*

The editors and publishers of *Ace, Broadway Laughs, Candid Annual, Cavalcade, Campus Howl, Collier's, Cosmopolitan, The Dude, Fun Parade, The Gent, Good Humor, Hello Buddies, Inside Story, Hi-Life, Joke Parade, King Annual, Ladies' Home Journal, Laugh Book, Man to Man, Man's Magazine, Modern Man, Modern Screen, Nugget, The Old Line, Orange Peel, Penn State Froth, Pic, Playboy, Reader's Digest, Scamp, Sir!, Swank, Texas Ranger, Touchstone, True, True Police Cases, The Watchman Examiner, The Wet Hen.*

Preface to the Second Edition

As noted in the Introduction, this book originally consisted of a study of American sex attitudes as shown in mass media published and produced early in 1950. When Grove Press became interested in re-issuing the book, I decided that not only would it be a good idea to bring the material up to date but that it would be fascinating to compare American sex views as they existed in the 1950's with those that exist today, in the 1960's.

Accordingly, the same kind of a study of American mass media that was done for the original edition of the book was done again in the beginning of 1960; and over 200 best-selling novels and non-fictional books, magazines, newspapers, and motion picture scripts were read to see what kinds of expressed and implied attitudes toward various modes of sex behavior they contained. The 1960 study was not exactly comparable to the original 1950 study, since many of the magazines originally investigated were no longer in existence a decade later and some of the media that were first surveyed—including plays and musical shows, radio and television programs, and scientific journals—were either not available or were, on the basis of previous experience, found to be relatively poor sources of information.

Actually, the 1960 mass media material was, on the whole, more indicative of American sex attitudes than was the 1950 material because, as a result of the previous experience, an effort was made to concentrate more specifically on highly popular outlets of mass communication in the latter decade and to include fewer of the less popular outlets. Thus, not only hard-cover novels were included in the 1960 sample, but best-selling paperbound novels as well. Fewer best-selling nonfiction works were surveyed in 1960 than in 1950, since most of these books have little sexual material in them. On the other hand, more newspapers were read and these were spread out over an entire month, instead of being concentrated on a single day, when they tend to be repetitious in their news stories.

In spite of the differences in some of the mass media material surveyed for the 1950 and 1960 studies, the two surveys were in the main quite comparable; and some legitimate comparisons between them are made throughout this revised edition and in the chapters on statistical considerations at the end of the book. Since the follow-up study did not, of course, in any way affect the original investigation of American mass media, I thought it best to reprint most of the material in the first edition of THE FOLKLORE OF SEX exactly as it had first been published and to add, at the end of each chapter, a section on sex attitudes in the 1960's. The only parts that have been rewritten in their entirety are Chapters 28 and 29 on statistical considerations: as these chapters now include comparative material on the original and the follow-up studies.

It has been a most interesting experience for me to do this second study of American sex folklore, as displayed in our most popular communicative media, and to be able to check up on my observations and conclusions of a decade ago. I really had little expectation of finding the remarkable changes in American attitudes that I actually did find taking place between the 1950's and the 1960's; but retrospective thinking—which is always so much safer than predictively sticking one's neck out!—easily recalls to mind that a nation which has changed in so many other significant ways in the last decade (and which is part of an equally rapidly changing world scheme of things) might easily have radically altered some of its fundamental sex views and practices. Apparently, as will be shown in many pages of this revised edition of THE FOLKLORE OF SEX, it has.

Introduction:
The Story of a Study

This study has a history, and that history itself would make an interesting story. Someday, perhaps, I shall write that story in detail; here I shall have to be content with giving its bare outlines.

The history of this study might be said to begin at one of several different places—with my own research interests in human sex and love behavior, which professionally began some eleven years ago; with my fortuitously meeting a well-known psychiatrist in Boston in 1948; with a publisher's unusual concern with scientific sex research; with—well, with endless other things which are too complicated and diverse to list here.

Anyway, let's start in Boston—one of the least appropriate places, one might think, for the inception of a book on sex. I had known for many years of the work and ideas of this particular psychiatrist but had never had the pleasure of meeting him. Then, at the annual meeting of the American Psychological Association in 1948, we did meet and, as luck would have it, rode back to New York in the same Pullman. We talked of many things, including the then recently published first volume of Dr. Alfred Kinsey's studies, and we saw eye to eye in much, if not all, of our discussion. We were especially concerned with Dr. Kinsey's being criticized for not doing detailed studies of sex attitudes, in addition to the painstaking researches into human sex behavior he was conducting; and we felt that he and his associates had every right to limit their investigations, at least for the present, to researches on male and female sex outlets rather than trying to cover every possible type of sex study that might be imagined.

At the same time, my psychiatric friend and I agreed that studies of present-day sex attitudes, feelings, beliefs, and myths were most important and should be done by competent scientific investigators. He perked up his ears when I told him that I, in fact, had already started some studies of human love attitudes and emotions and that I was interested in carrying them further. The trouble was, I said, that getting the backing for, or even an interested publisher for, this kind of sexuo-amative study was not very easy. No, he agreed, it certainly was not; but if I were really interested in going on with such work, perhaps he could refer me to some people who would be helpful. Fine, I said; but, knowing the usual value of such vaguely voiced promises, I did not take him too seriously.

Well, I was wrong. When I returned to my office I mailed this

11

psychiatrist some reprints of my researches on love which had appeared in scientific journals and then gave him and our Pullman conversation very little thought. As a full year went by, I had almost forgotten what we had talked about, although I pleasantly remembered our encounter. Then, in the winter of 1949, I was quite surprised to hear from a publisher who had been told about my research ideas by my Boston-met psychiatric friend, and who was quite eager to discuss them with me.

Having once worked for a book publisher myself, and knowing full well the pressures which induce publishers to present shoddy but salable rather than profound but unpopular volumes, my confidence in the scientific soundness of book hucksters is not high. My first meeting, therefore, with the publisher to whom the psychiatrist referred me was approached with a skeptically cautious attitude; and it was only after many minutes of conversation with him that I began to realize what a real, if belated, service my psychiatric friend had rendered me. For this particular publisher, it appeared, was sincerely interested in a sexuo-amative study for its own sake and not merely for the sake of its potential sales appeal. Moreover, he seemed to know what he was talking about and to have a grasp of the problems of psychosociological research, which is not overly common among the heads of publishing enterprises.

While at first the publisher and I hardly harmonized on every detail of the study I proposed, we did agree that what seemed to be most needed at the present time was a thoroughgoing study of sex *attitudes* rather than the field of sex *behavior*, which Dr. Kinsey and his associates have particularly selected as their focal point of investigation.

All right, then, it was agreed: I would do a scientific study of American attitudes toward sex, love, and marriage. The next question was: How?

It immediately became apparent that the study of American attitudes toward sex, love, and marriage is, if adequately done, a lifetime research in itself. And that, added to the studies on human love relationships and on psychoanalysis which I already had in progress, made three lifetime studies—at least. This, of course, did not noticeably daunt me, since when one is inured to being able to do only a small fraction of the research work one would like to do in one's lifetime, the thought of decreasing that fraction still further loses its ability to terrify.

Granted, then, that the study of sexuo-amative human attitudes was a devilish enough job for a crew of researchers to spend several decades at, the only truly relevant question was: Where to begin? The publisher and I kicked that question around for a few days, and it was finally decided that, for a starter, I would make a study of American attitudes toward sex, love, and marriage as these are expressed in popular mass media. For not only could such a study be done with fairly limited man power and financial resources, but it would also provide a great deal of valuable material for drawing up interview schedules, attitudinal tests, projective techniques of personality investigation, and other research procedures with which later and more comprehensive studies of sex, love, and marriage attitudes could be done.

Well, that did it: I was left with the specific task of drawing up and executing a study of American attitudes, feelings, beliefs, and myths on sex, love, and marriage which are normally expressed in our most popular mass media. I was given carte blanche to solve the problem as best I saw fit—and let the headaches fall where they might.

Assuming that I was going to investigate American sexuo-amative attitudes which are expressed or implied in our frightfully popular publications and communications, the very first detailed question to arrive was: *What* media? And the obvious answer seemed to be: Mass media, of course, such as newspapers, magazines, radio and television shows, movies, stage shows, popular songs, and best-selling novels and nonfiction books. For if one discovers what types of sex attitudes *these* media express, one surely has a representative sample of those found in the most popular American mass media.

Very well. But is that all? Are these the only media to be investigated? What about other media, for example, such as the ballet, night-club shows, sermons, sports, et cetera? Should they be included in the analyses as well?

After much deliberation it was decided not to include such additional media. For one thing, some of them—e.g., sermons—were found to be difficult to obtain, and contained very little material on sex, love, and marriage when they were obtained. Other media, like the ballet, were not verbal enough to be objectively analyzed for their sex content. Media like night-club shows were not considered popular or widespread enough to be deemed true *mass* media and therefore were eliminated from the study.

In the final analysis, then, it was decided to investigate the mass media listed above: newspapers, magazines, radio and television shows, movies, stage productions, popular songs, and popular novels and nonfiction books. Now the second important procedural question reared its ungainly head: Which *specific* newspapers, magazines, radio and television shows, and so on, were to be investigated? Obviously, especially if one goes back a few years, thousands upon thousands of these publications and productions may be obtained for purposes of analyzing their sex, love, and marriage contents; and at that rate the contemplated study would never end. What, therefore, was the specific *sample* of these productions to be investigated?

At first I tended to think in terms of a whole year's output of mass media, but it quickly became apparent that much too much material would be provided for analysis in even that comparatively short time. Besides, how could any random selection of the year's productions be made to insure, for purposes of research, that no special biases were evident in the selection of this sample?

Then I thought in terms of a single month's productions—and of getting, examining, and analyzing *all* the chosen mass media produced during that month. This would give what is statistically termed a 100-per-cent sample—which is most desirable for many research purposes. The trouble was, however, that there was still, on this basis, too much material to be examined and analyzed. Even, for example, if New York newspapers alone were investigated in the course of the study, a month's supply of all New York news-sheets runs to several hundred pages; and a month's coverage of network radio and television shows is staggering to contemplate.

Suddenly a pertinent thought struck me. The publisher and I discussed the research in November of 1949, and by the time we agreed on what kind of study, in general, I was to do, it was the middle of December. Coming up, obviously, was the new year—1950—which, according to conventional modes of calculation, was generally considered to be the turn of the half century. And coming up, more specifically, was New Year's Day, January 1, 1950. The thing to do, patently, was to try obtain a 100-per-cent sample of American mass media produced or published on January 1, 1950—the day on which the second half of the twentieth century officially, according to most conventional authorities, began. (Technically, according to a minority of authorities, the first day of the half century should be January 1, 1951, but very few contemporary Americans consider it as such.)

That, then, was the thing to do; and that is what I immediately proceeded to do: to collect a 100-per-cent sample of mass media extant on January 1, 1950, and to analyze these media for their sex, love, and marriage content. Actually, of course, it is not possible to get a true 100-per-cent sample of these media, for several reasons: (1) It is not possible to define, exactly, which medium is truly a *mass* one and which isn't. (2) Some mass media are not available for analysis. Scripts of certain stage productions, for example, which are playing on Broadway on January 1, but which go off the boards shortly thereafter, may not be made available for analysis by the producers. (3) Some mass media, even for a single day of the year, are too numerous to be covered in any practical research. Hundreds of newspapers, for instance, are published every day in America, and it would be virtually

14

impossible to read all of them for a psychosociological study.

For reasons such as these, a perfect 100-per-cent sample of the mass media examined in this study could not be obtained; but, within certain practical limits, a near 100-per-cent sample was obtained in every case. Thus all the plays and musical shows playing on Broadway on January 1, 1950, were either viewed or read, with the exception of a few which could not be seen and whose producers or authors refused to provide scripts. In addition, all the radio and television scripts for January 1 which could be obtained from two of the largest networks were read and analyzed, with the exception of a few programs whose sponsors refused permission for reading them.

Where 100-per-cent samples were not practical—as in the case of the newspapers—restricted 100-per-cent samples were taken. Thus not all American newspapers for January 1, 1950, could be read, but all the New York newspapers for this date were examined, as well as a sizable sample of newspapers from a good many other leading American cities. Again, not all magazines on the newsstands on January 1 could be perused, but the most popular magazines in every important class of magazine were read. This included general magazines, true-story publications, men's magazines, digests, quality magazines, little magazines, picture magazines, comic books, humor magazines, college magazines, hobby magazines, home magazines, organizational magazines, religious magazines, popular psychology magazines, fan magazines, pulp magazines, detective-story magazines, news magazines, and poetry magazines.

The general principles used in selecting the specific mass media to be examined in the course of this study were: (a) to obtain a full 100-per-cent sample wherever possible; (b) to obtain a near 100-per-cent sample where a full one was not entirely possible; (c) to reject media only because they were unavailable or because a sufficient number of the most popular media in their class had already been examined; and (d) not to be biased in the selection of the media by any other factors than practical limitations. The result of these selective principles would appear to be the examining, for the purposes of this research, of a near 100-per-cent sample of media which were extant on January 1, 1950, and which were most representative of the popular media in each of the areas selected for study. In other words, I, as the originator of this study, feel that the media examined were truly representative of American mass media published on January 1, 1950. While not perfect, the selection was a good one and was not specifically biased in any direction as far as could be determined.

The specific media examined for this study included: (1) all best-selling fiction and nonfiction books listed in the New York *Times* and the New York *Herald Tribune* on January 1, 1950. (2) All New

York newspapers for that day and a sampling of representative newspapers from every other major section of the United States. (3) All motion pictures playing on (or around) Broadway on January 1. (4) All stage productions playing on Broadway on that date. (5) All available radio and television shows broadcast by the National Broadcasting Company and the Columbia Broadcasting System, and a representative sampling of shows broadcast over the American Broadcasting Company and the Mutual Broadcasting System. (6) A representative selection of all types of popular magazines on the newsstands. January issues were used in all cases, except where the magazines (such as bimonthly and quarterly periodicals) had no January issues, in which case the first issues of the year were examined. (7) All "Hit Parade" songs listed in *Billboard* magazine for the first week in January, as well as popular songs printed in song-lyric magazines for January.

In addition to the mass media examined, a representative list of scientific journals in the fields of sociology, psychology, psychiatry, and anthropology was also included in the study for purposes of comparison. These scientific journals, of course, are not *mass* media in the usual sense of this term. All the other publications and productions examined are true mass media, although some of them—such as the religious magazines, the college magazines, and the humor magazines—seem to have a considerably smaller distribution than do many others of the mass media examined—such as best-selling books, newspapers, and films.

The next question that arose, after the media in question had been selected and examined, was: What about foreign material or material that has a distinctly historical slant? Since this study purports to be one of *American* attitudes on sex, and of *contemporary* ones, would this foreign and historical material be relevant? Included on the best-selling fiction lists, for example, were several novels by non-Americans; e.g., Waltari's *The Egyptian* and Moravia's *The Woman of Rome*. Also included were novels like O'Hara's *A Rage to Live* and Wilson's *Abe Lincoln of Pigeon Creek*, which were written by Americans all right, but which related historical tales and attitudes.

It was finally decided not to eliminate these novels (and plays and films) from the list examined, but to include their references to sex, love, and marriage *only* when these references were obviously *not* rooted in the past or in foreign climates, and only when they contained sex attitudes and references which were clearly similar to those which are found in novels by Americans about contemporary America. Thus O'Hara's book is clearly ultramodern in most of its sex, love, and marriage references, even though much of its plot is laid early in this century; and Waltari's and Moravia's books, while written by foreigners about foreign environments, differ very little in much of (though not, of course, all) their sex material from the sex treatment employed in thoroughly American fiction. It must be remembered in this connection that all the foreign or historical fiction analyzed and at times quoted in this study is fiction that on January 1, 1950, was extremely popular in America, and contained sex references that are quite in keeping with contemporary American tastes and may be called typically American. It should also be noted that, altogether, the foreign and historical fiction employed in this study comprises about 3 per cent of the reading material examined and the sex references found in the research.

A final important question which arose in relation to this study was: Should the research be confined to investigating American sex attitudes alone, or should it include attitudes on love, marriage, and family affairs as well? The answer to this question was easy, since the author feels that sex attitudes and acts do not exist in themselves and cannot be isolated from contemporary love, marriage, and family codes and practices, or from the general personality structure of the individuals having sex thoughts, feelings, and activities. Consequently, this study was designed to examine and analyze all the love, marriage, and family attitudes found in American mass media as well as sex attitudes therein discovered. Owing to limitations of space, however, the present volume will present only those findings relating to sex attitudes, while a second volume will present those findings of the study relating to love, marriage, and family attitudes.

So much, then, for the outline history of this study. Once conceived, the study made satisfactory progress, especially owing to the kind cooperation of many radio stations, advertisers, film companies, play producers, newspapers, publishers, and authors, who were very generous of their time and courtesy. To all these co-operative firms and individuals, my grateful thanks.

I also wish to thank Charles Boni, Ruth R. Doorbar, and Dr. LeMon Clark, who read the manuscript of this volume and made pertinent and valuable editorial suggestions.

The uniqueness of the present study would appear to lie in the fact that, for what seems to be the first time, all sex references in a broad and unbiased selection of some of the most popular and widely representative mass media are minutely examined to see what are the sexual attitudes and effects expressed in these media. The assumption is that the sex beliefs and usages delineated and implied in these public communications reflect to a considerable degree the basic sex attitudes of a sizable segment of the American populace; and where they do not accurately reflect public opinions, these mass-media expressions certainly tend to influence importantly such opinions. It is intended, in future studies in this series, to investigate American sex, love, marriage, and family attitudes and beliefs more directly by means of interviews, attitude scales, projective techniques, and other psychological and sociological research procedures. This preliminary study, it is to be hoped, will in some ways set the stage for further researches on the vitally interesting and important questions of what people *think* and *feel* about sex, love, and marriage, whatever their actual sexuo-amative behavior may be.

ALBERT ELLIS

CHAPTER 1

Fornication

FORNICATION: Illicit sexual intercourse on the part of an unmarried person.
—*Webster's International Dictionary.*

To what extent, in the last half of the twentieth century, Americans engage in fornicative or premarital sex relations—that is for Dr. Kinsey and other students of American sex behavior to say. To what degree they show, in their popular publications and productions, disapproving, approving, and conflicting attitudes toward fornication—that is what we shall now attempt to discover.

First, as to disapproval. Do contemporary Americans, to any appreciable degree, disfavor premarital sex relations? Most certainly, if we are to give credence to the views expressed and implied in their widely disseminated newspapers, magazines, books, plays, songs, movies, and radio and television broadcasts, they do.

To begin with, we find religious objections to fornication forthrightly, and not at all inconspicuously, proclaimed. Thus the *Catholic Digest* carries the plea of His Holiness, Pope Pius XII, giving his Prayer for Peace for the Holy Year: "Give to the ailing fortitude and health; to the young, strength of faith; to maidens, purity. . . ." And Father Connell, quoted in Blanshard's *American Freedom and Catholic Power*, makes it clear that it is far better for a woman to marry a venereally diseased man than to continue in an unmarried state after fornicating with him. Says Father Connell: "All the physical afflictions that can ensue from the marriage of a diseased person, both to the healthy consort and to the offspring, are an immeasurably lesser evil than one mortal sin which the marriage could avert."

Nor do American Catholics have any monopoly on extolling the virtue of virtue. Norman Vincent Peale, a prominent minister, relates in his best-selling *Guide to Confident Living* the story of one of his female parishioners who once, out of sincere love for a man of her acquaintance, "verged on the commission of a sex sin." But Dr. Peale goes on to quote his communicant: " 'I read in the Bible "That whosoever looketh on a woman to lust after her hath committed adultery with her already in his heart." So I saw at once my guilt. I had not performed this act, but it had been my desire, therefore I was just as guilty as if I had done so. All my life long,' she concluded, 'I have lived a clean, righteous life, but in this I sinned and it has haunted me and I know that when I die, I will be damned.' "

Fulton Oursler, in another best-selling volume, this one a retelling of the story of the New Testament in basic terms and tenets, also makes it clear that thoughts of lust "are the same as *acts* of lust." And, consistently following Paul of Tarsus's dictum of the first century, Oursler claims that celibacy is an even higher state than marriage and is for those select individuals "who choose to be free of family ties and obligations and the tyranny of the senses, in order to carry on the Master's work."

Secular religionists, as well, in the last half of the twentieth century, stoutly defend premarital celibacy and chastity. Writing in the bible of the physical culturists, *New Physical Culture* magazine, a Miss (?) Dorothy Zackary assures her readers that "a consciousness of health enables a man or woman to resist temptations of dissipations more readily than the emaciated creature. Seldom does a bridegroom worry about the past of his healthy bride. Virtue and good health are companions." Obviously, in the era we are examining, fornication is anathema to Bernarr Macfadden as it is to God.

Close on the heels of the religious upholders of premarital celibacy are those who might be called sexual conventionalists. These individuals, who seem to be legion, apparently believe that fornication is wicked because—well, its wickedness was good enough for their parents, so it must be good enough for them. Without having recourse necessarily to any authority save authority, they fill numberless ems of print with direct and circuitous attacks on would-be and had-been fornicators and fornicatrices, of which the following may serve as examples.

In the immensely popular and critic-acclaimed film, *All the King's Men*, the climax of the plot comes when the highly civilized and sensitive Dr. Adam Powell brutally annihilates the politician, Willie Stark, not because Willie is patently a murderer, thief, charlatan, and generalized cad, but because this murderer, thief, charlatan, and generalized cad has been sufficiently dastard to devirginize Adam's all-too-willing sister, Ann.

Laugh Book magazine prints the wheeze about the beautiful Indian girl who, after a sojourn of several months in a nearby village, returned to her parents' tepee. As she entered, she raised her hand and said: "How!" "Ugh," said her father, "me know how. Who?"

In a story in *Intimate Romances* the landlady catches the heroine in bed with the hero (to whom, of course, she happens to be secretly married). Quoth the landlady "in a cold, harsh voice, 'I guess that's one on me, Norma. I'd have sworn you were a decent girl. Well, I want you and that man, whoever he is, out of here by noon. I'll come by and lock up. Leave the key on the table, please.' "

Theodora Abel and Natalie Joffe, in a study of female puberty published in the *American Journal of Psychotherapy*, point out that not only do millions of our girls refuse to use tampons because they feel that by their use "virginity is in some way tampered with," but that some American physicians object to the use of tampons by young girls for the same reason.

In a story in *My Secret Romance* magazine a girl is accused of being a fornicatrix because she dates two men at the same time; and she sobbingly tells us that "when my virtue was questioned, I knew that I had ruined my life."

The *Ladies' Home Journal*, in a "Profile of Youth" biographical feature on Maxine Myers, presumably a typical high school girl from Corinth, Mississippi, quotes Maxine: "If a girl is smart she remembers that sex is for married people only. I think that's the way most girls feel around here."

True Story magazine reports a special survey of the views of young people obtained by a polling organization employing teenage interviewers. The pollsters found that only 14 per cent of several hundred young people who were queried believed "that petting or closer intimacy is permissible between steady couples. ... Most of this fourteen per cent are boys, in the proportion of about three to one." With noteworthy devotion to the ideals of objective commentary unvarnished by prejudice, the president of the polling organization, in apprising the *True Story* readers of the results of the poll, remarks: "The existence of such a group, even though it is small compared to all the other teen-agers who would not indulge in such liberties, is certainly a black mark against adolescent society. No parent can be quite certain that his son or daughter does not belong to this minority."

Closely allied to the conventional objections to fornication which stud present-day public utterances are what might be labeled social proscriptions against premarital copulation. Thus a commentator in his radio column of Hollywood gossip broadcast on New Year's Day, insisted that an affair between a well-known movie actress and her companion was "an ugly mess" from the day they began traveling around the world in unwedded bliss—because, presumably, they made no attempt to dissemble their affairs and the whole world knew their (premarital) intentions.

In a *Personal Romances* story the heroine gaspingly pushes away her fiercely kissing lover, who is "making the blood rush through my veins ... I knew that if he kissed me again I would be *lost*. I knew we were on the verge of *disaster*" (italics ours). Lost before whom? Disaster in whose eyes? The eyes of the (American) world, you may be sure.

One more illustration of anti-fornicative attitudes born of social pressures should suffice here. Henry, of a *Saturday Evening Post* story, who is stoutly helping care for his boss's infant with little co-operation from the boss's sister-in-law, who happens (coincidentally enough) to be snowbound in the house with him, indignantly replies to the boss's telephoned innuendoes: " 'Being with me, Mr. Champion,' said Henry grimly, 'is like your sister-in-law is locked up in a convent. She is safe as a statue. What kind of a guy does your wife think I am, Mr. Champion, to play around with the boss's sister-in-law?' "

Not only are premarital sex affairs today condemned on religious, conventional, moral, and social grounds, but they are also disapproved by many who consider themselves neither religious nor conventional and who are by no means noted for bowing or scraping for social approval. "Sophisticated" and "modern" circles, too, apparently have their share of anti-fornicative attitudes.

In the motion picture *East Side, West Side*, for example, which depicts the antics of worldly-wise, upper-class New York society, a playboy husband meets a ravishingly lovely, smart model at a bar. "You're a very nice girl," he tells her after a minute or two of conversation (while his wife is biting her nails to the knuckle, feverishly waiting for him to come home). "And I'll thank you to remember it!" she gaily raps back, letting him know just how he may (not) expect to get on with her.

Again, in an ultra-sophisticated international spy thriller, Van Wyck Mason's widely read *Dardanelles Derelict*, the hero (Major North) and heroine (Jingles Lawson), who have been madly in love with each other for several years, are alone together in her hotel room. To convince some spies who are watching them from the veranda that he has come to her room to make love to her, they snap off the lights; and twenty minutes later, the author tells us, "when he snapped on the illumination Jingles Lawson was engaged in pretending to re-secure a garter catch; otherwise, her lamé gown looked interestingly wrinkled and she presented a vision of disheveled loveliness. North arose, commenced to do up the tie he had just jerked loose. Then, when she departed to the bathroom, he smiled like Casanova fresh from another conquest and moodily ran fingers through his crisp black hair." It is made clear, of course, that Miss Lawson and Major North couldn't possibly have had *legitimate* reasons for redressing, bathroom visiting, and Casanova-like smiling on this occasion.

Today's most sophisticated anti-fornicative attitudes may be found in our psychiatric, psychological, and sociological literature. Thus we find writers like Harry A. Overstreet (in *The Mature Mind*), Janet Fowler Nelson (quoted in *Woman's Life* magazine), and Judson T. Landis (digested by *Your Marriage*) all subtly insinuating that any Americans who engage in premarital sex relations are "immature," "neurotic," or totally unsuited for subsequent marriages.

22

It can readily be seen, then, that pro-celibate and anti-fornicative views are overtly and underlyingly omnipresent in our culture and that a massive weight of religious, conventional, social, and even professional authority is being continually brought to bear against the espousal or practice of premarital sex relations.

At the same time, confusingly enough, our public presses and other media of mass communication keep turning out a profusion of material that, with attitudes ranging from utter frankness to the most ambiguous kind of innuendo, distinctly favors premarital sex relations.

For the frankest acceptance of liberal sex attitudes take, for example, Nelson Algren's best-selling novel, *The Man with the Golden Arm*, whose portrayals of everyday Americans won unusual critical acclaim for its fidelity to life. We learn that the hero of the book, Frankie Machine, ignored his girl friend, Sophie, "for a month just to show her he didn't care one way or another. Until she'd asked him straight out if they were still sleeping together on Saturday nights or not."

In one of the most raved-about and hard-to-get-tickets-to Broadway shows of the century, *South Pacific*, American Seabees unabashedly talk about the young Frenchwomen who may be had for the asking on Bali Ha'i; they sing about feeling restless, blue, and lonely without women and of feeding "every kind of feelin' but the feelin' of relief"; they—and obviously their audiences—take very much in their stride Lieutenant Cable's reaping the maidenhead of Liat, a lovely island maid.

In the extravagantly turned-out film musical, *On the Town*, two unusually attractive girls expend enormous energies trying to induce two dubiously attractive sailors to "come up to my place"; and one, having induced her lad to come to her apartment, almost gets into a fist fight with her roommate, whom she unexpectedly finds there.

In the popular radio serial, *Our Miss Brooks*, we hear about Miss Brooks's difficulty in inducing her boy friend, Boynton, to spend New Year's Eve alone with her; and when he finally agrees and innocently remarks that, this being New Year's Eve, he can take a certain liberty, she pertly snaps back (to the great delight, no doubt, of twoscore million or so radio fans): "Liberty? You can take shore leave!"

"ALL WOMEN CAN BE CAUGHT," runs the headline of an advertisement in *Beauty Parade* magazine. "Even one you expect to say 'No' will surprise you." The ad, with a suggestive full length cut of an almost nude man and woman unequivocally getting down to brass tacks, tells how only $1.98 will bring the postman and Ovid's *Art of Love* to the reader's door. It ends with this clincher: "*Get the kick of your life or pay nothing!*"

The same magazine, in the same issue, also features an article with the unsubtle title and subtitle, respectively: "No Babe Is Hard to Get!"

23

and "If You Have the Key to Her Heart, Bud, It'll Probably Open Her Apartment."

Even—one might almost say especially—modern detective stories are replete with frank acceptances of fornication. Thus in a syndicated detective novel published in the Amarillo *Sunday News-Globe*, a girl who has just met the hero of the tale lures him up to her room, does her best to rape him, and glows with hatred when he refuses to have her. In *Private Detective* magazine the hero of one story meets a beautiful girl on the beach, is up in her room about five minutes later, and within a few score seconds more her body, lightly covered with "lacy underthings ... dropped into my arms and I kissed the smoothness of her throat. She whispered, 'Don't be rough, big boy. Think I could be the right girl for you? ...' I said she could. It was two hours later when I went down to my own room."

A few more excerpts from humor magazines should suffice to show how premarital intercourse is, in some quarters, looked upon with a quite unjaundiced eye.

From *Laugh Book*: "Evolution of an office girl: First year—She thinks men are nice. Second year—She thinks some men are nice. Third year—She thinks most men aren't nice. Fourth year—She knows men aren't nice. Fifth year—She's glad men aren't nice."

From *Touchstone*: "A blanket party is where they count all the people coming and bring half that many blankets."

From *Penn State Froth*:

> There was a young lady from Lynn
> Who thought that to love was a sin,
> But when she was tight
> It seemed quite all right—
> So everyone filled her with gin.

In addition to our frank acceptance of fornication is the lefthanded acceptance of it which seems to be expressed in the attitude: Premarital sex relations may be naughty, but their naughtiness is oh, so nice!

The staid *Reader's Digest*, by way of illustration, prints an anecdote contributed by Loring Raines giving a schoolboy's description of Rebecca's courage in resisting Bois Guilbert's advances in *Ivanhoe*: "The Knight Templar leered as he asked Rebecca to be his mistress, but the brave girl reclined to do so." *Variety* runs an ad from Universal Pictures ballyhooing the fact that in her new picture, *South Sea Sinner*, Shelley Winters is, once again, "that wonderful bad girl at her BEST!" *Cosmopolitan* magazine publishes a poem in which the authoress tells us that if she watches her diet, takes her vitamins, never flirts with married gents, and so on, "I'll likely live much longer, but heaven knows for what!" The *Wisconsin Country Magazine* defines a pessimist as a man who feels all women are bad, and an optimist as one who hopes so. The *Ram-Buller* has one coed asking another if she had a good time last night, and the second coed replying that, no, she had too much will power. *Fun Parade* exhumes the joke: "Little Mary: Where do bad girls go? Mother: Everywhere, dear!"

Oh yes, all these publications are, consciously or not, unmistakably saying: fornication is simply awful—nice.

A third kind of liberal sex attitude which is prevalent in contemporary public sexpression is a more sophisticated type of espousal of premarital sex relations. Underlying this attitude seems to be the notion that not only is it pleasurable and proper to seek out sex satisfactions prior to marriage, but that he who does not do so is not smart, not *de rigueur*, not really a man.

Ensign Pulver, in the stage version of *Mister Roberts*, for example, is not merely frank about his sex affairs: his narrations of his feats, as the ship's doctor puts it, border on the supernatural: "It seems that on a certain cold and wintry night in November 1939... he rendered pregnant three girls in Washington, D.C., caught the eleven forty-five train, and an hour later performed the same service for a young lady in Baltimore."

The heroine of Frank G. Slaughter's novel, *Divine Mistress*, whose heroine baits the hero as follows: "'That *is* what men want in a mistress, isn't it?' 'Why ask me?' Antonio said severely. 'I have no mistress....' 'Aren't you a man?' Lucia asked sweetly....'"

Another rationalization for premarital copulation which is common today may be called the romantic espousal of fornication. The romantic attitude seems to be that, under normal circumstances, premarital sex affairs should be verboten, but that a great love or fondness between a man and a woman makes fornication permissible and desirable.

Thus in the film, *The Facts of Love*, Joan and her fiancé agree that, because of their great love for each other, going to bed together while her parents are away is a perfectly natural thing for them to do. When he asks her if she'll later be sorry for having sex relations with him, Joan looks at her fiancé most lovingly and says: "I can't imagine myself being sorry."

Even more explicitly, the beautiful artist's model, Clarice, in the novel, *Divine Mistress*, speaks in this wise to the religious-minded Antonio, whom she has just initiated into the rites of fornication: "'Forget the church for a minute, Tonio, and think of yourself. Last night you needed me and I was glad, even proud, that I could give you what you needed.' She lifted shining eyes to him. 'I don't think the Creator ever meant to forbid two people who are as fond of each other as we are from finding real happiness in each other's arms, do

25

you?' Instinctively Antonio realized that Clarice was right and that the happiness and release from tension he had discovered in her arms could not really be sinful."

To recapitulate: twentieth-century attitudes toward fornication are certainly disapproving enough if we are to believe some of the most authoritative and widely read, seen, and heard sources of the day; but at the same time these identical sources leave ample room for the inclusion of attitudes that are often frankly, insinuatingly, sophisticatedly, or romantically pro-fornicative.

To confuse the issue still further, a considerable portion of the published and broadcast literature of today seems to have accomplished the noteworthy feat of, in precisely one and the same breath, accepting *and* rejecting premarital sex relations.

By way of illustration:

The New York *Compass* features a story which shows how movie actor Errol Flynn can be criticized and haled into court on the charge of not conforming to certain sexual conventions, and then idolized by millions of picture fans—most of whom appear to be very conventional females!

The St. Paul *Sunday Pioneer Press* (along with scores of other American newspapers) features, as one of the biggest news stories of the year, the romance of two very prominent people, whom, it is noted, "newsmen followed ... almost around the world before their courtship culminated in marriage in France." The main reason for these two celebrities being thus reportorially plagued seems to have been (a) the sheer sinfulness of their flagrant premarital sex relations combined with (b) the sheer determination of millions of newspaper readers not to miss the slightest delicious morsel of this sinfulness.

In the syndicated comic strip, *Mitzi McCoy*, Mitzi (a gorgeous blonde) learns that wolves in Scott County are killing livestock and that some men are going out to hunt them. Says Mitzi: "If you're hunting wolves, I'm going too. It will be nice to reverse the field." Thus does our gal Mitzi, without so much as splitting a single larynx muscle, neatly epitomize the ubiquitous twentieth-century squibs about "wolves"; meaning, of course, men who make such a pleasant game of trying to seduce women that it is only they, and rarely their victims, who do the howling.

In the New York *Post* a serialized news story entitled "The Belvidere Morals Case" is emblazoned across column after column for many days. The case concerns six adolescent girls who were discovered, in Belvidere, Illinois, to have had sex "orgies" with fifteen men. The *Post* strongly implies in its stories (a) that heinous is the word for the affairs of the six Belvidere girls; (b) that Belvidere is "no different from any other [town]. The same things go on here as in your town—only this time the girls and fellows were caught"; and (c) that anyone who misses a word of this thrilling, exciting case, as minutely detailed in the *Post*, can hardly be said to be living at all.

Taking a leaf from the newspapers' Jekyll-Hyde attitudes toward fornication, the magazines are not far behind. *Fun Parade*, for example, publishes this masterpiece of now-you-condemn-it-and-now-you-don't appraisal of premarital sex relations: "Trudy: They say such terrible things about Mary. Can any of them be true? Rudy: I'm afraid not."

Reader's Digest, following suit, quotes from Daniel A. Lord in *Catholic Opinion* this anecdote showing how good—and bad—it is for a girl to remain chaste: "A non-Catholic who is thinking seriously of joining the Church asked a convert, 'Did becoming a Catholic stop your sinning?' 'No,' she replied, 'but it complicated it considerably.' "

Further ambivalence is found in the double-barreled inconsistency expressed and implied by many characters in contemporary novels. In Edison Marshall's *Gypsy Sixpence* the hero boasts about his many affairs with housemaids, barmaids, and bumboat girls, many of whom "were kind and good and will make good wives for men of their own station." The implication here is that fornication is a fine thing for women—of the lower classes, and for men of all classes.

In A. B. Guthrie's *The Way West* the heroine lets herself be seduced and then admits to her seducer: "I knowed it wasn't right." Oh no, says he, "I'm to blame." Then, a hundred pages later, the author has Dick Summers, master scout, think in this wise when asked for advice by the boy, Brownie, who loves the heroine and is troubled about marrying her because of her previous lapse from chastity: "And the rules that people set and broke and suffered from in the breaking? Like the rule against naturalness that animals had more sense than to deny? Like the rule that a girl couldn't lie with a man unless a preacher said amen? Big as it was now, how big would the lying seem to Brownie when the years had rubbed the fuzz off of him? ... A man was a man by the nature of him and, grown up, knew himself in secret for what he was, unless he had an extra-sore religion."

If we would note the full fury of confusion between the acceptance and rejection of fornication in twentieth-century sexpression, we need only turn to some of the best and most popular dramatic productions of that era. For example, take Garson Kanin's *Born Yesterday*, which on New Year's Eve, 1950, rang up its 1642d performance. In a notable scene in the play the junk tycoon, Brock, brashly checks into the leading hotel in Washington, D.C., with his entourage, including his luscious mistress, Billie, in tow. The assistant manager of the hotel, mistaking Billie for the woman she obviously is not, remarks: "Mrs. Brock seems delighted with the bedchambers." Brock, making no bones about it: "It's not Mrs. Brock." The assistant manager, gulping: "I see."

Later on in the same play Billie, who is quite unashamed of her relations with Brock, and who coolly explains how, when she wants to get anything out of him, she refuses to come across until he does, talks about her father: "He said I should write him again and I should have a hot lunch every day and I should let him know how I am but that he didn't want to see me if I was still living the life of a concubine."

In Sidney Kingsley's ultra-realistic play, *Detective Story*, the hard-boiled Irish detectives consistently work on the assumption that every girl in the city of New York likes nothing better than to raise her skirts for the first good-looking man who passes, and that any male who refused such an offer undoubtedly would be an idiot or a lunatic. But the great dramatic crisis of the play revolves around one of the detectives, McLeod, who suddenly discovers not that his wife has ever been unfaithful to him since they were married, but merely that she has been sexually intimate with one other man before their marriage. Whereupon this old-time, hardened detective bursts out: "I'd sooner go to jail for twenty years than find out this way that my wife was a whore." "Don't say that, Jim," she begs him. But he, adamantly: "That's the word; I didn't invent it. That's what they call it."

In Benn W. Levy's play *Clutterbuck*, and in Joseph Field's and Anita Loos's musical comedy, *Gentlemen Prefer Blondes*, the seesawings, from line to line, between accepting and rejecting attitudes toward fornication are so continual and prolonged as to make the poor auditor positively dizzy. The three wives in *Clutterbuck* are as unashamed *and* ashamed about their premarital sex affairs as it is conceivably possible for anyone to be; and Lorelei Lee of *Gentlemen Prefer Blondes* describes her devirginization in Little Rock in the most prudish-lascivious terms imaginable.

The epitome of double-dyed confusion as regards American attitudes toward fornication is brilliantly portrayed in two short excerpts from one of the most highly praised and most popular plays of the century, Arthur Miller's *Death of a Salesman*. In one of the scenes in this play the salesman's two sons, neither of whom is any longer a youngster, are talking:

HAPPY: You still run around a lot?
BIFF: Naa. I'd like to find a girl—steady, somebody with substance.
HAPPY: That's what I long for.
BIFF: Go on! You'd never come home.
HAPPY: I would! Somebody with character, with resistance! Like Mom, y'know. You're gonna call me a bastard when I tell you

28

this. That girl Charlotte I was with tonight is engaged to be married in five weeks.

A few scenes and girls later. Happy is trying to cheer up Biff.

HAPPY: That's the talk, Biff, that's the first time I've heard the old confidence out of you! You're gonna live with me, kid, and any babe you want just say the word. . . .

There, succinctly, we have it: the common man of the twentieth century—he who feels that he and his fornicating partner are without character or honor; and he who, simultaneously, feels that life without fornication is ridiculous, unlivable, worthless, grim, and stupid.

Or let us put it this way. Premarital sex relations today are widely believed to be bad, silly, and pointless; *but* thoroughly enjoyable; *but* normal and natural; *but* necessary for healthful living; *but* smart, gay, and sophisticated; *but* romantically permissible and thrilling; *but* adventurous and exciting; *but* inevitable in this all-too-fleshly world, and so on.

At the same time, prenuptial sex affairs, in our day and age, are commonly thought to be good, right, and proper; *but* likely to get you into trouble with your society; *but* predisposing to neurosis; *but* largely for the lower classes; *but* something, of course, *my* wife never practiced; *but* decidedly inferior to marital sex relations; *but* affairs which you engage in only as a last resort, and so forth.

In consequence, it may well be surmised that the average twentieth-century man (or woman) is as confused in his attitudes toward fornication as it is possible for a mortal to be. Consciously he desires to be a fornicator—and is guilty if he is one. Or he keeps strictly away from premarital sex relations—and is ashamed to admit his inexperience to his friends. Or he finds an excuse for his own fornicative adventures—and roundly condemns his fiancée's or his son's. Or he regularly, without qualms, seduces one girl after another—and then insists on marrying a virgin. Or he rigorously keeps himself pure for his bride—and openly envies the Casanovas of his day.

On an unconscious level, we may well be sure, contemporary conflicts over pro- and anti-fornicative attitudes are even worse. Legion is the number of those men who madly jump into the arms of the first girl who will have them—only to find themselves psychically impotent. Or who resist all temptations to go out with girls—only to find themselves compulsively exhibiting their genitals before, or even raping, teen-age girls. And multitudinous are those girls who break off their engagements because their fiances insist on their having premarital sex

29

relations, only to wind up with psychosomatically caused allergies, high blood pressure, or other symptoms. Or who gaily copulated with half-a-dozen boys before their marriage—only to acquire an acute case of dyspareunia (painful intercourse) on their wedding night.

Precisely what, today, are the absolute and relative incidences of fornication among various American regional, social, and educational groups may, despite the valiant efforts of Dr. Kinsey and his associates, be not soon determined. But this much seems certain, if we are to give any credence whatever to the ideas expressed and implied in our popular communications: that fornication is ubiquitously exposited and discussed; that the indited and declaimed attitudes toward it are neither universally pro nor con; that group agreement on its value is slight and individual accordance nil; that both interpersonal and intrapersonal consistency regarding its espousal and/or practice are more honored in the breach than in the act; and that the whole business of belief and non-belief in the goodness of prenuptial chastity is, to put it mildly, one damned big mess.

Attitudes Toward Fornication in the 1960's

During the 1960's attitudes toward premarital sex relations in American mass media began to swing definitely toward the liberal side, whereas they had been about evenly divided between conservative and liberal views in the 1950's. Although the material in the general magazines, the newspapers, and particularly the women's magazines tended to be critical and negative in regard to fornicative behavior, attitudes expressed and implied in the best-selling fiction, the humorous periodicals, and the men's magazines tended not only to be favorable but often consisted of enthusiastic espousals of premarital affairs. Moreover, where the 1950 endorsements of fornication tended to be of those kinds of affairs which were distinctly linked with love between the unmarried partners, the 1960 endorsements were frequently of premarital sex for sex's sake, with little or no thought of amative tie-ins.

On the disapproving side, many of the 1960 statements and implications were as clearly and comprehensively puritanical as they had ever been in the past. As just noted, the material in the women's magazines led all the rest in this respect. Thus, in a *Teen Secrets* story, a father "was furious and wanted to strap" his daughter who almost, but not quite, had intercourse with a boy; and she says that "I couldn't show my face after that. I couldn't go back to school. I wanted to die with shame." In a *True Confessions* tale, a boy says that "I should be shot!" for having relations with his sweetheart. In a *Real Confessions* piece, a fornicating girl is considered "unfit to work" in a department store. In a *Cosmopolitan* story, a father lashes his daughter's boy friend with his strap and buckle when he merely suspected that they might be having an affair. A waitress in a *Secrets* tale is called on the carpet for being suspected of having affairs with the customers in her diner. A *Ladies' Home Journal* heroine proudly tells her suitor that "there are a terrible lot of girls who'd give their souls to be able to say, 'The first man who really made love to me is the man I married,' the way I can." A boy in a story in *My Love Secret* is revolted by the idea of his sister's even knowing about the existence of premarital affairs. In a *Today's Romances* piece, a male who has just had intercourse with his sweetheart reacts in this wise: "There was a look almost of horror in his eyes. 'My God, what have I done?' he cried. He ran his hands through his hair as if he'd like to pull it out."

Other kinds of mass media were found to have equally disapproving attitudes toward premarital sex affairs. *Top Stars* wondered whether a young and beautiful actress was "really headed toward disaster as so many people believe," as a result of her "fantastic dates." *Inside Story* insisted that another young actress's closest friends were profoundly shocked by her round-the-world romance with a noted playboy. *Stardust* severely chastised a famous male singing and film star for his "kissing everyone, everywhere" and posing with a strip tease dancer. The same magazine also insisted that some mere rumors about many Hollywood stars "very nearly ruined their reputations and wrecked their lives." *Starlife* quoted no less an authority as Jayne Mansfield as follows: "You must have the strength to save yourself for the beauty and deep satisfaction of lasting love! A few short moments of physical satisfaction just aren't worth the lifetime of shame that sometimes follows."

A few other illustrations of anti-fornicative attitudes in the mass media of the 1960's may be quoted from the scores which were found in the present follow-up study. In an *Off-Beat Detective* story a father and son whose main business consists of capturing and tricking escaped chain gang convicts and selling them back to their captors are horrified when one of their victims copulates with their very willing daughter. In William Inge's play, *A Loss of Roses*, published in *Esquire*, a delinquent, work-evading boy confesses that "I'm allus afraid I'm gonna hurt a girl like that, or get her dirty, or something." In Robert Ruark's novel, *Poor No More*, a brother of a girl tells the hero who is dating this girl: "If you do anything at all to this kid, anything at *all*, I'll kill you. Painfully as possible." And the hero replies, "I wouldn't mind if you did. I'd rate it. Or I might even save you the trouble and do it myself."

In *For Two Cents Plain*, a best-selling non-fiction book, the author, Harry Golden, proudly tells how when he managed a hotel he refused to rent rooms to single women, forbade females to visit male guests in their rooms, and kept couples from registering unless they had genuine baggage. In the fabulously popular novel, *Exodus*, young Dov and Karen sorrowfully keep away from each other sexually, even though they are shiningly in love, because, as Dov says, "I'm not going to do what's wrong for you." In the *New York Times* of January and February, 1960, there are several reports of students being arrested at Yale University for having premarital sex relations; and a final report, as a result of these doings, with this headline: "F.B.I. MAN TO HEAD SECURITY AT YALE. Will Oversee Campus Police and Consult With Town—Made Associate Dean."

In the motion picture, *Because They're Young*, a high school boy is horrified and turns to delinquent behavior because his divorced mother has a lover. "Don't touch me," he tells the girl he loves, "you'll get dirty. Just like me—like my mother. A dirty, filthy, rotten—!" In the *New York Daily News*, columnist Doris Blake warns divorcees that when men make passes at them they must "slap them down verbally so that no doubt is left in their minds that you are both offended and annoyed." In his highly salacious novel, *The Cave*, Robert Penn Warren has Miss Abernathy tell her young boarder, Celia Hornby, when she finds that Celia is interested in the blacksmith, Jack Harrick: "You know what! He is shameless. It is the shameless —it is the shameful things he does to—to women."

In a review of Abigail Van Buren's *Dear Teenager*, appearing in the *Nation*, the reviewer notes that Miss Van Buren, like Dick Clark and Pat Boone (whose new books she also reviews), "advocates continence; but she is a great deal more persuasive about it." In her own current column in the *New York Daily Mirror*, Miss Van Buren bears out the *Nation's* reviewer by advising a correspondent who asks about marrying a man who snores: "There is no sure cure for snoring. Find out if the gentlemen snores before you get romantically involved with him. But be careful how you find out!" Finally, in a more humorous but still anti-fornicative mood, *Campus Howl* reprints the joke from the *CCNY Mercury* about the farmer who says to his wife, "It shore is too bad about our two daughters layin' up thar in that cemetery." "Shore is, Paw. Sometimes I wish they wuz dead!"

So much for some typical representatives of the many attitudes against premarital sex relations which were still found to be prevalent in the 1960's. On the other side of the fence, however, mass media attitudes favoring fornication were discovered to be surprisingly many and definite. First, for a few samples from the men's magazines.

From *Rapture*: An article tells the male reader how to become a great seducer of females by foregoing haircut and manicure for an appearance of real raunchiness: "'I could go for a man like you,' she says with feeling, reaching across and stroking your arm. 'Why don't you then.' She sets down the drink deliberately and slides over on the divan. Her skirt works its way up to the middle of her thigh, and you can catch the beginnings of the top of her stockings. Impulsively, you place your hand on the rough-smooth surface of the nylon above her knee. She smiles and moves in more. Your hand goes up until it is touching bare skin. . . . 'Don't tear it,' she says moments later, helping you with the bra catch. 'You don't have to hurry. We have all night.' The strap loosens and falls away, revealing the promised land beyond, standing like mountains in the sun. Much later, lying in the darkness, talking quietly, she tells you how she had misunderstood your impeccable nature—how much she enjoys your new-found raunchiness."

From *Off-Beat Detective*: A gangster has been painfully wounded by a girl, Bunny, who has been sent to kill him and has induced her to help him murder the man who sent her. She is so beautiful, he can't stop thinking of her and asks, reluctantly, where his intended victim is. " 'At one of his clubs, I guess.' She leaned close. Her fingers worked their way up the back of his neck and disappeared in his thick black hair. 'It's only ten, Bunny. We have loads of time.' 'That's exactly what I was thinking. . . .' Three hours later they entered Baron Kroneck's [the victim's] lavish apartment."

From *Playboy*: Sam, a brilliant inventor, shows a visitor in his combined living quarters and laboratory a cozy alcove. "There, stretched out on a divan, was a dazzling blonde, as nubile and as nude as any the visitor had ever seen. In her hand she held a glass, empty except for two ice cubes. 'This is my latest and greatest invention,' the genius beamed proudly. 'I call it instant sex. You just add Scotch.' "

From *Revels*: In an article on decorating a man's boudoir, the reader is cautioned: "Some colors do not blend at all well. If one decides to mix blonde, redhead and brunette at the same time for an evening of kaleidoscopic effects, it might do well to dilute each first with alcohol preferably martinis—so they develop a common denominator. Otherwise, fireworks might well result. . . . Also, if you feel your decorating scheme for the boudoir requires the mixing of these three shades, we'd suggest you get a king-size bed. You'd look pretty damned silly sleeping on the couch in the living room. One final word of instruction: there are things more important in selecting inspiring boudoir decorations than color and grace of line. If exceeding care is not exercised, you may find yourself replacing the wallpaper with wallflowers. And that would be one hellish way to spend any night!"

From *Modern Man*: "There had been a weird moment when the gears of his mind seemed to shift into high speed. Hal opened his eyes, drowsy with the warmth of the girl beside him, conscious of the soft resilence of her bare breast. . . . Hal's eyes popped wide. Then what set of breasts were nudging into his *left* side? Whose hair was puddled over his *left* shoulder? Somehow—impossibly and unbelievably—there was another woman in bed with Joyce Lind and himself." And when Hal realized that he was able to create, whenever he wished, two girls for the price of one, he did so endlessly and enjoyed himself incredibly —right up to and including the end of this story.

From *Bare*: "There is the dream of every girl that sooner or later just the right guy will come along. When she is sure the man is the right one, what has she got to lose? Joy while it lasts is better than wondering what it would be like! Most [girls]—regardless of how musically inclined—have come to the opinion that a guitar will never replace a man, when it comes to something to play around with."

From *Swank*: A cab-driver picks up a fare, Whit Skinner, and insists on taking him home to his lonely sister. " 'Go on,' the cabbie said, 'It's like an act of mercy' 'Yes,' Whit said, and walked in. At first, he couldn't see the face of the girl seated at the plastic-covered kitchen table; her black hair cascaded across her cheek. She was wearing a black dress that was a size or two smaller than it should have been, but the effect was to emphasize fullness here and roundness there, and to create an overwhelming impression of such voluptuous beauty that Whit Skinner's spotless eyeglass lenses clouded. Then she looked up, and he saw the deep luminous eyes and moist red mouth.

" 'Mumumumum,' Whit said. 'I—I—I—'

"He didn't have to find words. Clara came out of the kitchen chair and thundered towards him like a wish-fulfillment in three-dimensions. The full red lips were parted, the eyes glowing with ecstasy, the body taut and quivering in expectation. She threw herself upon him; at first, he was tense, then he relaxed. Relaxation was wonderful. He never knew *how* wonderful before. He didn't even hear Fundello leave."

Easily rivaling the unashamed approval of premarital sex relations in today's men's magazines is the enthusiastic approbation given fornication in many best-selling novels. Thus, in Michener's *Hawaii*, Captain Hoxworth takes his thirteen-year-old son, Whip, to a brothel because, he explains, "at thirteen it's high time a man gets to know what delicious things women are." In Faulkner's *The Mansion*, Montgomery Ward Snopes ridicules his kinsman, Flem, for being a virgin. "You never had a lay in your life, did you? You even waited to get married until you found a woman who not only was already knocked up, she wouldn't even let you run your hand up her dress. Jesus, you do want to stay alive, don't you? Only, *why*?" In Warren's *The Cave*, the males who discover that Jasper Herrick has copulated with Jo-Lea and got her pregnant are lasciviously jealous. " 'Diggity,' Jebb Holloway said, 'I shore bet it was juicy.' 'As a peach,' Isaac Sumpter said, and was overcome by a painful, inexorable envy for Jasper Herrick."

In John Hersey's *The War Lover*, the hero remembers his girl friend, Daphne, "sitting down at her mirror, the first time she'd locked the door of her room in Cambridge, with me in it, and looking at herself as if to say, 'Aren't I the clever one?'" In Ruark's *Poor No More*, a physician informs the protagonist, Craig, that he does not have gonorrhea and says: "'Just go ahead and screw what you can catch. If you collect a bug come see me, but don't let it spoil the fun. I had the clap three times when I was an intern, and every time it was a nurse. Quit worrying. It wrecks the sport. That'll be two dollars. After hours.' Craig paid him. The doctor looked at the bills as if they were a new culture under a slide. He shook his head, and handed them back to Craig. 'I suggest,' he said, 'that you run over to Durham and get yourself properly laid. Be my guest. Maybe your girl friend will like you better as a result. Good night, son.'"

In Rona Jaffe's *The Best of Everything*, Dexter tells his girl friend, April, that of course he'd marry a girl who was not a virgin. "'I hate going to bed with a virgin,' Dexter said firmly. 'They think they're giving you the greatest thing they have to give in their whole lives. What are they giving you? It hurts them, they don't know one thing about how to conduct themselves in the sack. . . . The whole procedure is a pain in the ass for the guy. If I know a girl's a virgin I won't even make a pass at her.'" In Jack Kerouac's *On the Road*, Dean says: "'Sal is here, this is my old buddy from New Yor-r-k, this is his first night in Denver and it's absolutely necessary for me to take him out and fix him up with a girl! . . . Sal, I have just the girl waiting for you at this very minute—if she's off duty. . . . A waitress, Rita Bettencourt, fine chick, slightly hung-up on a few sexual difficulties which I've tried to straighten up and I think you can manage, you fine gone daddy you. So we'll go there at once—we must bring beer, no, they have some themselves, and damn! I've just got to get into her sister Mary to-night.'"

Even the religious-oriented and politically high-minded contemporary novels manage to get in some favorable assessments of fornication. Thus, in Morris L. West's *The Devil's Advocate*, Dr. Aldo Meyer carefully explains to the bastard, Paolo, that he is to think of his mother as a good woman—"ten times better than those who put this name [of whore] on her"—because she fornicated with the boy's father for love. In Leon Uris's *Exodus*, the dedicated fighters for Israel, David and Jordana, slip away from their fellows, spread a blanket on the earth, embrace, and love each other. "His hand felt for the smoothness of her body. She took the clothing from her to ease his way, and they pressed against each other and she asked to be taken and they blended into one." Even in the fanatically religious novel by Eugene Vale, *The Thirteenth Apostle*, the heroine visits the hero in his apartment and the inevitable takes place: "He drew her close—and suddenly all hesitation fell from them. Suddenly there was only the great want of two beings, surrendering at last, embracing each other, finding one another outside of time and place, far from the brooding stare of fate and its mysteries and all its unresolved intents. Her indistinct face, turned to him afterwards on the pillow, reflected neither confusion nor regret."

To return for a moment to the men's magazines, we find an almost incredible amount of additional material which loudly and almost proudly endorses fornication. In a *Men's Digest* story, the heroine practically forces the hero to have "lusty fun" with her when she finally gets him alone in his home. *Twenty-One* goes out of its way to reprint a forty-year-old excerpt from Edward Westermarck's *History of Human Marriage* dealing with the joys of *jus primae noctis*, the right of an ancient lord to devirginize all the girls on his estate. *Confidential* features the story of the late Errol Flynn's not remembering one of his old girl friends until she reminded him that they had copulated on a gravestone so that he could thereby "fulfill a lifelong ambition." The *National Enquirer* serializes Beverly Aadland's proud tale of "My Life of Luxury on Errol's Yacht." *True* runs a condensed version of Flynn's own autobiography, *My Wicked, Wicked Ways*, which boastingly tells of his innumerable affairs from the age of twelve onward. *Monsieur* insists that not only will the Greenwich Village girl quickly invite you to her bed, but "if her roommate happens to be asleep on the other side of the room when she brings you back to her pad, you're expected to go on with the show just the same." *Revels* encourages its male readers to rush to West Berlin for their vacations, because girls there go to bed with a man literally at first sight. *Man's Conquest* quotes a young teenage girl who was a member of a sex club as saying "I just minded my P's and Q's... I kept to home and with boys my own age. They got more energy anyway—."

Confidential Tattler, a periodical published in Canada and widely distributed in the United States, goes just about as far as one can go in espousing premarital sex relations. Thus, in the January 16, 1960 issue it first notes that one of the most famous movie stars "hasn't let a little matter like marriage stop him" and quotes one of his friends as saying " 'He likes girls, period. So what are you going to do with a guy like that, psychoanalyze him? He's normal.' " In another article, the magazine quotes a famous female stage and screen star who hasn't married: " 'The real reason,' says she, is 'Men are my hobby. If I ever got married I'd have to give it up.' Makes sense, doesn't it?" In its *Personals* column, *Confidential Tattler* features many ads which are nothing but frank invitations to fornication. For example: "Young gentleman, seeks attractive, broadminded singles, modern couples anxious to form 'Fun Club,' enjoy house parties, photography, etc. What's your pleasure? Strict confidence. Snap, phone number for quick reply. New York City area."

Other kinds of publications, in a somewhat more muted way, also publish articles, stories, cartoons, jokes, or advertisements which clearly favor the joys of premarital love. Included among these periodicals in the early 1960's were the *New York Times*, the *Saturday Evening Post*, *Popular Medicine*, *Mystery Digest*, *Fantasy and Science Fiction*, and *Commentary*. In the last named publication, for example, Paul Goodman has an article on "Youth in the Organized Society" in which he strongly protests against adults trying to persuade a boy that his sexual adventures are bad and that some different behavior is much better when "he knows by the evidence of his senses that nothing could be better."

Even in the motion pictures of the 1960's, which still tend to be heavily censored under the production code, premarital sex relations are frequently accepted lightly or heartily approved. In *Never So Few*, the heroine, Carla, already has one affair going when she gets involved with Captain Con Reynolds, the hero, though she has known him only a short while. In *Heller in Pink Tights*, Angela has one heller of a time keeping out of the arms of the killer, Mabry, even though she is presumably madly in love with the hero, Healy. In *Can-Can*, the heroine, Simone, runs a cafe where "lewd and lascivious" can-can dancing takes place. But, a synopsis published in *Screen Stories* informs us, "Simone had been getting away with it for a long time. Thanks to her lawyer, François Durnais, she had what was called 'protection.' And when her lawyer wasn't advising her about writs and torts, he was very often kissing the back of her neck. That's right, François and Simone were sweethearts. Furthermore, François was on terribly good terms with the President of the court in that district, Paul Barrière, who believed people should live and let live. It looked as if nothing could go wrong with the Bal Du Paradis. The Can-Can would flourish, and Simone would grow rich." Multiple fornication, anyone?

For a final look at some of the highly permissive attitudes toward premarital relations that are being published in the 1960's, we print a small sampling of the scores of jokes and cartoons that were found in contemporary periodicals.

From *Candid*: "He: Do you believe in free love? She: Have I ever given you a bill?"

From *Texas Ranger*: "A girl was telling a boy friend that she realized she was very popular, but she didn't know why. 'Do you suppose it's my complexion?' she asked. 'No.' 'My figure?' 'No.' 'My personality?' 'No.' 'I give up.' 'That's it.' "

From *Jest*: "Young lady to the male she is entertaining at home: 'I'll be back in a minute. I'm going to change into something more comfortable to get out of!'"

From *For Laughing Out Loud*: "Rich old gentleman to bartender: 'I suppose that there must be more to life than just gadding about with one beautiful girl after another, but if there is I don't want to know about it.'"

From *Campus Howl*, quoting from the *Florida Orange Peel*: "Girl: 'I'd like to see the captain of the ship.' Gob: 'He's forward.' Girl: 'That's all right. This is a pleasure trip.'"

From *Scamp*: "Our art director swears that he saw a movie at a drive-in theater the other night that was so exciting, so thrilling, so breathtaking that six couples actually stopped to watch it."

From *Nugget*: "Young bachelor to his girl friend, as they are lying in bed looking at a football game over the TV set: 'Isn't this better than sitting in some drafty stadium?'"

As might be expected, in the light of the foregoing disapproving and approving attitudes toward fornication that are prevalent in the 1960 publications, many periodicals include material in the same issue, or often on the same page or in the same line of the same page, that is strikingly pro- *and* anti-fornicative. Thus, in *Tan* the heroine of one story relates: "That's how I came to meet Tommy. He was fun for awhile, and helped to take my mind off things back in Detroit." But then, three paragraphs later, she is tragically noting: "And so I have consigned myself to a world of lost women—the women who love foolishly, and through that foolish love find themselves ruined forever."

In *True Story*, a girl who cannot marry her sweetheart moans, as he says he had better not stay and have sex relations with her, "No—no—no! Stay with me, John—please, please—stay with me!" "I knew I was wrong," she goes on to tell her readers, "but I didn't care. I'd been denied everything else, why shouldn't I have the wedding night we'd dreamed of?" Then, in the very next paragraph, she continues: "Looking back, I realize the blame was entirely mine."

In Washington, D. C., *Confidential Tattler* tells us, when a G-girl (that is, a girl who works in a government position) goes to a cocktail bar: "Some are afraid they will. Others are afraid they won't."

In a *McCall's* serial, the hero confesses that there's never been another woman in his sexual life other than the heroine; and when she hesitates to believe this, he confesses that he has boasted about phantom conquests previously because he had been ashamed, in front of his friends, to be so virginal.

In a *Personal Romances* story, a girl has intercourse with a man she does not love because "We needed each other. Needed each other."

38

But, as usual, in the very next paragraph she is "staring up at the starry night in numb anguish. How could I? How could I be so easy with a man I didn't love, or hadn't known much over a month?"

In the film, *Happy Anniversary*, a husband humorously needles his in-laws about the "very beautiful romance" he and his wife had before they were married. "And here it is fourteen years later, and we're celebrating our thirteenth anniversary. If music be the food of love, play on!" But when his teenage daughter says, on a TV broadcast, that her grandparents discovered that her mother and father had premarital relations, this husband and father is so upset that he breaks the TV set over which he is witnessing the broadcast.

In William Inge's play, *A Loss of Roses*, printed in *Esquire*, Lila tells her friend Helen that Helen is just wonderful for understanding about Lila's affair with her boy friend, Rick. But a few lines later we note: "LILA (*in a mood for repentance*): Helen . . . I hope you don't think I'm too terrible, me and Rick."

So it goes: with one mass media outlet after another steadily displaying attitudes toward fornication which are, at one and the same time, incredibly liberal *and* reactionary. As usual, the epitome of these double-dyed contradictory attitudes may be seen in some of the more popular jokes of our day. Here is a small sampling:

From *Comedy*: "Beautiful young girl who is about to leave old bachelor's apartment: I'm sorry that I can't stay, Mr. Jones, but first, I'm a decent girl and, second, I forgot my pajamas."

From *Jest*: "Sergeant, I'm making a classified list of all the girls in town. Ah, good for you. No, Sir. The bad for me; the good for you!"

From *Texas Rangers*: "She: Do you know what they've been saying about me? He: What do you think I'm here for?"

From *Cavalcade*: "Horrified mother, to her daughter who lives alone in the big city and who has told her about a date: 'You didn't allow that man into your apartment, did you?' Daughter: 'Oh, no. We went to his apartment. Let *his* mother worry.' "

To summarize: Everything that has been said in the first part of this chapter about the utterly conflicting attitudes toward premarital sex relations that were prevalent in the public media of the 1950's can be repeated about the thoroughly contradictory attitudes toward fornication that are still prevalent in the popular media of the 1960's. The words may have changed a little (on the more liberal side); but the tune's still the same.

CHAPTER 2

Adultery

It is easier to find frank expression of anti-adulterous attitudes in contemporary publications than it is to find negative attitudes to virtually any other mode of sex behavior. Indeed, if adultery were to be accepted unequivocally as a good and proper act, a very large proportion of our popular stories, novels, films, plays, and radio dramas would automatically become plotless.

Much to the average writer's good fortune, however, anti-adulterous attitudes, and the complications in human lives to which they lead, are still very much with us. A sampling of views on adultery taken from contemporary magazine stories reveals the following notions:

1. The worst thing that can possibly happen to a married man is for him to fall in love with a young woman and, simultaneously, to learn of his twenty-one-year-old daughter's adulterous affair with the father of two children (*Cosmopolitan* magazine).

2. Any woman who kills her lover to prevent her husband's finding out about her adultery will, even if her husband discovers the murder and helps her to hide it from the authorities, be seen by him for the rest of his life with "hidden reproach," and will continually experience "the sourness of shame and regret"—not, mind you, because of her murder, but because of their mutual remembrance of her act of infidelity (*Argosy*).

3. Any woman who takes back an adulterous husband may be expected to have her friends discuss her in this wise: " 'And the disgraceful part of it is,' Harriet said, 'that Caroline took him back, just as if nothing had happened.' Edna squinted a little as she threaded her needle against the light. 'You'd think she'd have more pride,' she said. 'You'd think any woman would' " (*Redbook*).

4. Any man who loves a woman other than his invalided, shrewish wife may well be suspected of murdering this wife when she finally dies (*American* magazine).

5. No wife who loves her husband can possibly live comfortably with him while he is carrying on an affair with another woman (*True Story*).

6. No husband can ever forgive his wife's having an affair with another man (*Real Romances*).

7. Any man who so much as kisses a girl other than his wife is "a cheap, unfaithful cheat," and is only fit to be horsewhipped (*Honeymoon*).

8. Any man who, in an explosive burst of temper, kills his wife's paramour should unquestionably be acquitted under the unwritten law (*Family Circle*).

9. An unfaithful husband is nothing but an "alley cat," and any woman who has sex relations with him, a "chippy" (*True Police Cases*).

10. A married man and a single girl who are desperately in love with each other have no right even to exchange a single kiss (*Secret Loves*).

11. A girl who once has a crush on a married man should pay for it the rest of her life (*All Love*).

12. A married woman who commits adultery because her husband is a hopeless cripple deserves to die a horrible death (*I Confess*).

13. A young wife who commits adultery while her ninety-year-old husband is deathly ill is unspeakably wicked (*Theatre Arts Monthly*).

Not to be outdone by their story-writing confreres, contemporary nonfiction contributors to current periodicals similarly condemn adultery. Thus we are told that adulterers and adulteresses

...are wholly unfair to their mates (*Judy's*).

...have no regard for anyone's feelings but their own (*Your Marriage*).

...are iniquitous marriage wreckers (*The Catholic Mind*).

...bring disaster on themselves and their children (*Woman's Life*).

...lose their own self-respect and the respect of their fellows (*Personal Romances*).

From all sides, and in all ways, in point of fact, public condemnation of adultery impinges on American readers and audiences. The adulterer or adulteress in our society is portrayed by some of our leading novel, book, play, scenario, script, and song writers as—

hideous (in the play, *That Lady*).

indecent (in the novel, *The Long Love*).

a dirty dog (in the book, *A Guide to Confident Living*).

reprehensible (in the play, *I Know My Love*).

shocking (in the novel, *Loving*).

wicked (in the book, *The Greatest Story Ever Told*).

incredibly arrogant (in the novel, *Never Dies the Dream*).

a nauseating intriguer (in the book, *The Aspirin Age*).

a phony little fake (in the play, *Death of a Salesman*).

a base philanderer (in the film, *East Side, West Side*).

a shameless hussy (in a Jimmie Fidler radio broadcast).

a cruel home wrecker (in the film, *Adam's Rib*).

Et cetera.

Even modern gag writers utilize negative attitudes toward adultery, as in this anecdote from *Joke Parade*: "The young husband, while traveling on business, was invited to join a fishing party. He had exceptionally good luck and proudly wrote to his wife, 'Landed a darling today. Really a beauty. Some struggle.' A few days later he received her reply: 'Don't think you can flaunt your conquests before me. Am leaving for Mother's tomorrow.'"

Finally, if we turn to current newspapers, we find that it is a commonplace occurrence for a woman to shoot her husband when she finds him kissing another woman (Amarillo *Sunday News-Globe*); that a man will pay thousands of dollars' blackmail to prevent his wife's being told of an illicit love affair he is having (Denver *Post*); and that the press and the public will not stand for a movie actress's leaving her husband to live with another man, and would rather see her brilliant screen career dead first (New York *Sunday Mirror*).

To doubt, in the face of all this evidence, that huge segments of the American public are unalterably opposed to and ashamed of adultery would be to admit one's candidacy for a hearing aid and a Seeing Eye dog.

There is, as usual, another side to the story. For at the same time that publicists are decrying the evils of adultery, attitudes which range from a mild acceptance to a wholehearted endorsement of it are far from being infrequently expressed or implied in American writings and performances. Thus, in the novel, *Gypsy Sixpence*, the hero not only tolerates, but actually encourages, an affair between his father and a housemaid. In the film, *Sands of Iwo Jima*, one of the soldiers tells how, since his wife no longer writes him, he's going to Hawaii after the war ends, "get me a little wahine, and settle down to a nice, quiet life in the sun." In the book, *Queen New Orleans*, the author pleasantly plays up the adulterous temperament of Bernard de Marigny, who had, he tells us, "all the vices of—of—a gentleman!"

And in a *Cosmopolitan* story it is frankly acknowledged that "no woman is attractive to one man forever." In a tale in the *Yale Literary Magazine* a wife matter-of-factly runs off with another man, and when her husband commits suicide she and the other man matter-of-factly return to live on his farm. In the film, *Prince of Foxes*, Cesare Borgia, in arranging for the hero, Orsini, to marry Cesare's sister, is quite undisturbed over the fact that Orsini will doubtlessly be unfaithful to her after the marriage. In a feature article in the Sunday magazine section of the New York *Journal American*, the extramarital affairs of a well-known socialite, "one of the most defiant and least conventional members of society," are most sympathetically recounted.

And in the novel, *The Man with the Golden Arm*, the adulterous relations between Violet and Sparrow, which are carried on literally under the husband's nose, are treated as if they are the most normal and commonplace affairs in the world. In a *Liberty* magazine story the hero calmly accepts a girl's proposal that she blackmail her husband into letting her have an affair with said hero. In a story in *McCall's* we have the heroine's reaction to discovering the infidelity of an acquaintance: "He is still playing around with Clare Dover, she thought, more factually than critically."

If adultery is often calmly accepted or outrightly approved in serious scenes in novels, plays, films, magazines, and newspapers, it is even more frequently and enthusiastically endorsed in humorous treatments in these same sources. Thus:

In an Amos 'n' Andy broadcast, when Kingfish is asked about showing interest in everyone but his own wife at a New Year's Eve party, he retorts: "All I kin say is when you finds yo'self wanderin' in a peach orchard, you don't go around lookin' for rutabagas!"

In a humorous story in the *Cornell Review*, the adultery of the heroine and her lover is made to seem like the most delectable preoccupation in the world.

In a syndicated column printed in the Tulsa *Sunday World* Earl Wilson writes: "About Ingrid Bergman, Benny Rubin said, 'Once every little Italian boy wanted to grow up to be like Mussolini. Now they all want to grow up to be like Rossellini.' "

The most undiluted acceptance of adultery in our culture may be found in the productions of our gag writers: according to most of whom faithful husbands and wives, in these United States, are (a) virtually non-existent and (b) missing all the fun out of life. Here, to illustrate, are some of their latest productions—and reproductions:

From *Pic*: "Another Hollywood yarn is about a movie star and his wife who were asleep. The wife dreamed she was in her secret lover's embrace when her husband walked in and caught them. She shouted in her sleep, 'My husband, my husband.' Her husband, hearing the shrieks, jumped out of bed and ran to the closet to hide."

From *Fun Parade*: "Marty: Your wife is a gorgeous gal! Is she faithful? Artie: My wife is too good to be true."

From *Joke Parade*: "Wife: Whenever you see an attractive woman, you completely forget about me. Husband: My dear, you are quite wrong—I only wish I could."

From *Good Housekeeping* (exhuming a century-old verse by Thomas Moore):

> "Come, come," said Tom's father, "at your time of life,
> There's no longer excuse for thus playing the rake.
> It is time you should think, boy, of taking a wife."
> "Why, so it is, Father—whose wife shall I take?"

Actually most humorous anecdotes concerning adultery, like those just quoted, include distinctly ambivalent attitudes toward it: since the whole point of these jokes is that adultery is good *because* the adulterer is getting away with it—that is, because it is bad! Thus in one anecdote a woman demands a divorce because her husband is psychopathic. "What makes you believe that?" asks her lawyer. "Oh, it's quite obvious," responds the young woman. "He flies into a towering rage every time he finds another man trying on his pajamas."

In another squib from *Joke Parade* we have this interchange: "Bob: I met my wife at dinner last night. Bill: How nice. Did you have an exciting time? Bob: Did I! I was supposed to be working late at the office."

The best example we could find of the consistently inconsistent attitudes toward adultery which are frequently displayed in our mass media are those exhibited in the prize-winning film, *Quartet*. In one of the four Somerset Maugham short stories portrayed in this picture a fairly prominent husband casually leaves his unloved wife at his country estate and goes to London to meet his young mistress. When his mistress happens to mention some of her friends he protests: "I'd just as soon you didn't talk about me to your friends." Whereupon she immediately retorts: "What do you take me for?" In other words, he has a perfectly easy conscience about carrying on an extramarital affair with her as far as his obligations to his wife are concerned—but at the same time he and his mistress clearly understand that there is something shameful about their affair which makes mention of it to her friends undesirable.

When this same adulterer discovers that his wife has published a narrative poem supposedly describing her passionate affair with a deceased lover, he is so shocked that he is afraid to ask her about the factual foundation of her poem. "I'm afraid she'll tell me the truth." But he simply *has* to find out. "I can't overlook a thing like that. I've been made a laughingstock ... I'll never forget it as long as I live ... For the past few days I have lived in a state of horror and utter shame."

Another ironic example of this dualistic attitude toward adultery may be found in Waltari's *The Egyptian*. Here the author goes to great lengths to describe the tale of Princess Baketamon, the consort of Egypt's great general, Horemheb, who taking no pleasure in her husband's bed, grants her bodily favors to all the fish marketers and street sweepers she meets, asking of them only some kind of stone in return. These market men, Waltari tells us, "left the streets unswept and followed her to the reed swamps, saying, 'Such a delicacy does not come the way of the poor every day. Her skin is not like that of our wives, and the scent of her is like the scent of the nobles. We

44

should be mad not to take the pleasure she offers us. . . .' Even respectable men left their wives and went to the taverns, and at night they took stones from Pharaoh's buildings so that next morning every man in Thebes went from market to market with a stone under his arm, impatiently awaiting the appearance of the catheaded one. . . ."

Then, later, the princess constructs a great building with the stones she got for granting her favors to these men and frankly tells her husband where and how she got her building material. Whereupon, we learn, Horemheb can do nothing, since "to tear the building down would have been to betray to everyone his knowledge that Baketamon had let all Thebes spit upon his couch, and he preferred laughter behind his back to open shame."

The profound irony here is that Horemheb has a great sense of shame because his wife has made him a cuckold behind his back; but none of her lovers, virtually all of whom seem to be married men, appear to have any feelings of guilt or shame whatever. In other words, Horemheb, who has done nothing shameful, is shamed in the eyes of his wife and many hundreds of men who have! And they, in turn, are rendered exceptionally happy about a deed which is made, to them, doubly good only by virtue of their considering it very bad!

We quote one more illustration of the completely ambivalent attitudes toward adultery which may frequently be found in American publications. A *Collier's* cartoon by William von Riegen shows a ravishing young thing luxuriantly reclining in her apartment, surrounded by gifts from her lover. She is having a leisurely morning conversation with one of her girl friends, to whom she is saying: "I suppose it's his wife who's spreading those nasty truths about me."

Need we say more?

Attitudes Toward Adultery in the 1960's

In the original study that was made of attitudes toward adultery in the 1950's, it was found that a considerable number of expressed and implied attitudes existed at that time and that these were fairly evenly divided between liberal and conservative sides of the fence. The same basic findings are evident in the 1960 study, except that the liberal attitudes seem to be somewhat stronger and less abashed than they were in the previous decade.

As might be expected, anti-adulterous views were found primarily in the women's magazines, newspapers, and motion pictures; a fairly even liberal-conservative split was found in the general magazines; and an overwhelming advocacy of adultery was prevalent in best-selling novels, humor magazines, and men's periodicals.

In regard to negative attitudes toward adultery, we find this facet of sex behavior given the following designations:

"... unnerving"—*True Police Stories.*
"... foolish"—*True Confessions* and *Personal Romances.*
"... shocking"—*Twenty-one.*
   ... a just cause for homicide—*Off-Beat Detective Story.*
"... shameful"—*Saga.*
"... appalling"—*Esquire.*
"... revolting"—*Confidential Tattler.*
"... selfish and messy"—*Pageant.*
"... immature"—*Coronet.*
"... sneaky"—*National Enquirer.*
"... irresponsible and cheap"—*Secrets.*
"... disgusting"—*Screen Parade.*
"... greedy"—*Real Secrets.*
"... inexcusable"—*Intimate Stories.*
"... irrational"—*McCalls.*
"... reprehensible"—*Redbook.*
"... unnice"—*True Story.*
"... a reason for one to live a slow death"—*Real Confessions.*
"... indecent"—*Today's Romances.*
   ... justifiable cause for rage and physical assault against the adulterer or adulteress—*My Love Secret*; *Redbook*; *Men's Digest.*

Even in the relatively liberal and sex-filled best-selling novels of our time, adultery is often severely condemned. In *Peyton Place*, Clayton Frazier refers to the adulterous Ginny Stearns as a "trollop" and a "whore." In *Exodus* "a scandal that rocked army circles for months" occurs when Brigadier Sutherland's wife runs off with a lover. In *On the Beach*, the heroine refuses to "do dirt" to the hero's wife by having an affair with him, even though his wife is undoubtedly dead and his thoughts about her being alive are entirely unrealistic.

In *Poor No More*, the highly skullduggerist business man, Craig Price, thinks of himself as a "cold-eyed son of a bitch" and an "impossible bastard" because he is being unfaithful to his thoroughly undesirable wife. In *The War Lover*, one of the Army pilots thinks his wife is a horrible whore and bitch because she confesses an affair to him by mail. In *The Mansion*, the family of Flem Snopes prefer to have Mrs. Snopes publicly notarized as a suicide than have her publicly condemned as a whore because of her adulterous affair with the town banker. In the *Best of Everything*, a young secretary is horrified to have her boss make a pass at her when he is "a married man! And right in front of his wife's picture on the desk!".

The epitome of negative attitudes toward adultery that are prevalent in the 1960's is perhaps shown in an article in *Men's Digest*. Several men on the street were asked: "What would you do if you found your wife in bed with another man?" All said they would be quite shocked and one gave this fairly typical answer: "I'd shoot her. I'd shoot the guy, too. I'm not kiddin' you. I'd be put in jail, sure, but I don't think I'd be convicted. I have a son and I know he'd understand. I think a judge and jury would understand, too. You can't really put a man in prison for killing his wife and her boy friend if you walk into your bedroom and find them in the hay together there. Even if I was convicted, even if I went to the electric chair, it'd be worth it. I wouldn't let her get away with that, believe me."

As for acceptances or endorsements of adultery, these were found to be a little more numerous and often just as vociferous, in the mass media of the 1960's, as the negative views were found to be. As usual, the men's magazines led all the rest of the media in this respect. *Calvalcade* enticingly featured "the true story of Elias 'Lucky' Baldwin, lover and financier without peer. He acquired six wives, uncounted mistresses and children, and $30 million." *True* brazenly presented Errol Flyn's autobiography, *My Wicked, Wicked Ways*, where he boasts of one adulterous affair after another. *Bare* included a story where a wife gives her husband a birthday present of a real, live call girl—so that he will purchase a male lover for her when her birthday arrives. *Scamp* featured a story where a mother tells her son that he will not commit incest if he has intercourse with one of his father's illegitimate daughters because he, the son, is really not his father's child but the child of one of her lover's.

A *Man's Daring* tale has a hero who insists that every married serviceman who's been overseas for awhile "eventually plays around. If he's a man he can't help it." A *Saga* story tells about a Colonel who attempted to requisition his wife for the post of second lieutenant under him, but when the Army shipped him a similar gal instead "it was at this particular point that the colonel demonstrated his adaptability: he accepted the substitute. Very shortly, he established her in the cozy domestic situation planned for his wife."

A *Bare* article encourages adulterers to use hotels and insists that the house detective will not molest them because "If you've paid the freight for two in a room, have signed the register as man and wife and don't start screaming at each other behind a closed transom, he couldn't care less." *Confidential Tattler*, outdoing itself in its personal column (which as we saw in the last chapter, featured pro-fornication ads), has several adultery-inviting advertisements, such as this one: "NICE COUPLE. Attractive, young broad-minded couple, wife 26, 5'5", 125 lbs. husband 33, 6', seeking attractive couples and single ladies who enjoy extremely different parties and stimulations. Name your desires. Photo, phone, address. New Jersey—New York City."

Contemporary novels add their frequent pro-adulterous attitudes to those of the men's magazines. One of the main protagonists of Kerouac's *On the Road*, Dean, is continually living it up with at least one wife and one girl friend, usually having children by both; and the narrator of the same novel has his best affair with a married Mexican girl who starts to live with him in mutually blissful unguiltiness the same night that he picks her up on a bus. Craig Price, the hero of Ruark's *Poor No More*, is practically dragged into bed by a succession of females who are not at all concerned that he is married. One of these women, a friend of his wife's and married herself, propositions him: "You'd find I'm not dull at all, Craig. If you'd care to investigate. Some afternoon, Craig, when work's slow at the office, if you'd like to call me. . . . Or if you'll just pull over into the first road for a minute right now I'll give you a sample of just how dull I'm *not*."

In *Lady Chatterley's Lover*, Connie's father, noticing that she does not seem to be getting along well with her crippled husband, asks her: "Why don't you get yourself a beau, Connie? Do you all the good in the world." When he later discovers she has a lover, he asks him: "Honor! How was the going, eh? Good, my boy, what?" "Good." "I'll bet it was! Ha-ha! My daughter, chip of the old block, what! I never went back on a good bit of fucking, myself."

In Gallico's *Too Many Ghosts*, Mrs. Wilson boldly propositions Hero, the male protagonist of the book; and he is excitedly willing. In Faulkner's *The Mansion*, we find this apotheosis of an adulteress: "When a community suddenly discovered that it has the sole ownership of Venus for however long it will last, she cannot, must not be a chaste wife or even a faithful mistress whether she is or not or really wants to be or not. That would be not only intolerable, but a really criminal waste; and for the community so accoladed to even condone, let alone, abet, the chastity, continence, would be an affront to the donors deserving their godlike vengeance."

Other mass media sources in the 1960's are also replete with pro-adulterous implied and expressed attitudes. In the motion picture *The Fugitive Kind*, Lady begs Val to live in her store while her husband is dying upstairs and, when he tries to leave, darts ahead of him, barring the way with her arms, and cries: "No, no, don't go! *I need you!* To live—to go on living." Never being able to turn his back on need, he stays. In the film, *Beloved Infidel*, F. Scott Fitzgerald's affair with Sheilah, while Fitzgerald is still married, is consistently depicted as one of the finest events of the century. In *Look Magazine*, W. Somerset Maugham is approvingly quoted as saying: "The fact is, two persons don't want to have intercourse with one another indefinitely. With few exceptions, the only way they can keep it (their marriage) going is for one or both to have some fun on the side."

Nugget, in the February 1960 issue, features an article by the present author emphasizing some of the advantages of polygamy; and the March issue of *Pageant* features another of my articles telling wives how to remain calm and collected if they discover that their husbands are engaging in adultery. This kind of sexually enlightened article, as I point out in one of the chapters on censorship in my book, *Sex Without Guilt*, would never have been published just a few years previously. And, almost as if in response to the *Nugget* article, an early 1960 issue of the *Realist* notes that, in spite of the fact that for 70 years the Mormon church and the United States government have forbidden the practice of polygamy among the Mormons, "it is believed that polygamists in Utah and neighboring Arizona and Idaho may number as many as ten thousand."

As ever, the popular jokes of the country, as published in the humor and men's magazines, as well as in many more staid periodicals, give an almost unqualified nod of approval to adulterous relations. Some of the jokes which were widely publicized in the 1960's were these:

From *Campus Howl*, quoting from the *Florida Orange Peel*: "He: Have you a room and bath for my wife and me? Hotel clerk: All we have left is a room with a double bed. He: Will that be all right with you, dearest? She: Yes, mister."

From *Snappy*: "Beautiful young thing as she is about to rent an apartment: Just how many men do you think I could hide in the clothes closet?"

From *Jest*: "Another beautiful young thing to her lover: If my husband should return unexpectedly, jump into the closet. I have it all stacked with provisions."

From *Cavalier*: "Father to his son who is about to get married: Let me give you just two pieces of advice. First, make clear to your bride that you reserve the right to spend one night a week out with the boys. Second, don't waste it on the boys."

From *Swank*: "Boss, to old male secretary, as he is seated with his beautiful new young female secretary on his lap: Harkins, for the past 37 years I've noticed your work has been unsatisfactory. I've hired Miss Wayne to replace you."

From *Rapture*: "She: Darling, will you still love me when we are married? He: I think so, dear. I've always been especially fond of married women."

From *Jest*: "Employee: I hate to bother you, but I need your advice. Would you cheat on your wife? Boss: Who else—on my mother-in-law?"

Attitudes toward adultery in the 1960's closely follow those toward premarital sex relations, according to the material surveyed, in that often a line, a paragraph, or a story contains both pro and con statements and implications. In a *McCall's* story, Mrs. James Barret is very sympathetically depicted as she carries on an affair with her lover, Philip; but, as one might expect, she manages to get herself in most serious difficulties by the end of the story. In the novel, *Peyton Place*, Jennifer is portrayed as a horrible bitch and a wonderfully highly-sexed female as she twits her husband about the possibility of her committing adultery. In the nonfiction best-seller, *For Two Cents Plain*, Harry Golden tells about the fat tycoons who delighted in having regular mistresses, but who took care to hire an "escort" when they took their mistresses out on the town, so that if their wives spotted them they could pretend that they just happened by while two handsome young people were having a good time.

In a feature story in the New York *World-Telegram*, the famous French film producer, Roger Vadim, notes that in Western civilization "men are permitted all sorts of excesses of behavior. If a married man is seen around with another girl we smile tolerantly. If a married woman does this people are easily shocked." In a *Revealing Romances* story, Phil Lansing tells how terribly dishonest and indecent he was —while he was wildly, joyously reacting to his adulterous affair with Peggy Welch. "By the glow of the light shining from the street lamp, I saw how blond curls looked outlined on a pillow, first in ecstasy, later in overwhelming shame and regret." In a tale in *Alfred Hitchcock's Mystery Magazine*, the narrator is so amazed that "my mouth dropped open" when one of his female friends confesses to being engaged in an affair with a married man of their acquaintance; but she, unrepentantly, exclaims: "You're not my—my guardian, Norman! You needn't be so righteous!"

In Lederer and Burdick's novel, *The Ugly American*, a visiting United States Senator says to an Army sergeant stationed in Vietnam, " 'Son, have you ever laid one of these Vietnamese girls. . . . Some of 'em look like pretty nice pieces.' 'Sir, we don't fraternize very much with the natives,' the sergeant answered. 'Hell, I didn't ask if you fraternized. I asked you if you ever laid them.' 'No, sir. I have my family out here,' the sergeant said." In a story in *Rapture*, the hero, Eddie, is continually propositioned by his beautiful secretary, in spite of the fact that she says she loves her husband, Harvey, and wouldn't do anything to hurt him. She finally gets Eddie into bed and the story climactically ends as follows:

" 'Eddie, Eddie darling,' she gasped incredulously as he began to make love to her again. Extravagantly, wildly, cruelly, he brought her to the very edge of abandonment, held her there for a long moment as she lay with her eyes wide open, waiting, almost pleading for him to give her release. And just when it seemed she was no longer capable of meeting his urgency, he swept her with such savagery that she was lifted, beyond her will, to a range of ecstasy bordering on hysterical collapse.

"Still breathing deeply, he looked at her in the scant light. Her face was still marked, as if by pain. Her hand twitched.

" 'You just think about that the next time you're with Harvey,' he said. 'Think about it and let me know how you feel.'

"And he knew damn well she wouldn't be feeling too good."

Vance Packard, in his best-selling book, *The Status Seekers*, sums up the current contradictory American attitudes toward adultery (as well as premarital intercourse) as follows: "Premarital intercourse for males is accepted as such a normal and natural occurence at the lower social levels that some lower-level clergymen, according to the Institute [of Sex Research, Inc. at Indiana University], preach against profanity, smoking, drinking, gambling, and infidelity, but will not include premarital sex in their listing of sins to guard against. Even in the matter of extra-marital sex relations there is general, if bitter, acceptance that, although such activity is disapproved, boys will be boys. Whyte made the same point about Cornerville men."

A final summing up may be given in the tragicomic poem from the Michigan State *Spartan*, quoted in *Campus Howl* magazine:

> "Beneath this stone lies Murphy.
> They buried him today.
> He lived the life of Riley,
> While Riley was away."

Precisely! To live the happy adulterous life and then to be guilty about or punished for being so sublimely happy—this is the American wish and reality today. A great formula, I have to admit, for supplying a steady flow of patients for my psychotherapeutic practice. But a little rough, I am afraid, on some of my best customers.

CHAPTER 3

Sexual Promiscuity

Perhaps the best indication of how sexual promiscuity is publicly regarded in America is the promiscuous manner in which the term is generally employed. According to dictionary usage, a promiscuous individual is one who engages in indiscriminate, casual, or irregular sexual union. According to common parlance, however, a promiscuous individual is virtually anyone who has, say, two or more successive or—especially!—simultaneous lovers.

Take, illustratively, a handsome, intelligent woman who is literally besieged with propositions by male aspirants for her favors. Suppose that, being quite particular, she finally selects one out of a hundred of such males and takes him as her paramour. Suppose she has sex relations with him for a year or so and then, for one reason or other, replaces him with another lover, whom she again selects, with much serious contemplation, from several score applicants. Suppose, finally, that every year or two she repeats this process, always entering a new amour after careful deliberation and the weighing of her would-be lovers' physical, mental, social, and other attributes.

Will this woman, under such circumstances, be having sex relations in an indiscriminate, casual, or irregular manner? Of course not. But will she, by most of the members—and especially the female members—of our society be labeled as a promiscuous woman? Of course.

Or suppose, if still another example is wanted, that the woman just hypothesized, instead of taking a new lover every year or two, takes only three or four inamoratos in her entire lifetime, and that she selects these from literally hundreds of candidates. But suppose, also, that she has all these sexual partners simultaneously, perhaps for a long period of years. Again, will she be in the least indiscriminate, casual, or irregular about her sex unions? Naturally not. But will she be labeled, by contemporary Americans, as promiscuous? Naturally.

In other words, the mores of our day seem to be so opposed to sexual promiscuity that virtually any kind of (successive or simultaneous) plural sex union, no matter how discriminatingly or selectively it may be indulged, is viewed as being a promiscuous one.

Nor is sexual promiscuity, in our culture, applied only to the female of the species. A *True Story* writer confesses: "I never thought he was a 'good' man. Even while he loved me, I knew he went out with other girls." And the hero of Damon Runyon's *The Brakeman's Daughter*, as dramatized over the Mutual Broadcasting System, ruefully observes about a girl he wishes to court: "A doll like that wouldn't go for a promiscuous 'hummingbird' like me, who flits from doll to doll."

Other examples of negative attitudes toward sexual promiscuity are fairly common in modern writings. Thus Marghanita Laski, in her story, *Little Boy Lost*, condensed in *Reader's Digest*, expresses a typical Anglo-American notion that any affair that is entered "without emotional involvement," for the purpose of mere sexual companionship, is a promiscuous one and is cheap and vulgar.

One of the popular songs of our day complains bitterly about a girl who is so popular that she has boy friends standing ten deep in line, but she is so fickle that the love light in her eyes lies, lies, and lies. Still another song laments that a girl's kisses are perfectly worthless because they are simply a dime a dozen.

In the *Aspirin Age*, Morris Markey refers to a promiscuous girl, as is common in modern American parlance, as a "*tramp*."

American attitudes toward promiscuity are usually so negative that even writers in scientific journals find it difficult to remain objective about this mode of sex behavior. In the *Educational Forum*, J. B. Shouse implies that all promiscuous girls are drifting, wayward, and lacking in self-respect. In the *Journal of Social Issues* four clinical psychologists contend that promiscuous behavior is "meaningless," as compared to presumably much more "meaningful" non-promiscuous sex activity. In the *American Journal of Psychotherapy* Renato J. Almansi insists that promiscuity must always be "emotionally shallow ... fails to give complete satisfaction ... [and] represents a neurotic manifestation." And in the *Journal of Venereal Disease Information* John Stokes confesses that he has grave fears that ridding the world of venereal disease will lead to "a world of accepted, universalized, safeguarded promiscuity." Some contend, says Dr. Stokes, that promiscuity is not to be accepted; to which contention, he affirms, "I say for myself, unhesitatingly, it should not be. ..." To find more distinctly anti-promiscuous attitudes than these would, naturally, be difficult.

It can hardly be doubted, therefore, that the official, conventional American attitude toward promiscuity, as expressed in contemporary mass media, is rabidly antagonistic. Any sex activity, by male or female, young or old, single or married, that is not strictly monogamous tends to be viewed as constituting rank promiscuity—and that, brother, is bad.

At the same time, the anti-promiscuity forces do not quite monopolize the field of American public writing; and pro-promiscuous attitudes tend to keep coming in, at least through the back door. Thus in a *Private Detective* story Our Hero casually informs us that "Jerry took Lorraine inside the salon and his blond girl came over to tell me I might give her a chance to keep her warm. She made a cozy armful all right." Then, a moment later, with a different girl, he tells us: "As soon as he was out of sight, I went over and picked her up bodily. She was nice to pick up, the way she was, soft and fragrant and warm."

The obvious tendency of modern romantic novels to play up the enjoyable promiscuity of their heroes and heroines is satirized in this note in *Touchstone*: "Then there's the great grandfather of Mudfence Q. Mudfence, who survived the war after having four horses and six nurses shot out from under him."

Pro-promiscuous attitudes are presented in several Broadway productions: notably in *Kiss Me, Kate*, where the hero, singing Cole Porter's "Where Is the Life That Late I Led?" enthusiastically thumbs through his address book and reels off girl after girl with whom he has relished carnal delights.

In a popular song, which praises the charms of Katrina, we are told that, despite the fact that said Katrina is a little coquette who will kiss and then run, one cannot resist losing one's heart to her.

As for the gag writers, they supply us with these items. From *Joke Parade*: "Mary: John dear, are you sure you love me? John: Why, of course, my darling. Let me tell you, you're one in a hundred." From *Good Humor*: " 'Last evening sir, I distinctly saw my daughter sitting in your lap. What explanation have you to make?' 'I got there early, sir, before the others.' "

Once again, then, we find an American sex practice—this time, promiscuity—which is overviolently condemned on the one hand, and then, on the other hand, blithely, matter-of-factly, or jocularly accepted. This ultra-ambivalent attitude toward promiscuous individuals is perhaps best exemplified in a statement which one of Nelson Algren's characters sees written on the wall of a Chicago jail: "Girls who would and girls who wouldn't. If they did they were no good and if they didn't what good were they?"

This view leads logically to the common contradictory attitude of young American males that (a) promiscuity is wrong, because a fellow should have some real feeling for the girl with whom he has sex relations; and (b) any fellow who has very limited sex experiences isn't really a man and had better pretend to a wider than actual knowledge if he is to gain and keep the respect of other fellows.

The detailed facts of sexual promiscuity in America are not at all clear at present; nor is it the purpose of this volume to survey them. From common observation, as well as from the studies of Kinsey and others, it is evident that many millions of Americans, at one time or another in their lives, engage in what millions of other Americans would doubtlessly deem promiscuous sexual behavior. It is also obvious that indubitable promiscuity—that is, sex acts performed in a non-discriminating and utterly casual manner—is also fairly prevalent among sizable segments of our population.

Not all contemporary American promiscuity can be laid at the door of anti-promiscuous attitudes, but part of it probably can be. Thus, overemphasizing monogamous sex affairs often would seem to make non-monogamous ones appear more novel, exciting, and adventurous. And banning promiscuity—like banning virtually any other sex act—sometimes puts a premium on getting away with it, and thereby gaining prestige by outwitting social codes and mores.

Less directly, it may be hypothesized that the general anti-sexual attitudes of which anti-promiscuous ones are representative create inner tensions and rigidities which encourage compulsive, neurotic outbursts on the part of many individuals which are likely to take ultra-varietist modes of expression. That is to say, whereas the average human being, if more freely allowed to give in to his sexual inclinations than he currently is permitted in our culture, might conceivably practice a mild form of sexual varietism, this same person, when refused any multiple sex outlets whatever, may acquire compulsive and extreme varietist desires. These desires, in turn, may induce him actually to practice a greater degree of promiscuity than, in a more permissive environment, he would spontaneously practice; or else, if he refuses overtly to give in to these desires, they may unconsciously overwhelm him and express themselves in numerous symbolic-neurotic aberrancies, such as an inability to stick to one job for any length of time, general loss of frustration tolerance, or a deep, unconscious hatred of an inamorata or spouse with whom he overtly has "satisfactory" monogamic relations.

Orthodox psychoanalysts are fond of tracing Don Juanism to latent homosexuality on the part of the Don Juans and their consequent compensatory overly heterosexual drives. This may well be true in the case of some unusually promiscuous males. The chances are, however, that the majority of notorious Don Juans are no more latently homosexual than other males but that many of them have, as a result of overrepressive attitudes toward sexual varietism in our culture, and because of general feelings of inadequacy on their own part, compulsively overreacted to inner sex and other tensions and become insatiable, ego-aggrandizing collectors of women's hearts and parts.

Viewing the matter broadly, it may be assumed that men and women either do not have fundamental varietist sexual needs or they do. If they do not have them, then anti-promiscuous attitudes, such as those which now are predominant in our literature, are superfluous and meaningless. If, however, human beings are basically promiscuous, then the type of anti-promiscuous attitudes which are now volubly expressed in our mass media are usually so rigid and unrealistic as to invite (a) failure to convince anyone; (b) the outcropping of balancing, contradictory attitudes on promiscuity; (c) the actual flouting of the anti-promiscuous tenets in modern sex living; and (d) the flourishing of deep-seated neurotic conflicts, guilt feelings, and even pro-promiscuous compulsions. The whole situation, in sum, is as confused, muddled, and unhealthy as—well, as almost every other sex situation in our society presently seems to be.

Attitudes Toward Promiscuity in the 1960's
In the course of the study of sex attitudes in the 1950's that was

made for the first edition of this book, it was found that our mass media included fairly many references to promiscuity and that these were preponderantly conservative. In the course of the follow-up study of sex attitudes in the 1960's, it was found that there still are a good number of expressed attitudes to promiscuity but that the majority tend to be liberal. Only the women's magazines, as usual, come out quite consistently against promiscuity; while the best-selling fiction works and the men's magazines are more often than not found to be distinctly in favor of promicuous sex relations.

On the negative side, we find the usual clear-cut condemnations of sexual promiscuity in a variety of different sources. In the introduction to the new uncensored edition of *Lady Chatterley's Lover*, D. H. Lawrence is quoted as saying, "God forbid that I should be taken as urging loose sex activity." In the movie, *The Fugitive Kind*, the highly-sexed Carol is ordered by the Sheriff and paid by her brother to stay out of the county because of her promiscuous affairs. In a *Real Confessions* article, a horrified look is taken at the "sex rampages," the "sex clubs," and the divorcing of "sex from any spiritual or love feelings" by many modern teenagers.

In Ruark's novel, *Poor No More*, Craig Price's best friend, Jimmy Wilbur, excoriates him severely because "your daughter Carol is a bum, like her mother is a tramp. And I blame you." Vance Packard tells us, in *The Status Seekers*, that "the most-sought girl for Cornerville boys to date casually, from a prestige standpoint, is what they call a 'one-man lay.' She is faithful for the time being, Preferably she should be as non-Italian looking as possible. The 'real McCoy' is a blonde of 'old Puritan stock.' Rated below the one-man lay in desirability are, in order, (1) the promiscuous girl, (2) the prostitute." The only solution for the sex problem of modern man, Harry Golden insists in *For Two Cents Plain*, is "not in one million years, through promiscuity" but only through a man's being thoroughly convinced by a single woman that he is indeed "all right."

So go the negative appraisals of sexual promiscuity in the 1960's. On the more positive side, frank espousals and endorsements of loose sex behavior are more frequent, particularly in the men's magazines. An article in *Revels* exults in the fact that in today's West Berlin a man can get any sex partner he wants by merely asking almost any woman on the street to go with him. In New York City, a *Man's Conquest* article informs us, "Not long ago, a gang of 50 girls and 50 boys were interrupted by police in the middle of a mass orgy. 'What the hell else is there in life?' was the reply one Stuyvesant High School youngster snapped."

Joy magazine features an article on the newer International Playgirls, who are promiscuously fornicating throughout Europe and

America; and the article concludes: "It might be fun, at that, to meet one some time." *Candid* includes a photo essay by the photographer, Ed Van Der Elsken, who, the magazine tells us, "spent over a year living with the left banks exiles watching their disordered lives, their impetuous quest for freedom to love and live in an encroachable paradise. His heroine, Anne, is poetically typical of the forlorn girl of the streets who sleeps in any pallet."

Man's Magazine includes the story of Monk Wallace, at whom the girls of the town of Broome "threw themselves with little trills of delight, kicking and gouging in the competition to attract him. He pushed them aside and whistled for his friends. 'Take your pick, boys. The girls are on Monk tonight.' It was a carnival of debauchery." *Harem* features an article on the Todas of Tibet, which describes in detail some of their sex orgies and then concludes: "Indolent, lazy, and sexually promiscuous they certainly are, and perhaps it is true that they have not progressed in any way for centuries. But what do we mean by progress? If we mean the attainment of a life of perfect contentment, then the Todas are far more progressive than any of us in the so-called civilized Western world."

As for the best-selling novels of the 1960's, they carry the delights-of-promiscuity theme even further, at times, than do the men's magazines. In *The Cave*, Robert Penn Warren zestfully gives a picture of what is happening sexually when a group of men and women get together to wait for a trapped man to be dug out of a deep cave. Says one of Warren's characters in the novel: "I went down in the woods a-ways, dark as the inside of a widow woman's best black silk bombazine bustle, and you could hear the brush crashing where they fell. I tell you, down yonder there is fraternizing amongst strangers. There is clap-swapping amongst the non-introduced. It is damned near like cordwood, the way they are stacked. . . . But not much harm going to be done."

In *The War Lover*, John Hersey indicates how Captain Marrow is so delightfully promiscuous that he will even take after an ugly girl who was "but for great bosoms attached to her like a mail carrier's endless burden surely a man. She was bound to be a man in disguise. Yet Marrow flirted with her as if his life depended on her charms. After a while he came over to me and confidentially said, 'You never can tell about those ugly ones. Sometimes they're hot as a pancake.'"

In James Michener's *Hawaii*, Captain Rafer Hoxworth tells his young grandson, Whip: "'Whip, you've tasted Chinese girls and Spaniards. There are a thousand more to sample. Try 'em all. That's the one thing you'll do in life that you'll never regret.'" And, true to this teaching, young Whip "enjoyed the wild companionship of strange women in most of the world's major ports. His entire earnings for seven years had been spent freely on these women and he regretted not a penny of his loss."

In Allen Drury's *Advise and Consent*, we are given this sympathetic portrait of the promiscuous young Seab Cooley: "At first in desperation but then in a more relaxed and pragmatic fashion, he turned to the easy sex of the town, and for a time that became the surest road back to sanity; he never regretted it or gave it a second thought, for he perceived instinctively that he needed it, indeed had to have it if he was to regain balance, and so went about it without compunction and without worry, violently though it flew in the face of his upbringing and earlier character."

In *Poor No More*, Robert Ruark has Craig Price's valet, Jazzbo, snickering with delight over his success in getting the Harlem girls to flip over him and the big Rolls-Royce he chauffeurs. " 'I thinks maybe us better buy us one of dem little foreign cars so's I knows whether de gals courtin' de car or me.' He chuckled. 'Man, it shootin' fish, jes' plain shootin' fish. How your huntin' comin' along, Boss?' "

In *On the Road*, Jack Kerouac lustfully reports: "And Dean told Carlo of unknown people in the West like Tommy Snark, the clubfooted poolhall rotation shark and cardplayer and queer saint. He told him of Roy Johnson, Big Ed Dunkel, his boyhood buddies, his street buddies, his unnumerable girls and sex-parties and pornographic pictures, his heroes, heroines, adventures."

Other sources, too, include pro-promiscuous attitudes. In the film *Can-Can*, Judge Philippe Forrestier proposes to the patently loosely-living Simone, who protests that he cannot possibly love a lascivious dance hall girl such as she is. Whereupon this delectable dialogue ensues:

Philippe: Are you a liar? Are you cheap? Are you a thief?
Simone: No.
Philippe: Then you're respectable. And decent. You're as good as anyone on earth and better than most, and I'll never let you forget it.

In *Newsweek*, in an article reviewing Errol Flynn's book, *My Wicked, Wicked Ways*, it is noted that "he carried on with women of varied races and came to the conclusion that the most satisfactory liaison was the one of least duration."

In the humorous magazine, *Jest*, we find this squib: "Are you a man of settled habits?" "I certainly am! I've settled down to a constant round of drinking, smoking, wenching, and clenching!"

When any group of publications and other means of mass communication is filled with pros and cons, favorable and unfavorable attitudes toward a mode of sex behavior such as promiscuity, it is inevitable that some sources will include statements that are, at one and the same time, for and against this kind of behavior. So it is in the public presenations of the 1960's. In the novel *Advise and Consent*, for example, the junior Senator from Iowa says, with a rather rueful grin, to the senior Senator from Utah: " 'I don't know. I was thinking as I came through own on my way out, and do you know, it's getting so I can't travel en blocks in Washington without passing three places where I've made love. It's a hell of a depressing thing when a town gets all filled up with memories of your one-night stands. I think I'll move out.' " Here, obviously, the junior Senator from Iowa is saying (a) I had one hell of a good time enjoying myself with one-night stands but (b) it's really wrong to go through life like this and I shouldn't have been so promiscuous.

Coronet, similarly, reprints from the American Association *Journal* the joke about the man who asks a very attractive tennis star about her training program for future tournaments. "She: I'm going to have to practice a lot. I need to improve my form and speed. He: If your form improves, you're going to need all the speed you can muster!"

Here again, the joke is saying (a) sexual promiscuity is such an enjoyable relationship that virtually every male who spies a very attractive girl will tend to try to get her to bed and (b) since promiscuity is an evil thing, especially for the girl involved in promiscuous affairs, any female who is propositioned had better learn to run like the devil.

In sum: the attitudinal situation in regard to sexual promiscuity, as revealed in American mass media of the 1960's, is somewhat more liberal but still almost as confused, muddled, and unhealthy as it was found to be in the 1950's.

CHAPTER 4

Prostitution

The official American attitude toward prostitution is unequivocally negative, since prostitutes and their accomplices, in every state of the Union, are arrestable, finable, and jailable. The World Almanac reports that some nine thousand annual arrests are made for prostitution and commercialized vice, including about fifty-five hundred women and thirty-six hundred men. And, according to the vice exposés by *Pace* magazine and other periodicals, it would appear that many, many times this number of arrests for prostitution would be made were not millions of dollars spent every year to purchase police protection.

Unofficially, American attitudes toward prostitution are often just as unfavorable as are legal prescriptions. In speaking of Mary Magdalen, for example, such widely different spokesmen as the Reverend Dr. W. Perry Crouch, Fulton Oursler, and Sholem Asch continually refer to her prostitution as "sinful" and "polluted." In radically differing novels like *Cry, the Beloved Country* and *The Woman of Rome*, exactly the same term—"bad woman"—is used to describe characters who are harlots. In the former novel the prostitute thus characterizes herself; while in the latter, a lying scoundrel, who becomes engaged to the heroine in order to seduce her (when he is already, in fact, married), refuses to let her associate with a kindly whore because "my fiancée must have nothing to do with bad women"!

An honest trollop, indeed, is in such disrepute in modern America that the term *prostitute* is continually used in an opprobrious way to designate any woman who has committed almost any atrocious (sexual or non-sexual) act. Thus in the film version of *All the King's Men*, Jack Burden, right-hand man to the dictatorial Willie Stark, wishing to hurt his former fiancée, Ann, as deeply as possible for her alliance with Willie (which she has obviously entered on a loving, non-prostitutional basis), bitterly comments: "There's no God but Willie Stark; I'm his prophet and you're his—!"

Again, in *Queen New Orleans*, Hartnett Kane tells the presumably true story of a member of the floor committee at an exclusive Mardi Gras affair who, in calling out the names of those present to announce their dances with members of the masked krewe, sportively called out the names of some famed New Orleans jades. "Later," reports Kane, "he was dropped by the krewe, to be restored to grace only after a season of penance."

In addition, we may note that prostitution is considered so scurrilous a trade by modern Americans that when the film, *Bicycle Thief*, included a mild-mannered scene of some *filles de joie* having Sunday-morning breakfast in a brothel, scores of church and other organizations immediately cried shame and induced the Motion Picture Association of America to ban the film as long as this scene was retained.

Obviously, therefore, the hard-working whore is persona non grata to a vast segment of the American public.

Curiously enough, however, disguised or undercover prostitution seems to be an American custom that is widely and quite approvingly accepted. An undercover harlot normally operates in one or both of two main ways: (1.) She selects as sex partners males who, while rarely directly giving her cash rewards, continually treat her to shows, night clubs, dinners, jewelry, fur coats, and what not. (2.) She marries, and continually beds with a man for whom she has little love or sex feeling but who is able to support her in a fairly comfortable style of life.

Undercover harlotry is well exemplified in two scenes from Amercan stage successes. In Giraudoux's *Madwoman of Chaillot* the Countess asks the Ragpicker, who is doing a take-off on a millionaire: "So you think there are no women with morals?" Says he: "I mix morals with mink—delicious combination. I drip pearls into protests. I adorn resistance with rubies. My touch is jeweled; my smile, a motorcar. What woman can withstand me? I lift my little finger—and do they fall? Like leaves in autumn—like tin cans from a second-story window."

In Garson Kanin's *Born Yesterday*, Billie, mistress of a junk tycoon, explains the secret of her power: "I got everything I want. Two mink coats. Everything. If there's somethin' I want, I ask. And if he don't come across—I don't come across. If you know what I mean."

One of the sharpest ironies of modern American life is that the undercover prostitute is rarely recognized for what she is. But her less shrewd sister, whose only recompense for copulating is her frank enjoyment of it, and who would not think of submitting sexually to a man, for any price, whose bed company she does not relish, is often labeled a whore. At the same time, the undercover strumpet (who more often than not is precisely the one who does this labeling) is deemed to be a sharp operator or an eminently respectable woman.

The good humor and envy with which the American public observes undercover prostitution is exemplified in an epidemic of cartoons dealing with this theme. Thus Peter Arno, in *Sizzling Platter*, depicts a pulse-raising blonde saying to an old man as he places an expensive necklace around her throat: "You certainly know my Achilles' heel, Mr. Benson." Gregory d'Alessio, in *Hello Buddies*, shows us two young misses, having cocktails, being observed by two males at another table. Says one miss to the other: "I haven't any money either . . . will you wink or shall I?" Hoff, in a national men's magazine, has a girl coming home to her hardworking mother, flashing an enormous diamond-studded bracelet on her arm and saying: "I'm afraid I'm going to have to tell you a white lie, Mama." Michael Berry, in *1,000 Jokes*, potrays an old duffer at the race track saying to a pert young thing who, behind his back, is scooting away as fast as she can, that even if he has lost all his money, he still has her.

Similarly, in musical comedies such as *Kiss Me, Kate*, and especially *Gentlemen Prefer Blondes*, the advantages of getting Cadillacs, diamonds, and other little knickknacks in exchange for sexual favors rendered are enthusiastically extolled. As Lorelei Lee remarks to her gift-bearing paramour: "You're just wonderful. You never forget a single holiday!"

Clearly: be an undercover trollop and the world laughs with you; be an honest whore and you weep alone.

Not always, however. Prostitution is so matter-of-factly accepted in many contemporary writings as to show unmistakably that by no means are all Americans opposed to it. In two leading war films, *Sands of Iwo Jima* and *Battleground*, and one popular stage play, *Mister Roberts*, the unmitigated relish of American soldiers and sailors for consorting with harlots is brashly depicted. In two best-selling novels, *The Woman of Rome* and *Mudlark*, the indubitable advantages of being a prostitute are zestfully and minutely detailed.

American humor also sometimes smiles at whoring, as in the anecdote from *Laugh Book* about the girl who, having returned to the farm after living in Hollywood, and finding her father saddled with a thirteen-thousand-dollar mortage, offers to pay it off. "Her father became quite surprised and asked if she had been a good girl while away from home. She replied, 'Father, to make thirteen thousand dollars in Hollywood a girl *has* to be good.' "

In real life, as well, evidences are found of Americans accepting prostitution. The staid New York *Times*, for example, in a *Sunday Magazine* feature, indicates that New Yorkers take Fifty-second Street's many prostitutes for granted. And *Pace* magazine tells us that when a madam, who was charged with operating Hollywood's most notorious bagnio, was brought before the grand jury probing into police-vice connections, she was cheered by "whistling, clamoring crowds."

We may note, in addition, the usual ambivalence which is shown in American attitudes toward prostitution by publications condemning it, on the one hand, but using it for reader bait on the other. Thus the New York *Post* takes the sorry tale of a minister who was forced to aid his wife to prostitute herself in order to support themselves and their three children on meager church pay, and headlines it: "MINISTER STOOD GUARD AS WIFE USED FAMILY AUTO FOR BROTHEL." *Picture Show* magazine, in an article entitled, "Love on Sin Street," ostensibly written to warn men against prostitutes, actually glamorizes the world's oldest profession. And several popular novels and plays (e.g., *One on the House and Detective Story*) use whores or whore houses in a sensational way to arouse their readers' interest.

A notable example of ambivalent American attitudes toward prostitution may be found in the fictionalized account of Lincoln's youth, *Abe Lincoln of Pigeon Creek*. In this novel the author implies on page 120 that prostitutes are no better than hardened criminals; and, on page 203, that they are good enough to serve Lincoln as a possible source of surcease from his sorrows after he has lost one of his girl friends.

Modern Americans, then, according to the views expressed and implied in their publications and dramatic productions, seem to believe:

That all prostitutes are sinners, and vice versa.

That women who enjoy men for their own sake are whores, and those who enjoy them only for their gifts, entertainments, and weekly pay checks are not.

That men have a better time in brothels than anywhere else, and that all brothels should be promptly closed.

That nothing raises newspaper and magazine circulation like a good exposure of whoring, and that films with mild references to a bagnio should be censored.

That vice is not nice—and is.

Attitudes Toward Prostitution in the 1960's

It was found, in the course of the study made for the original edition of this book, that American mass media included relatively many expressed and implied attitudes toward prostitution and that these attitudes were fairly evenly divided on the liberal and conservative sides. In the follow-up study of views on prostitution in the 1960's, a good many more references were discovered than were turned up in the previous decade; and these were overwhelmingly in favor of prostitution.

The main reason for this increase in both the number and liberality of the allusions to harlotry was clearly the significant changes that had taken place in the men's magazines between 1950 and 1960. Whereas there had been many of these publications in the earlier period and they had been reasonably bold and permissive in the sex views expressed in them, by the time the 1960's arrived these men's magazines had mushroomed in numbers and they were printing highly spiced words and pictures that would never have been permitted ten years previously. Even though many of the boldest of these periodicals were not included in the present study, since they had been banned from the newsstands in New York City where the study was made, those that were available were still salacious enough to include scores of features which went out of their way to emphasize the thrills and pleasures of prostitution.

Thus, in a single month's issues of men's magazines that were surveyed, nonfiction articles on prostitution were found in *Cavalcade*, *Man's Conquest*, *Man's Magazine*, *Confidential*, *Candid*, *Climax*, *Confidential Tattler*, *Zest*, *Swank*, *Men's Digest*, and *Twenty-One*. During the same period, articles on prostitution were also found in *Life*, *Sexology*, and the *New York Times*.

Considering that relatively little prostitution now actually exists in the United States (because of the competition of the "amateurs" whom the professional girls are always complaining about), it is amazing to what lengths some of these magazines go to dig up what seems to be, for them, at least one standard story per issue on harlots or call girls. Mexico, the Middle East, the Barbary Coast of the 1890's, 18th-century France—apparently no place is too far and no time too distant to be employed by these magazines as the focus point for a highly revelatory, sizzlingly orgiastic article on the world's oldest profession. Obviously, their readers demand this kind of material; and they are more than willing to cater to these demands.

In addition to the non-fictional stories on prostitution current in modern mass media, there are a considerable number of fictional variations on the same whoring theme. Thus, tales about trollops or courtesans were found in *Mystery Digest*, *Hi-Life*, *Ace*, *Bare*, *Twenty-One*, *Joy*, *True*, *Men's Digest*, *Swank*, *The Dude*, and *Esquire*. Oh, yes: also in the woman's magazine, *Real Secrets*.

Virtually all these articles and stories on prostitution baldly state or slyly imply that harlotry is one of the finest imaginable institutions and that males could hardly get along very happily in life without its beneficent administrations. Thus, in a *Mystery Digest* story, we are told that Miss Claire D'Amour was so beautiful that "there wasn't a man in the world who wouldn't have given a fortune to spend one evening with her." In a *Swank* article, the author chop-lickingly tells about the delights of spending a night in a $2,000 a night brothel on the French Riviera. "Damned good," he relates. "I'll never forget it. It had been terrific—from start to finish." Only, he laments, it's now going to be tough going through life just being his ordinary dull self "and wishing that I could really be Abdul, the son of Sheik Ismail [his host at the bordello], wishing that I had a million bucks and knowing where I'd spend an awful large chunk of it."

In a story in *Bare*, a wife saves her house money for a year to get her husband a wonderful present—a date with a call girl; and he is most thankful and appreciative after he enjoys her present. In a *Twenty-One* article, we read a New York plainclothesman's description of how a call girl makes herself desirable to her customer:

" 'Fifteen bucks—' were her first words. When I nodded in agreement, she kissed me long and lingeringly on the mouth. Then, without conversation, she sat down on the bed and proceeded to undress. All her movements were practiced. Undressing was a ritual to excite. She removed a dress and red silk slip. Another kiss followed. The transparent bra came off, the red net panties. . . . The idea of all this being, obviously, to bring the man to a state of such excitation by the time she was completely naked, that the sex act would be im-

64

mediately consummated. In this way, such girls are able to keep as many as ten appointments a night."

So much for the light reading material of the magazines. Included among the somewhat more serious reading material of some of the best-selling novels of the 1960's are equally favorable attitudes toward prostitution. For example:

From John Hersey's *The War Lover*: "We walked along Bond Street, where we'd heard there were some French ones, and soon a pair of babes stepped out of the shadows, and Max had one of those little pencil flashlights, he was a systematic bastard, maybe he'd brought it from the States for this purpose, and he shined it in their faces, and they were crusty old dreadnoughts, and we sniffed and walked on. But we'd had a lot of brandy; libido lived where judgment had vacated. After a few steps, Max said, 'Oh, well, they prolly need the money.' So we went back, and they were Flo and Rose."

From Vladimir Nabokov's *Lolita*: "I let myself go with her more completely than I had with any young lady before, and my last vision that night of long-lashed Monique is touched up with a gaiety that I find seldom associated with any event in my humiliating, sordid, taciturn love life. She looked tremendously pleased with the bonus of fifty I gave her as she trotted out into the April night drizzle with Humbert Humbert lumbering in her narrow wake."

From Jack Kerouac's *On the Road*: "As in a dream, to the din and roar of more loudspeakers inside, we made the bed bounce a half hour.... My girl charged 30 pesos, or about three dollars and a half, and begged for an extra 10 pesos and gave a long story about something. I didn't know the value of Mexican money; for all I knew I had a million pesos. I threw money at her."

Popular jokes of the 1960's were, as usual, found to be another form of public dissemination which often contained pro-prostitutional attitudes. Witness these examples:

From *Ace*: "One imaginative shoe manufacturer, according to the gossip in his trade, will put out a line of orthopedic shoes for streetwalkers."

From *Scamp*: "According to a publicity release that never got out, a famous Hollywood actress last year made four pictures, two directors and two producers."

From *Hi-Life*: "Madame of a brothel to her girls: Remember girls, the game isn't over until the last man is out."

From *Rapture*: "The best way to approach a woman with a past is with a present."

From *1,000 Jokes*: "There's many a girl with an expensive wardrobe who started out with just a little slip."

From *Nugget*: "One call girl to another: Sondra's status seeking will be the end of her. Whoever heard of a call girl with an unlisted number?"

From *Comedy*: "Employer (to pretty applicant for a job): What wages did you get in your last place? Girl: I received fifty dollars a week. Employer: We'll pay you that with pleasure. Girl: Oh, with pleasure it will be seventy-five dollars a week!"

Even though the present follow-up study showed considerably more pro- than anti-prostitutional attitudes existing in our mass media in the 1960's, a number of distinctly negative attitudes were also expectably present. In the film, *Happy Anniversary*, a mother and grandmother of a teenage daughter are shocked when she uses the word *prostitute* to describe a loose woman. An Albany judge, the *New York Post* tells us, threw out a police court conviction against a whore in order to spare the embarrassment of the man who otherwise would have had to testify against her in court. In a *Mystery Digest* story, the narrator moralizes: "How can a man stoop so low and visit a bordello? ... This disgraceful situation will go on forever, I suppose, as long as there are men who are haunted by the mad passion of sick brains. Proprietors of these houses who take advantage of the demand are worse than the owners of slaves."

When the writer of a *Secrets* tale discovers that her roommate is accepting money for sex favors, she exclaims to herself: "Oh, God, what kind of a monster was she?" And she deals this way with the horrible offender: " 'You filthy creature!' I screamed. 'You animal!' Lucy winced. I was savagely glad my words had hurt her."

Some of the same novels which we saw, a few pages back, including quite favorable attitudes toward prostitution also take a distinctly negative view of harlotry as well. In Ruark's *Poor No More*, when the beautiful secretary, Libby, is accused of being a company pimp and whore because she is having an affair with her boss, Craig Price, with whom she is madly in love, she is horrified and is sure that she will never be able to live this accusation down. In Kerouac's *On the Road*, the greatest whoremaster, fornicator, and adulterer of all the characters in the book, Dean, suspects one of his girl friends of being a prostitute, and he keeps compulsively following her around, to see whether his awful suspicion is true.

In the more conservative novel, Vale's *Thirteenth Apostle*, Webb hates himself so much for his misdeeds that he deliberately seeks out a brothel. "He stumbled ahead, insanely choosing among the painted faces, seeking the one who would make him despise himself the most."

Double-dyed hypocritical attitudes toward prostitution, where there is both an accepting and a condemning attitude toward it, are also still existent in our mass media. In Nevada, a *Man's Magazine* article relates, prostitution is openly practiced; and even though it is not considered the nicest profession in the world, it "even enjoys a certain social acceptance. ... The general civic attitude—and rarely does anyone talk about the houses—is live and let live. Many house owners, in fact, belong to the local Chamber of Commerce. And, a promotion brochure called 'Vacation Guide to Nevada' points out, the people of the state display 'an urgent lack of concern for the morals, backgrounds or affairs' of others."

In a story in *The Dude*, a girl calmly saves up eighty-five thousand dollars (tax free) by being a high-class whore in order to pay her way to stardom in a film production. She has no particular guilt about earning the money this way; but in telling her adventure to the narrator of the story she says: " 'And nobody has to know it but you and me.' I smiled. 'Don't you worry, baby, Nobody's going to know.' She looked relieved."

Harry Golden, talking about the closing of the brothels in New York City after World War I writes: "The brothel prostitute was plagued with the amateur competition which eventually destroyed her profession. The amateur began to call it 'dating' and she was grossly insulted if you offered her cash. Instead, she accepted the equivalent in the form of a present. This helped her maintain the amateur standing and remove the stigma. The Puritan strain in our culture hounded the professional out of the brothel and forced her to move into an apartment next door, where she quickly became the best tenant. She gave the janitor a dollar every day. You gave him a dollar at Christmas time. But we all felt better when we closed up the red-light district and created for ourselves the illusion that the whole thing doesn't exist."

True magazine prints a story about a call girl who thought that one of her customers had given her a Mexican silver dollar, but discovered that it was really some sort of medal, not worth anything. Instead of being angry, she was delighted. " 'I'll be damned,' she laughed. I done it for lots of things, but this is the first time I ever got a MEDAL for it!' "

As noted, then, in the original edition of this book, contemporary American views on prostitution are still consistently inconsistent. If anything, they have become somewhat more liberalized during the last decade. Vice has become a little nicer. But, no matter how you slice it, it's still considered to be plenty wicked.

CHAPTER 5

Venereal Disease

Everyone, of course, is against venereal diseases, but the interesting question is: Who is against being against them? And the surprising answer is: Quite a few Americans.

Many religionists, for example, are quite opposed to anti-venereal disease education because it encourages men and women to have extramarital sex relations and because it will inevitably lead to compulsory health examinations—which in turn may lead to forbidding diseased persons to marry and thus abet fornication. The attitude of these religionists is, in other words, that it is far better for people to have syphilis or gonorrhea than to live quite healthfully in "sin."

Nor are religionists alone in this attitude, since a good many of the social-hygiene people in both America and England have for many years been more concerned with preventing the spread of sin than of syphilis and have consistently disfavored attempts by organizations like the American armed forces to take effective measures—especially the issuing of condoms to soldiers, sailors, and marines—which would enable people to "sin" freely without suffering the "natural" consequences of their acts. Regarding this concept of natural punishment for sexual iniquity, we may quote from a story in *I Confess* magazine. In this story a man and woman love each other and have sex relations in spite of the fact that the woman is still married to a hopelessly crippled and impotent husband. When it appears that they both may have syphilis she says to her lover: "This is our punishment, Dick. Yours and mine. God has visited this plague upon us for the terrible sin we committed."

This same type of attitude toward the ridding of the world of syphilis and gonorrhea is, surprisingly enough, shown in a statement of Dr. John F. Stokes, one of America's leading syphilologists, in the *Journal of Venereal Disease Information*. Says Dr. Stokes: "Were venereal diseases wiped out . . . the accomplishment would have heavy costs in the social, moral, and material life of man. . . . It is a reasonable question, whether by eliminating disease, without commensurate attention to the development of human idealism, self-control, and responsibility in the sexual life, we are not bringing mankind to its fall instead of its fulfillment." In other words, Dr. Stokes fears that a syphilis-free world will be a sexually lighthearted one: which, of course, would be horrible to behold.

Toward venereal disease publicity the American public has also traditionally taken a super-scared and pussyfooting attitude, but this has recently been somewhat modified. Thus *Newsweek* blithely prints an account of the effective treatment of syphilis by a new antibiotic—an account that just a decade or so ago would never have been published in any leading American magazine. The same story in *I Confess* referred to above also very frankly and casually handles the medical treatment of syphilis. At the same time, however, the hero of this story goes to a quack to be treated because he is too ashamed to let his own doctor know that he is afflicted with syphilis; and the heroine commits suicide when she learns that she may be venereally infected.

In another popular modern tale, the best-selling novel, *Earth Abides*, one of the characters is utterly despised by the others because "he's rotten inside as a ten-day fish. Diseases, Cupid's diseases, I mean. Hell, he's got all of them there are!"

On the other hand, in the play version of *Mister Roberts*, venereal disease is handled in a casual, humorous manner—with obvious undertones. Thus when the ship's doctor sees the men going for their first shore leave in many months, he says that he is going to give them "little favors from the Doc. I'm going to put one in each man's hand, and when he wakes up he'll find pinned to his shirt full instructions for its use. I think it'll save me a lot of work later on."

A little later on in the same play, when Doc asks Mr. Roberts how one of the other officers could possibly obtain some fulminate of mercury aboard the ship, Roberts replies: "I don't know. He's pretty resourceful. Where did he get clap last year?"

Once again, in Mary Lasswell's popular novel, *One on the House*, we find this exchange of dialogue: " 'God loves the American sailor because his heart is pure,' Miss Tinkham said. 'Even if it ain't always true of his blood stream!' Mrs. Feeley said."

From these few open references to venereal disease—which were all that could be found in the media studied—it can be seen that the basic American attitudes toward it run quite closely to those about other modes of sex behavior. That is to say, on the one hand, venereal disease is considered to be so awful that anyone who is inflicted with it may well refuse to let his family doctor know about it, or may commit suicide, or may stoically accept it as punishment of his sins. On the other hand, venereal disease is considered to be commonplace, a laughing matter, and an excellent excuse for salacious comment.

In the face of these conflicting attitudes, great hordes of Americans continue to suffer and die from venereal diseases. According to the *Journal of Venereal Disease Information*, some sixty-nine thousand cases of syphilis and seventy-seven thousand cases of gonorrhea are still reported every three months in America. As Walter Clarke editorially states in the *Journal of Social Hygiene*: "In 1950 syphilis and gonorrhea, though robbed of much of their killing and crippling power, still rank first among serious communicable diseases in our country."

Obviously, then, the notion that *not* effectively attacking the venereal disease problem will deter people from engaging in illicit sex unions is convincingly demonstrated to be pitifully erroneous. Indeed, the pussyfooters of anti-venereal disease action not only effectively abet continued high rates of gonorrhea and syphilis in our country, but make the victims of these diseases doubly suffer: first, through the ravages of syphilis or gonorrhea; and second, through the victims' (conscious or unconscious) guilt about acquiring these diseases.

Actually, it would be medically simple to eradicate venereal diseases completely in a few years' time—merely by making it mandatory for all Americans to be examined annually and treated when evidences of syphilis or gonorrhea are found. But this is precisely what violent anti-sexualist lobbies try to prevent, and moves for a thoroughly realistic and ruthlessly logical medical attack on venereal disease are always promptly massacred. Thus, according to the *Journal of Social Hygiene*, the First Regional Conference of the International Union against Venereal Disease, held in New York City on October 23, 1949, passed strong resolutions against prostitution and specifically excoriated Italian brothels; but as far as tracing sources of venereal infection and promptly doing something about them was concerned, it voiced this impotent resolution: "It is understood that each government, by arrangements in accordance with its own national customs, can adopt such measures as it considers necessary to trace and treat all individuals, whoever they may be, found after medical examination to be infected and capable of transmitting infection."

In other words, this International Union against Venereal Disease, sparked by the views of the American delegates, deliberately shirked the responsibility of calling for mandatory examination and treatment of all potentially and actually diseased individuals and left proper venereal disease action to the sabotaging "national customs" of each member nation. As scientists, the delegates to the union's First Regional Conference obviously capitulated to the prim, negativistic sex *attitudes* of the people in their homelands—including, especially, the people of our own country.

When given the choice, then, between venereal disease and venereal ease, Americans officially take the former. Here, out of deep-lying fear of and guilt about sexuality, they grimly face the (wholly unnecessary) consequences of their sex acts.

Attitudes Toward Venereal Disease in the 1960's

In the study of American sex attitudes that was made in 1950 it was found that there were very few references to venereal disease published in our mass media and that these were preponderantly conservative. In the present follow-up study on 1960 attitudes, a considerably greater number of expressed and implied attitudes toward syphilis and gonorrhea have been revealed; and, as might be expected, these are still for the most part on the conservative side.

More references to venereal disease were turned up in the novels of the 1960's than in any other popular media. Thus, in Metalious' *Peyton Place*, Selena's mother keeps thinking and talking to herself about getting the clap from her husband. In Warren's *The Cave*, John Harrick confesses to his wife that when he ran off to Chattanooga for awhile he got drunk, lay around with whores in alleys, hotels, and whorehouses, and got the clap. And in Ruark's *Poor No More* there are several open references to venereal diseases, including this description of the time when Craig Price thinks that he has contracted gonorrhea:

"By God, they were right. Four days later he knew it. He had it. He had to have it. The thing his mother said had told him he had it. What the drunks said told him he had it. There was that itching, the burning, the discharge. And she had been such a wonderful girl, too. It couldn't be possible that Mary Frances had given him—you had to face the dirty word—the clap. The plain old clap. Not that sweetly held body, not that yearning face, not those lips which blotted out all thinking. Gonorrhea? Great God. Mary Frances. Clap? *Christ.*"

It is fairly obvious that references such as these to venereal disease are being used in contemporary fiction largely for shock appeal. Having by now employed almost every possible allusion to normal and abnormal sex activity, modern authors are running out of the usual stimulating material; so they are resorting to sex diseases, disorders, and anomalies in some instances. This is in accordance with the general literary trend of the last half century. Where detailed descriptions of normal intercourse would once give a highly sexualized flavor to a novel, this kind of material has now become almost boring to jaded readers; so that more unusual aspects of sexuality are being increasingly employed for lascivious intent.

Other references to venereal disease in 1960 publications, most of them conservative or objective, were found in such widely differing publications as *My Love Secret*, the *New York Times*, *Tomorrow's Man*, the *National Enquirer*, *Sexology*, and *Realife Guide*. Several more liberal references were also found. In Hersey's novel, *The War Lover*, a film on venereal disease is shown to the officers in a flying squadron and we are told that "Doc showed us a movie on how to catch a dose. We got cheering for the microbes, as if they were the Good Guys."

· In Robert Ruark's *Poor No More*, this entrancing dialogue takes place between Craig Price and Phillippe duFresne:

" 'Then you have never been to Paris?'

" 'No. I've never been anywhere. Is it nice?'

"Philippe rolled his eyes ecstatically. '*Magnifique*. But wonderful. The women—ahh. *Magnifique*. I caught the clap in Paris,' this with great pride.

" 'You caught the clap?'

" '*Alors, oui*. It was nothing. No worse than a bad cold. We say in Charleston a man is not a man until he has caught the clap, screwed a nigger, and gone with a woman who is having a monthly.' "

In a *Man's Magazine* story on prostitution in Nevada, we learn that "Disease is not a problem. The author talked to doctors who handle more than 80 per cent of the weekly examinations; many of them had never found an infected girl, except perhaps one applying for the first work-permit in Nevada. The incidence of venereal disease among girls on the job is less than one in 2,000 examinations. Even in these rare cases, the sanitary and prophylactic measures the girls employ on their customers are such that not one doctor had ever heard of a man who had contracted VD from a legal prostitute. Nor does the State Health Department know of a single proved case."

All told, it is fairly clear from these typical excerpts from mass media in the 1960's that although enthusiastic endorsement of venereal disease is hardly the rule and while acceptance of this unpleasant aspect of sex behavior is not likely ever to be overly favorable, mentions of the subject have increased and distinctly negative, moralistic attitudes in regard to syphilis and gonorrhea seem to have become ameliorated. Nothing too effective has yet been done to stamp out venereal diseases completely; but perhaps a little progress toward that eventual goal has been made in terms of a liberalizing of public attitudes.

CHAPTER 6

Kissing

Two items in *True Story* magazine nicely sum up the traditional American twentieth-century attitudes toward kissing. In the first item, a story, the sixteen-year-old heroine, Tibby, whose "mouth seemed afire with a new strange burning" when her young lover introduced her to the osculatory art, gets some advice from her mother: "If a boy tries to kiss you—or—or if you want to let him kiss you, then—*then*

72

you'd better stop seeing that boy right away. Do you understand, Tibby?" Not wanting to understand, Tibby rushes to her favorite schoolteacher, Miss Reynolds, and asks: "If a girl is sixteen and she wants a boy to kiss her, I mean wants it a lot, how bad is that?" "It isn't bad at all," Miss Reynolds reassures her. "It's perfectly natural, if she likes the boy."

In the very same issue of *True Story* a poll of American teenagers shows that "a very few boys, and almost no girls, approve kissing on the first date." But, the pollsters discreetly admit, "three quarters of all teenagers interviewed believe that steady couples have a right to indulge in mild love-making—kisses, embraces.... Almost no teenagers believe that steady couples should *never* kiss."

Also concurring in this cautious attitude toward kissing we find (a) a storyteller in *Love Novels* magazine, whose hero remarks to his girl friend: "Why, to a girl like you, a kiss should be a sacred thing"; (b) a *Seventeen* author, one of whose characters objects to her granddaughter's lips being touched in a kisslike fashion by her boy friend's fingers; (c) a *Ladies' Home Journal* writer who advises young males to wait at least till the third date to attempt to kiss a girl; (d) a New York *Journal American* columnist who points out that some teenagers abjure kissing games at parties because "they give a girl a bad reputation"; (e) the publishers of "America's favorite teen-ager" comic book, *Buzzy*, who on the front cover feature the horrendous shock of Suzie's father when he overhears her ask: "Would you like a kiss, Buzzy?" not realizing that she means (of course!) a candy kiss from a box she is offering him; and (f) the Kansas Public Health Service and the United States Public Health Service who (according to *Woman's Life* magazine) published a list of "Rules for Kissing" which started off: "1. If you must practice the art of kissing, do it on the quiet and do not tempt others."

That, presumably, makes it virtually unanimous. Kissing, today, is apparently a sport barely tolerated by conservative mores—and then only for lads and lassies who have shown at least some signs of marital proclivities.

One of the predictable effects of this semi-official ban on or delimitation of kissing is to endow osculatory practices with a super-romanticized aura that lifts them almost entirely from this earthly vale and wafts them to the most ethereal heights of sentimentality. The underlying philosophy behind this spiritualizing of labial grazing seems to be the notion that, since kissing is not of and by itself a healthy, recommendable practice, let's see what we can do to bind it intrinsically to a less suspect aspect of heterosexual relationships—e.g., romantic love. Encouraged by this notion, there seems to have developed a romantic entrapment of mutual lip-lapping which has saturated the literary productions of true confessor after true confessor, and innumerable sophisticated-enough-to-know-better tale tellers as well. We note in the literature, for example, statements of extravagant beliefs like these:

1. The kiss of your true lover, as you may recognize at first brush, is entirely different from that of him who does not truly adore you. ("But this kiss—this kiss was different. It had sun and moon and wind and flame in it—and a little dynamite, too."—*Intimate Romances*.)

2. The kiss of him who pretends to love you but really and truly does not is flat, tasteless, and easily recognized for its (non-) true worth. ("She looked up at Jeffry for a minute, wondering if his charm had diminished or if she was really seeing him for the first time. Then she reached up, took his coat lapels in her hands, and pulled his head down until his lips met hers. It was amazing! No thrills—no nothing."—*Gay Love Stories*. "When Larry kissed me. I felt none of that ecstasy that Brad's kisses gave me."—*I Loved*.)

3. Your truelove's kisses give you sexual feelings that no other's kisses could ever possibly convey. ("Oh, John darling ... Why does your kiss electrify me and fill me with a thrill never known before?"—*Revealing Love Stories*. "A divine warmth, unlike anything she had known before in her life, flooded her."—*Gay Love Stories*.)

4. Kissing someone who attracts you but for whom you do not cross-your-heart-and-hope-to-die care is entirely devoid of meaning and pleasure. ("If girls would always be duly cautious and thoughtful before letting a man kiss them, there wouldn't be so many meaningless kisses, life and love would be more romantic, and when a girl got kissed she'd really know why."—*Woman's Life*.)

5. Your truelove's kiss can always tell you more, in one single stroke, than a million million words could ever say. ("Sherry kissed her—a long, long kiss in which heart spoke to heart, crying out its need and the hopelessness of its love."—*Gay Love Stories*.)

6. One single kiss of your true, true love, even though two minutes ago you never knew of his existence, will undeniably tell you that you were born for each other. ("'So!' His blue eyes twinkled. 'I'm forward and impudent, am I?' 'Yes, you are!' The next instant he had tilted up her face and pressed her mouth firmly and definitely against his own. It was a kiss of black magic and unexpected shock. It changed her crazy heart into a zooming rocket ship that went whizzing away to nowhere, leaving her groping breathlessly in a sea of bright pink clouds."—*New Love Magazine*.)

7. Once you find your true beloved and let him know you are his, one perfect kiss will cement your love (marriage, family, and parenthood) forever. ("He kissed her, his mouth fiercely, savagely, covering

hers, putting his mark on her, branding her."—*New Love Magazine*. "Then he gave a schoolboyish whoop of exultation and swept her into his arms for a kiss that threatened to last forever. A getting-married kiss. A living-happily-forever-after kiss!"—*Gay Love Stories*.)

The foregoing attitudes toward kissing, and many more like them, are not, as you might expect, offered up for discussion or debate; they are given axiomatically. For who, indeed, could possibly doubt their truth?

Conservative anti-kissing mores, aside from inspiring super-romantic ideologies, have had at least two sequelae which their pure-minded promulgators probably never predicted. The first of these seems to be attributable to the fact that, precisely because kissing has been given some polite sanction as a restricted mode of premarital heterosexual experience (while "heavy necking" and more direct modes of sexual contact have been given no official sanction whatever), the kissing scenes in contemporary stories, novels, movies, and plays have tended to take on an element of orgiastic sexuality which puts some of the love play in the erotic classics almost to shame. The orgasm-like feelings and movements which modern lasses go through as their lipstick begins to smudge are, if we are to believe their fictional portrayers, so graphically experienced that one begins to wonder what more could possibly happen if (after all legal formalities had been duly complied with, of course) their lovers ever actually got them to bed.

Here, illustratively, are some choice magazine and novel passages in this connection:

From *Gay Love Stories*: "His mouth was hot and furious and passionate on hers. She almost swooned at the wonder of that kiss. She forgot all about why he was kissing her, and just gave him back his kiss with all the ardor of her loving nature."

From *Private Detective* magazine: "Gloria relaxed and offered her moist red lips. Jerry jammed his mouth down on the hot softness. An unbelievable thrill shot through him, leaving him tingling, at the contact. Then she pulled away, but the fire in her eyes and the uncontrolled gasping of breath indicated internal tumult."

From Edison Marshall's *Gypsy Sixpence*: "Then we were kissing in hunger and deep thirst, all else paled into eclipse. I did not doubt this was the first burst of her fountains. By the sudden freeing of their long, aching curb, they leaped like geysers."

From Alberto Moravia's *The Woman of Rome*: "Something cool and living pressed against my teeth and when I unclenched them I felt his tongue, that had caressed my ears so long with the sweetness of his words, now penetrating wordlessly into my mouth to reveal to me another sweetness I had never suspected. I did not know people could kiss in that way for so long, and I was soon breathless and half intoxicated. In the end, when we broke away from one another, I was obliged to lean back against the seat with my eyes closed and my mind hazy, as if I were going to faint."

From *Love Short Novels*, page 30: "He kissed her, and she kissed him back, with the little Christmas bells ringing a paean of ecstasy in her head." Page 44: "No kiss had ever been like this before. No kiss could ever be like it again. This was the ultimate, a tingling wonderful emotion that left Lorna dizzy. The air was bubbling like champagne." Page 59: "He drew her up so closely she couldn't possibly escape, and his lips came down like wings of flame against hers, holding them, burning them, while her breath was swept away and meteors spun in dizzy, flashing spirals in her heart." Page 71: "The kiss went on. It lost all gentleness, burning on her soft mouth until she felt her veins traced with a silvery thrill like witchfire."

And all these effects—mind you—merely result from *kissing*!

The second important effect of restricting people's freedom to kiss members of the other sex seems to be to cause them not only to view puckering up as a highly enjoyable pastime, but actually to make them considerably overvalue it.

Thus we have the custom of kissing under the mistletoe, which is made the subject of endless jokes and comments every Christmastide, and which graphically shows how seriously twentieth-century inhabitants can take interpersonal pecking—even when it is quite divorced from embracing, petting, and other more sexual followups. For example, on the opening day of the second half of the century we find mistletoe kissing emphasized in two Sunday comics, *Terry and the Pirates* and the *Sad Sack*; in a popular song, the "Mistletoe Kiss Polka"; and on the Amos 'n' Andy radio program, where Sapphire sarcastically remarks about the antics of her husband, Kingfish, at a New Year's Eve party: "A great big man like you walkin' around wid a piece o' mistletoe taped to yo' head!"

All this childish emphasis on momentary kissing once a year under a sprig of mistletoe can only mean that the populace making such an emphasis is (a) kiss-starved, (b) kiss-scared, and (c) kiss-crazy. It may serve as a classic illustration of the almost invariant rule that the more a certain sexual or semi-sexual mode of behavior is banned, and the more ashamed of it people become, the more glamorous its surreptitious expression seems, the more pleasurable its indulgence becomes, and the more desirable it appears in the inner hearts, if not the outer admissions, of the members of that populace. Or, in other words, the most predictable effect of banning or limiting a given sex activity in a civilized culture seems to be the inhabitants' acquiring pronouncedly ambivalent attitudes toward it.

Further examples of American opinions which clearly imply that, while kissing is just not the thing to do, not to do it is just simply awful may be noted in the following anecdotes from popular magazines.

From *Laugh Book*: " 'Sweetheart, let me kiss those tears away,' he begged. He was very busy for some time, but still the tears flowed. 'Will nothing stop them?' he asked. 'No,' she murmured. 'It's hay fever, but go on with your treatment.' "

From *Judy's* (quoting from the *Ladies' Home Journal*): "John L. Lewis and another labor leader, in Washington for a conference, watched as two very pretty young girls met on the street and kissed each other rapturously. 'There's another of those things that are so unfair,' remarked Lewis dourly. 'What do you mean?' asked his companion. Lewis pointed to the scene and said, 'Women doing men's work.' "

From *Good Humor*: "If you weren't in a canoe, I'd kiss you!' 'Sir, I demand to be taken ashore immediately.' "

From *Joke Parade*: "Mother: Now, dear, there are many young couples who *don't* kiss one another on park benches. Daughter: Oh, I know—they go to the movies—but John and I are trying to save money."

All of which may be epitomized by the observation that to kiss or not to kiss is one of the most important questions of the twentieth century: a question which is normally answered no and acted yes.

Attitudes Toward Kissing in the 1960's

Comparing the attitudes toward kissing in the 1960's with those that were previously found in the 1950's, little change is found. In the earlier period, it was observed that there were relatively many references to kissing in American mass media and that these were preponderantly favorable or liberal. Exactly the same findings are to be noted in the follow-up study of attitudes today.

On the anti-kissing side of the fence, only a few references could be found; and some of these were equivocal. In Faulkner's novel, *The Mansion*, Essie Meadowfill says to her father: " 'Papa, this is McKinley Smith. We're going to be married.' Then walking back out to the street with him five minutes later and there, in full view of whoever wanted to look, kissing him—maybe not the first time she ever kissed him but probably the first time she ever kissed anyone without bothering (more, caring) whether or not it was a sin."

In Elsa Maxwell's column in the *New York Journal American* we read: "One of the funniest things I've heard was when Bootsie Hearst told me that her older son, Willie, hates to kiss anyone. His father often has to bribe him by paying a nickel for a kiss. When his father asked young Willie why he hated kissing so, the boy answered, 'Aw, cowboys hate kissing,' showing the influence of the Westerns."

The only real dyed-in-the-wool anti-kissing attitude that was found in the course of the present follow-up study was noted in a story in *Personal Romances*, where the narrator writes: " 'Never let a boy touch you or kiss you,' Mom would tell me over and over again, almost hysterically. 'A kiss can lead to having a baby.' I didn't know any of the facts of life. I asked Mom once how a kiss could make you have a baby. She burst into tears and said I was too young and innocent to talk about it."

On the other hand, long and highly favorable and desire-arousing descriptions of kissing are often found in the public media of the 1960's, just as they were found in the previous decade. Here are a few examples from contemporary best-selling novels:

From *Peyton Place*: " 'Aw, come on, Betty. Don't be like that. Kiss me a little.' Betty lifted her head and Rodney quickly covered her mouth with his. She could kiss, thought Rodney, like no one else in the world. She didn't kiss with just her lips, but with her teeth and her tongue, and all the while she made noises deep in her throat, and her fingernails dug into his shoulders. 'Oh, honey, honey,' whispered Rodney, and that was all he could say before Betty's tongue went between his teeth again."

From *Exodus*: " 'No, dammit! I can't be away from you for two years! I can't even take it for two days any more.' He [Dov] stood and seized her [Karen] in his arms and covered her mouth with kisses and she returned kiss for kiss and both of them cried, 'I love you' over and over and their cheeks were wet with perspiration and tears and their hands felt for each other's bodies and they slipped to the floor."

From *The Best of Everything*: "He strode to her and put his arms around her, and before she knew what was happening he was kissing her. This wasn't like the last kiss she had received, from that dirty Mr. Shalimar, and it wasn't like any kiss she remembered from the boys at home. It was magic, a pounding of the heart and a touch of something that was like silk and warmth; a kiss she couldn't remember the moment afterward because it was so emotional for her."

From *Lolita*: "Not daring really to kiss her, I touched her hot, opening lips with the utmost piety, tiny sips, nothing salacious; but she, with an impatient wriggle, pressed her mouth to mine so hard that I felt her big front teeth and shared in the peppermint taste of her saliva."

Other mass media than best-selling novels also contain many favorable and desire-arousing descriptions of or allusions to kissing. In a *True Confessions* story, Jeff kisses Maggie "so hard that my whole body went limp." And in another story in the issue of the same magazine, we are told that "Once, after one of Greg's kisses, I had the feeling that my heart was going to burst into a million pieces. I felt all shivery too and my body seemed to tingle with a funny kind of afterglow."

Intimate Story magazine also has a batch of tales in the same issue which relate the glories of kissing. In one, the female narrator states that "Boys had kissed me before, of course, but I hadn't been *kissed*! Not till now! I knew that I would never forget this first kiss of Dirk Wellston's. Why, my whole body was throbbing and spinning. I felt like I was riding in a car going a hundred miles an hour and feeling every vibration of the springs and motor and as though I were— well—whirling off into space myself." In another story in the same issue, the heroine narrates: "Yes, he finally got around to kissing me, and when he did, my head would spin, my knees would turn to butter, and my insides would catch on fire. What a crazy feeling, I thought. I liked that feeling, and I knew it meant I was in love. This was truly what made the world go 'round."

In other stories, songs, and articles, we learn that kissing makes "wild bells begin to ring" (*Good Housekeeping*); "sent my blood singing through my veins and my whole body seemed to be on fire" (*Today's Romances*); makes one's heart suddenly soar (*Girl's Romances*); brings a "storm of sweetness and thrill that went through me" (*True Confessions*); makes "the world turn upside down" (song; "How About That"); and is quite the natural thing to do between doctors and their female patients and nurses and their male patients (movie: *Suddenly Last Summer*, and comic strip: *Little Annie Rooney*).

A final look at modern pro-kissing attitudes may be taken at some of the jokes and cartoon gag lines published in mass media of the 1960's:

From *Comedy*: "He: I've been out with a hundred different girls and never kissed one yet. She: Which one was that?"

From *For Laughing Out Loud*: "A stenographer who was transferred to the New York office of a large company was told by her male supervisor that she would find the work the same as in the firm's Chicago office: Fine, she said, kiss me and let's get started."

From *Snappy*: "Man to beautiful young neighbor who is watering her garden: Pardon me, but my wife, who always greets me at the door with a kiss when I arrive home from work, is out of town today. I was wondering if I could borrow one of yours."

From *For Laughing out Loud*: "A handsome farm boy was walking along the road with a young woman but was quite occupied in carrying a pail on his back, holding a chicken in one hand, a cane in the other, and leading a goat. When they came to a dark lane the girl said: I'm afraid you might try to kiss me here. Said the boy: How could I with all these things I'm carrying? Well, replied the girl, you might stick the cane in the ground, tie the goat to it, and put the chicken under the pail."

Kissing, if we are to go by this kind of material, may not be entirely approved under all circumstances in the 1960's; but the situations in which it is highly disapproved are rapidly dwindling to zero.

CHAPTER 7

Petting

Never let it be said that American attitudes toward petting or necking are unequivocally hostile; they are quite equivocally so.

Practically all serious public pronouncements on petting take the form of *yes—but* arguments. Yes, of course petting has its good points, is almost universally practiced, constitutes part of the regular growing-up process, does little harm, has always been with us—*but* ... And then the extenuations begin to fly thick and fast.

Concretely, if we are to accept the points of view overtly and implicitly presented in current American publications, then we must believe that petting, while not entirely shameful and wrong, will:

... give you only a false popularity with the members of the other sex and actually make you less popular with them (*Woman's Life*).

... make you incapable of real love relationships and cause you to fritter away valuable time (*Family Circle*).

... produce internal conflict and sabotage your personality development (*Your Psychology*).

... ruin your reputation irreparably (*True Story*).

... drive you to drink (*Integrity*).

... keep you from doing your work properly (*American Legion* magazine).

... draw down the wrath of the community on you (*Joke Parade*).

... invite complete emotional and physical disaster (*I Confess*).

Is there, then, no good word to be said for petting? There certainly is—and how! In fact, in reviewing the material for this study, many more favorable than unfavorable attitudes toward petting were found in American publications and productions. For every writer who pointed out its disadvantages, there appeared to be two or three who made no cavil with its essential enjoyability and goodness. In reading these pro-pettingites, however, one quickly was struck by a curious coincidence: they were all, every ex-petter's son of them, humorists.

Take, for example, the movies. One might not expect to find in present-day America the Production Code bound motion pictures frankly stating that necking is one of the best and most desirable pastimes imaginable. Yet—and in just so many words—one finds precisely that in the film, *On the Town*, where is one scene a sailor says that he doesn't want to dance with his girl because the dance floor is so crowded that they might get crushed to death. Whereupon she most ecstatically replies: "What a way to die!" In the same picture a girl who has lured her sailor boy friend up to her room pointedly remarks to her unwelcome roommate, who has suggested that if she had a camera she could get the two of them together: "You could do that by just leaving the room!"

Ah well, you may say, you never can trust the movies. But take the radio, now: you'd never find a thing like that *there*. No? Well, in a favorite family program titled *Our Miss Brooks* we find the hero noting to O.M.B. that the only fun a bachelor can have is really to let go once in a while; whereupon she, disappointed with his kid-glove handling of the situation, retorts: "It might also be fun to hold on once in a while!"

Obviously, even the heavily censored movies and the closely watched radio shows manage to get in some pro-petting propaganda—as long as they keep it light and breezy.

Another mass medium known for its romanticism rather than its sexiness is popular song writing. But here, too, we find petting getting an unabashed—though once again humorous-plug in the song "Please Take Me Home This Moment." For, after insisting that petting in public is not nice and that her boy friend had better take her home immediately, the heroine of the song ends up with her real reason for wanting to be taken home: because there's no one home that night.

As for the magazines, no holds seem to be barred in connection with abetting petting; and the non-petter is made to look like a cold and hungry waif plaintively watching a Christmas party through the brightly lit windows of a magnificent warm house. To illustrate:

From *Fun Parade*: "As they walked down the street she said to him, 'Now, before we go any further, I want you to know that I don't permit anyone to kiss me, put his arm around me, or even hold my hand. Is that clear?' 'Yes,' he said. 'Now that that's settled,' she continued, 'where are you taking me?' 'Home,' he replied."

From *Laugh Book*: "There are two kinds of flat tires, and both make you stop."

From *Joke Parade*: "English bobby, halting recklessly driven car in which young couple were driving: See here, young fellow, why don't you use both hands? Youthful Driver: By George, you're an understanding chap—but I can't, you know. I've got to keep one hand on the wheel."

From *Modern Screen*: One young thing to another, as they are entering a movie: "I came here last night with Bill, so I thought I'd come tonight and see what the picture was like."

From *Touchstone*: "I don't smoke, drink, or neck. I lead a nice, clean, monotonous life!"

From *Broadway Laughs*: "A beautiful June moon shone down on the parked car in which sat Sadie and her bashful boy friend. 'Dear, you remind me of Don Juan, the great lover,' murmured Sadie. 'Why?' he asked hopefully. 'For one thing,' snapped Sadie, 'he's been dead for years and years.' "

From *Man to Man*: Girl to fellow who is sitting far away from her on the sofa: "If you don't come any closer, I'll scream!"

This, then, would seem to make it almost unanimous. Petting is continually described as a thoroughly enjoyable, inviting, worthwhile pastime—in American humor. In more serious handlings of the subject, however, it is accepted, if at all, only in an entirely equivocal, wishy-washy fashion.

And, as we must consistently ask, the result? Exactly what we might expect at this stage of our study. The same petting which in serious writings is reviled or apologetically accepted, and which is so enthusiastically approved in the humorous folklore of contemporary America, is, as far as the behavior of our young people is concerned, apparently rife. Thus the conservative *Reader's Digest* has no hesitation in printing Geoffrey Gorer's observation that in American boy-girl relations "it is usual ... intimacies should increase with each successive 'date' with the same partner, up to, but seldom including, actual intercourse." And the *Ladies' Home Journal* notes that in the drive-in theaters which have recently become so popular in this country "everybody is too busy necking to watch the movie."

The cycle, in regard to petting (as to many another tabooed sex act), is then complete: In morals, we reprove it; in humor, we approve it; in action, we improve it. Thus round and round we go, savagely biting our own tail.

Attitudes Toward Petting in the 1960's

In the study that was made for the original edition of this book it was found that during the 1950's there were relatively many attitudes toward petting in American mass media and that these were preponderantly liberal. The follow-up study of public means of communication in the 1960's shows even more expressed and implied attitudes toward petting and an overwhelming proportion of pro-petting attitudes among them. As expected, the most favorable references to this form of sex behavior are found in the best-selling novels, the men's magazines, and the humor magazines.

Among the anti-petting attitudes (only seven, all told, among scores of books and magazines investigated) are the following:

From Robert Penn Warren's *The Cave*: "I really am a virgin. I haven't been loved up much even, not even after dances in the back of a car. I never even let a hand go between my legs, the way some nice girls do—yes, they do, they've told me."

From *Newsweek*: "Mount Moriah's (Missouri) first dance was held one happy evening in mid-October. The village pastors were quick with their denunciations. 'It's evil,' complained the Rev. Gene Hays, a Southern Baptist. 'It's the tool of the Devil.' The Rev. Edward Lathrop, a Methodist, warned that 'many unwed mothers across the nation . . . are victims of the school dance.' "

From *My Love Secret*: "Do you have a sense of guilt or shame about any petting you have already done? Suppose your mother, or some other older person whose opinion you respect and whose approval you sincerely desire, knew absolutely everything that has taken place on your dates. Would you be *ashamed* of yourself and your boy friend because of some of the things you have done together? Also, if you do pet, are you sure you're not overdoing it?"

From *Teen Secrets*: "Prolonged 'necking' and petting' should have no place in a teenager's life. This type of activity should be reserved for marriage. This extreme form of teenage lovemaking can lead to various types of temporary nervous disorders."

From *For Laughing Out Loud*: "I help keep sex out of the movies." "You mean you're a censor?" "No, I'm a balcony usher."

As can fairly easily be seen, the foregoing attitudes toward petting are rather definite; and yet they are still, for the most part, relatively mild. Compared to the negative attitudes that existed on the same subject and were published in our mass media ten and twenty years ago, they are indeed moderate. On the positive side, however, attitudes toward petting are getting, one might say, more and more immoderate; and fairly enthusiastic endorsements are becoming increasingly common in the popular literature of the 1960's.

Exhibit A in this connection is the contemporary novel. In Kerouac's *On the Road* the characters are always petting with each other, even in the most public places; and at one point we are told that "Dean stood googing around with a towel [in a diner, as they helped the owner wash his dishes], so did Marylou. Finally they started necking among the pots and pans; they withdrew to a dark corner in the pantry. The counterman was satisfied as long as Ed and I did the dishes."

In West's *The Devil's Advocate* we read "She put her arms round his neck and pressed her lips on his, and when he tried to resist, she held him more tightly; and when he felt her breasts against him through the shirt, he decided that it was pleasant after all. And he began to kiss her, too."

In *Lolita*, Vladimir Nabokov gives us many detailed, ecstatic descriptions of petting affairs between his hero and several girls, particularly the young Lolita. Some of his descriptions in this respect have probably never been surpassed, for their joyful lasciviousness, in all of ancient and modern literature.

Other public sources also contain highly favorable and sexually exciting depictions of and attitudes toward petting. *Revels*, for example, has an article titled "Sports Cars Are Too Small for Crashin' or for Passion." Since, this article points out, small sports cars are too small to do any amount of heavy petting in, "the new sales approach is that a man should have two cars: one for sport and one for sporting. The canny Europeans have viewed this trend with some degree of alarm, of course, and already have started a counter-measure. They realize that front seat fondling is a grand old American custom and is not likely to be done away with in favor of automotive fashion. ... So don't be surprised if the new imported models suddenly appear with double sleeping bag. ..."

Both the men's and the humor magazines are replete with jokes and cartoons whose main points are pro-petting attitudes. For instance:

From *Swank*: "Chauffeur to wealthy boss, who has a willing girl in the back seat with him: This looks like a nice spot, shall I run out of gas, sir?"

From *Cavalcade*: "Policeman: You claim this fella here stole your money out of your stocking? Pretty gal: Yes, Officer. Policeman: Well, why didn't you scream, or put up a fight? Pretty gal: I didn't know he was after my money."

From *Inside Story*: "An elderly lady was visiting a Rehab Hospital in Kansas City. Stopping at the bed of a convalescing GI who's been wounded she said: Poor lad you must have had some pretty tight squeezes. At this, the soldier replied: Well, madam, the nurses here have been pretty good to me for a fact."

Even in the quite respectable mass magazines jokes with a pro-petting gag line are quite frequent. In a *Saturday Evening Post* cartoon a gypsy is shown playing his violin in a restaurant where all the couples are madly embracing. "If I must say so myself," he is saying to the waiter, "I'm really in great form tonight." The *Reader's Digest* includes the story of the girl who went to Alaska and married a man on very brief acquaintance. When asked why their courtship had been so short she replied: "When it was dark enough to park, it was too cold; and when it was warm enough, it was too light." *Coronet*, quoting from the *American Mercury*, reprints the notice that was posted on a private road: "All people using our drive as a lovers' lane please observe these rules: Participants park on the right, spectators on the left."

In sum: contradictory, inconsistent attitudes toward petting are still rampant in the United States in the 1960's; but the pro-petters seem to be making significant gains and may soon have the (indoor and outdoor) playing fields practically to themselves.

CHAPTER 8

Masturbation

If this chapter were to rely only on the data gathered in the course of this study from surveying American mass media, it would almost end right here: for exactly four references were found to masturbation in the course of the study.

The first of these references is an unmistakably negative one. It consists of an advertisement in *Your Physique* which reads in part: "TIME FOR YOU TO READ 'SEX AND EXERCISE' by George F. Jowett... HOW TO OVERCOME SECRET HABITS which have robbed thousands of fine bodies of their natural health and sex vigor, causing fear and shame. For them, the instruction contained in this great book, and the COURSE ON EXERCISE VIRILITY, teaches HOW TO OVERCOME HIDDEN HABITS, and restore healthful virile manhood."

This ad, obviously, is referring to the supposed harm of masturbation; and it and the book advertised seem to be typical of a large number of existing texts which either directly or indirectly condemn the practice. The usual wont of even the most up to date of these books is to say that masturbation is not a harmful practice in itself—*but* it has various grave disadvantages, such as isolation, introversion, alleged interference with heterosexual relations, harmful overindulgence, et cetera. Thus the second reference to masturbation found in the course of this study is an article by Winfield S. Pugh in *Sexology* magazine. Dr. Pugh states that masturbation "will cause no harm as long as it is not done to excess." He significantly fails to state that performing masturbation "to excess" is, for the normal male, almost impossible, and that this notion of "overindulgence" is largely a chimerical bugaboo invented as a last resort by anti-sexual die-hards who could not find anything bad to say about masturbation from a scientific standpoint but who still could not bring themselves to favor it.

The third reference on masturbation found in contemporary publications is included in an article in *Your Physique* entitled "Exposing

Body-Building Superstitions." This article points out that loss of semen through nocturnal emission or masturbation, although once erroneously believed to be harmful to the human body, is now known to be harmless. The article thus indirectly favors masturbation—or, more accurately, it at least says nothing against it.

The fourth, and final, reference to masturbation found in the course of our study is one by a psychiatrist, Alexander Wolf. In an article on group psychotherapy in the *American Journal of Psychotherapy* Dr. Wolf notes that after a certain amount of participation in group therapy the patient "is able to relinquish his detached, masturbatory and individually enterprising 'freedom'—which amounted to nothing less than neurotic enslavement—for gregarious, heterosexual, and communal relationships." Dr. Wolf, in other words, distinctly implies that masturbation is equivalent to detachment and neurotic enslavement and that "normal" individuals never resort to it. While it is doubtlessly true that *some* neurotics avoid heterosexual relationships in favor of masturbation, and thus defend themselves against emotional involvements with other individuals, it would also appear to be true that the vast majority of masturbators in our society are driven to autoerotic practices because of the dangers or difficulties of their engaging in heterosexual relationships; and this point is, unfortunately, ignored by many orthodox psychoanalysts and psychiatrists, like Dr. Wolf, who overemphasize the neurotic aspects of masturbation and who largely ignore its normality *in our society*.

Aside from the four references to masturbation just reviewed, no mention of autoerotic sex practices was found in our public writings— and that, actually, tells us more about American attitudes toward this sex act than the few overt references to it that could be discovered. For while literally scores of stories were found in which the central characters were sexually excited and were debating with themselves whether or not to give in to their desires by having sex relations with members of the other sex, none of these characters, apparently, even considered the possibility of masturbation.

On the nonfictional side, while a good many articles dealing with the pros and cons of petting, kissing, and even premarital sex relations were found in our study, including several attempts to gain public-opinion-poll samplings of American feelings and activities in these connections, all such articles signally failed to discuss or inquire into the incidence or propriety of masturbation. It would seem that either American writers now take masturbation so much for granted as a good and proper sex act that they simply find no need to discuss it—or else they dare not even touch upon the subject in popular literature. Of these two hypotheses, the latter appears to be somewhat the more likely explanation of the observed facts.

One would think that the sexual conventionalists would in some ways favor masturbation, since it would appear to be one of the most effective means, if it were frankly and publicly espoused, of minimizing fornication, adultery, prostitution, illegitimacy, and many other unconventional sex outlets. Apparently, however, once an anti-sexualist, consistently an anti-sexualist; for there seems to be a tendency for the same individuals who are conventional in other sex respects *also* to be negativistic as regards masturbation.

In actual practice, as virtually every competent sexologist has known for half a century, and as Kinsey and his associates are more accurately now rediscovering, masturbation is almost universal among young males and females; so that here we have a classic example of an enormous chasm between modern sex attitudes and practice. The average American, at one time or another during his or her life, and often for many years at a stretch, certainly masturbates. And this same average American continually sees attitudes on masturbation expressed or evaded in the public prints which, at best, accept it most halfheartedly and at worst soundly excoriate it. Wherever may the twain, the masturbator and the imbiber of anti-masturbatory viewpoints, meet? Worse yet: how, since the twain are inescapably one, may they possibly separate?

With even the outlet of masturbation directly or indirectly condemned, the outcome can only be that huge numbers of Americans —including all the unmarried, widowed, separated, and divorced, and many of the married (e.g., those whose spouses are ill or away)—find themselves denied any legal or acceptable sex outlet whatever. And since several thousand years of recorded history conclusively show that complete sexual abstinence, especially on the part of males, is rarely achieved, the result can only be the acquiring of sex outlets by men and women *in spite of* the public condemnation of these outlets. This has certainly been, and still very much seems to be, the case with masturbation. Millions, apparently, like it and do it—but do not like the likes of their doing it. Which is, from the standpoint of effective mental hygiene, precisely as it shouldn't be.

Attitudes Toward Masturbation in the 1960's

As was true in the course of the study made of sex attitudes in American mass media during the 1950's, it was again found that only a few references were made to masturbation in the follow-up study of attitudes in the 1960's. In the latter period, however, most of the references that were found were on the liberal side, in contradistinction to the unanimous conservatism found in the earlier period.

In the two anti-masturbatory attitudes that were discovered in the follow-up study, there is only a mildly anti flavor. Thus, in Robert

Penn Warren's novel, *The Cave*, Goldie objects to Ikey's having se[x] relations with her when he obviously no longer is keenly interested i[n] her; and she says: "I love you and I'm sorry but I'm not going to le[t] you just use me some way because you're all fussed up. I'm just no[t] going to let you use me for some kind of Grade-A masturbation—o[r] whatever the hell it amounts to that you were trying to use me for.' Here there is but a backhanded slap at masturbation; and no clearcu[t] condemnation of it.

In Rona Jaffe's novel, *The Best of Everything*, Caroline asks Mik[e] what he does for sex satisfaction when he does not have a woma[n] and he tells her he masturbates. We read: "She was appalled. 'Why?' he asked. 'But that's so ... that's for children. Little boys. Adoles cents. ...' 'Caroline, when will you learn that nothing two people d[o] when they love each other is wrong?' 'That's just it; it isn't tw[o] people, it's you by yourself. It's dreadful. It's so isolated.' 'It isn'[t] isolated because it brings me closer to you.' " Here we have a some what disapproving but also a distinctly accepting attitude towar[d] autoerotism.

In the other references that were found to sexual self-stimulation more positive attitudes toward it were expressed or implied. Dr Benjamin Spock, in the latest best-selling edition of his famous book *Baby and Child Care*, goes out of his way to point out that fa thers should not only tell their young sons that masturbation is per fectly normal but should take care not to tell them that the practice i[s] harmful if they do it too often. "I think it's a mistake for a paren[t] to set a limit even though it may sound sensible. The trouble is tha[t] an adolescent easily becomes worried about his sexuality, easily imagines he is 'different' or abnormal."

Dr. James R. Sauls, Jr., in an article in the popular magazine, *Realife Guide*, discusses masturbation by a homosexual patient with out any moralism whatever. And the medical editor of the same magazine, in an answer to a question from one of the readers, shows that it may be normal for an individual to masturbate seldom or fre quently and that "it is impossible to establish a norm" in this respect.

Not only masturbation but nocturnal seminal emissions appeared to be discussed more openly and permissively in the literature of 1960 than in that of 1950. In fact, during the earlier period its mention was conspicuously absent from popular media. At least two best- selling novels of 1960 feature nocturnal emissions. In Grace Metalious's *Peyton Place*, there is a long passage describing Norman's dream about Miss Hester and Allison MacKenzie; and in his dream of being pursued by poisonous worms coming from Allison's abdomen, "most of the time he succeeded in reaching the arms of his mother before he awoke. It was always at that moment, when he reached his mother, that Norman reached a climax in the excitement engendered by Allison. At such times, Norman awoke to warmth and wetness and a sense that his mother had saved him from a terrible danger."

In Nabokov's *Lolita*, we are frankly told that "the dimmest of my pollutive dreams was a thousand times more dazzling than all the adultery the most virile writer of genius or the most talented impotent might imagine."

All told, the number of references to sexual self-stimulation in the literature of the 1960's, as well as the permissive salacious tone taken in regard to these references, tends to show that the subject is now being approached in a less hush-hush manner and that anti-masturbatory expressions are on the decrease. The millions of Americans who were found in the first edition of this book to be masturbating, but not to be liking the likes of their doing so, apparently are still engaged in the same activity but many of these are distinctly less ashamed of being so engaged.

CHAPTER 9

Illegitimacy

In more ways than one American attitudes toward illegitimacy are peculiarly topsy-turvy. In the first place, the so-called "illegitimate" child appears to be almost the only *victim* of an illicit sex act who is not only punished but is frequently penalized far more than is the perpetrator of the act. For in actual practice many unmarried mothers seem to avoid responsibility for their "love children" in one way or another and, except for the burden of their own consciences, escape almost scot-free from the consequences of their sex behavior. But their offspring often carry around the scars of their "illegitimacy" for the rest of their lives and are frequently excruciatingly pained and plagued because of the conditions of their birth.

Another irony to be noted about illegitimacy is that it is a sex act which, while having virtually no legal penalties attached to it, is more bitterly viewed by society than many specifically jailable offenses. Thus, while most states in the United States make sex behavior such as adultery, nudity, and dissemination of "obscene" literature a distinct misdemeanor or felony, our gendarmerie rarely actually arrests anyone for perpetrating these illegal acts. Instead, millions of our citizens, rather than looking down on adulterers, strip teasers, and publishers of bawdy tales, seem either to envy them or view them as public benefactors.

Illegitimacy, on the other hand, when the unwed mother is of legal age, seems to be practically never punishable by American law. But in the public's eyes the woman who has an illegitimate child seems to be regarded as a spineless, worthless, "fallen" woman who is a terrible menace to society and who should be ostracized for the rest of her days for the frightful crime she has committed.

Graphic examples of the horror with which illegitimate motherhood is viewed in our culture may be seen in the consistent depictions in American publications of the cold terror which strikes a woman when she learns that she is going to be blessed with one child too many and one husband too few. Thus, we are continually told, the unwed mother-to-be suffers "nerve-racking torture" (*Your Psychology*), is "terribly alone, afraid, and so ashamed" (*Real Romances*), and becomes absolutely desperate in her attempts "to hide my mistake in marriage and get a name for my baby" (*I Confess*).

This "get-a-name-for-my-baby" theme is almost ubiquitous in modern magazine writing, and time after time we note that for this reason alone forced marriages between pregnant girls and the putative fathers of their children are advocated or condoned. In the same month we find almost identical belaborings of this theme in stories in *Redbook*, *The Saturday Evening Post*, and *I Confess*; in articles in the *Ladies' Home Journal* and *True Story*; and in a full-page advertisement for the film, *My Foolish Heart*, published in several leading magazines.

Another convincing illustration of the horror with which our society looks upon illegitimacy is shown in the frequent references to girls, when they are about to give birth to illegitimate children, going away to some place where they can obtain "confidential seclusion" during their pregnancy and childbirth. A single issue of the Denver *Post* contains no less than four classified advertisements for such "strictly confidential" services.

If any more examples are needed to show how violently opposed to illegitimacy so many of our publicists are, here are a few attitudes culled from popular magazines, books, and radio programs:

1. Any man who gets a girl pregnant and refuses to marry her literally deserves to be shot (*The Saturday Evening Post*).

2. A girl who has an illegitimate child cannot possibly return to her home town to face the censure of her neighbors (Van Wyck Mason's *Dardanelles Derelict*).

3. Any girl who becomes illicitly pregnant will of course not be invited to the wedding of one of her ex-boy friends (*Your Psychology*).

4. Parents who discover their daughter's pregnancy will naturally force her child's father to marry her against his and/or her will (*True Story*).

5. A girl cannot possibly tell her own father, to whom she normally tells everything, that she is illegitimately pregnant (*I Confess*).

6. The most shocking headline of the year is that which announces that a famous movie actress is about to have a child by a man other than her husband (Sheilah Graham in a Mutual Broadcasting System radio broadcast).

7. A girl who becomes illegitimately pregnant and then marries to give her child a name will have all her neighbors watching to see whether her child is at least a month "premature," and she will greatly lose caste in their eyes if it is (*I Confess*).

This type of negative attitude toward illegitimacy is even carried into popular anecdotes, as in this one from *Joke Parade*: "He: Who was your mother before she was married? She: How dare you insinuate such a thing!" And Peter Arno, in *Sizzling Platter*, depicts a movie director saying to an obviously pampered, overfed, spoiled darling: "You're unhappy, see? You're an unwanted child. You were born out of wedlock."

Has, then, no one a good word to say for illegitimacy? Not a very good one, according to the results of our survey. For in all the hundreds of writings and productions seen and viewed for this study, only two unequivocal defenses of unwed mothers could be found:

1. In William E. Wilson's novel, *Abe Lincoln of Pigeon Creek*, Abe's mother tells him that her own mother was not married and that she is, in consequence, base-born. Whereupon, we learn: "Abe was not shocked or frightened. Lots of folks were base-born, he reckoned; and if his mother was, then it was a fine thing to be."

2. In Ludwig Bemelmans' *The Eye of God* we are told that when Marusja, one of the girls in the novel, had an illegitimate child, "the whole village, with the exception of Big and Little Hedwig [her parents], was happy about the event—one more added to the local single children bothered no one."

It is notable that in these two wholehearted acceptances of illegitimacy one takes place in America of a century ago and is an idealization of the actual illegitimacy of a President's mother, while the other scene is laid in a Bavarian village. It is difficult to imagine these authors taking illegitimacy so lightly if they were portraying American reactions of today.

Clearly ambivalent attitudes toward illegitimacy were easier to find in the course of our survey. Thus, in Ardyth Kennelly's *The Peaceable Kingdom*, Mrs. Sterling is both despised and respected by her women friends when she induces a Mormon preacher, Brother Bell, to give her a house and a thousand dollars by pretending that she is pregnant by him, when she is actually illegitimately pregnant by another man, whom she marries on the bounty Brother Bell bestows on her. In Edison Marshall's *Gypsy Sixpence*, the hero, Rom, is not at all ashamed of his illegitimacy, nor is his father; but many other characters in this novel hold his illegitimate birth against him. In Robert L. Taylor's biography of W. C. Fields the comedian's liaison with a Ziegfeld girl and his having an illegitimate son by her is reported in a matter-of-fact manner, with the implications that (a) it was unconventional and daredevilish of Fields to live sinfully with his mistress and to have an illegitimate son by her and (b) it was darned nice of him to contribute to the support of his son over a period of years. In S. N. Behrman's play, *I Know My Love*, the illegitimate pregnancy of one of the girls in the play is accepted by her very understanding mother—but the fear and dismay of this mother on learning of the pregnancy are also made very clear.

All told, it would appear that while twentieth-century American publicists do not always handle illegitimacy as if it were the most horrendous crime imaginable, they generally come fairly close to doing so. At best, they seem to *forgive* illicit birth and rarely to condone or approve it.

This means that although American mass media—as we have seen in other chapters of this book—frequently encourage or tolerate fornicative and adulterous behavior on the part of men and women, they virtually never approve the possible pregnancies to which these acts may lead. Or, more pointedly stated, the same girl whose sex habits may be tolerantly viewed by her friends, associates, and lovers while her stomach remains appropriately flattened may be in for the severest kind of censure once she begins to stock up on maternity dresses.

At the same time, as we might at this stage of our study begin to suspect before even viewing the facts, illegitimacy is employed for lascivious purposes by a good many American mass media—particularly by humorous anecdotes dealing with marriageless pregnancies:

From *Wet Hen*: "And then, of course, there's the one about the coed who had to leave school because her slip was beginning to show."

From *Laugh Book*: "The prodigal son returned to the homestead. He was empty-handed. The prodigal daughter returned. She had her hands full."

From the *Ram-Buller*: "Wife of Oriental, when he remarks on the whiteness of their children: Occidents will happen."

We find, then, that the inconsistency between American public attitudes toward premarital and extramarital sex relations which effectively and non-effectively employ contraceptive devices is enormous; and that the usual inconsistencies between actions and words, and between conscious and unconscious attitudes, exist in regard to illegitimacy as well as in regard to various other kinds of American sex behavior. The present-day citizen of our land who truly knows his

92

own mind and consistently acts accordingly in relation to so-called illegitimate pregnancy is indeed a rare phenomenon.

Attitudes Toward Illegitimacy in the 1960's

In the beginning of the 1950's it was found that expressed and implied attitudes toward illegitimacy in American mass media were very few and that they were mainly conservative or condemnatory. In the beginning of the 1960's, we see that considerably more attitudes toward illegitimacy are being published or otherwise publicly displayed and that although the majority of such attitudes are still (as one would expect) opposed to unwed mothers and their children, a larger minority of attitudes which are on the more liberal side also finds expression.

Women's magazines, as usual, include more than their share of anti-illegitimacy attitudes. In this class of publication, we find these kinds of reactions to the discovery of pregnancies in unwed mothers: "revolting" (*Revealing Romances*); "heartbreaking" (*Real Confessions*); "shocking" (*Real Confessions*); "ruinous" (*True Confessions*); "gruesome" (*Secrets*); "awful" (*Personal Romances*); "terrible, bad, and wrong" (*Today's Romances*); "insane" (*Intimate Story*).

In contemporary best-selling novels, equally moralistic attitudes about unwed motherhood are frequently found. In *The Cave*, Mary Tillyard cannot tell her father when she becomes illegitimately pregnant because he would not be able to accept such a frightful occurrence. In *Poor No More*, old Holmes McCadden, when he discovered that John Grimes had impregnated his only daughter, "took down his shotgun and went looking for his son-in-law. He found John Grimes. There was a big to-do. Old Mac was so upset he died of a heart attack just after the child—the girl—got born."

"In the town of Peyton Place," we are told in the novel of the same name, "there were three sources of scandal: suicide, murder, and the impregnation of an unmarried girl." When Elizabeth Standish becomes illegitimately pregnant, she goes to the greatest possible lengths to hide from the people of the town, and from the child herself, that any illegitimacy ever occurred; and she invents a fictitious husband to document her lie. Flem Snopes, in *The Mansion*, gets to marry the most beautiful and richest girl in town because he agrees to wed her "in time to save her from dropping a bastard."

Other anti-illegitimacy attitudes are to be found in a wide variety of public sources, including *Man's Magazine*, *True Police Stories*, *Ace*, *Confidential Tattler*, and *Starlife*. American views in this connection are to some extent summarized in *The Realist*, where we note that the "National Assn. of Social Workers, meeting in Washington last month, considered the problem of the increasing number of illegitimate babies. The director of a home for children in that city said that the public 'now rests comfortably isolated from responsibility' by making the unwed mother 'a faceless stereotype upon whom we can heap our anger.' "

All, however, is not negative in regard to illegitimacy in our public press and other means of mass communication. *Cavalcade* quite favorably reviews the life of Lucky Baldwin, who is supposed to have left some thirty million dollars to his many legitimate and illegitimate children in the early part of this century. The same magazine also nonchalantly reports the paternity suit brought by a girl against one of the sons of a famous screen and TV star.

Popular Medicine features an article on the Child Adoption Service of the State Charities Aid Association and quotes its director, Mrs. Amelia Igel Sternau as saying: "No girl in trouble need go to a stranger —and she won't if she knows the kind of help and protection available to her" at this Service.

In the motion picture film, *The Fugitive Kind*, the heroine, Lady, is very proud of her first illegitimate pregnancy, by David Cutrere. And, when she has a miscarriage with this child, she gets into an affair with Val Xavier, though she is married to Jabe Torrance at the time, and is delighted to become, by him, illegitimately pregnant for the second time.

In the nonfiction best-seller, *For Two Cents Plain*, Harry Golden includes this defense of illegitimacy: "Alexander Hamilton, Leonardo da Vinci, Jean Duvois (who fought arm in arm with Joan of Arc), and Nancy Hanks (Lincoln's mother) were all illegitimate. One can't help thinking of these heroic figures every two years when Senator Wilbur Jolly of the North Carolina Legislature tosses in his usual bill proposing sterilization of mothers who have had two or more children out of wedlock. Jolly's folly was aided in 1959 by Dr. Rachel Davis, a freshman legislator. The bill they jointly propose has its humane aspects. Twins don't count as two births—but as one. Jolly. What a wonderful, happy name. How can a man with the name of Jolly want to mutilate young bodies or deny a girl the possibility of a happy married life?"

In contemporary novels—some of which we just saw containing anti-illegitimacy attitudes—there are a surprisingly large number of pro-bastardy references. In *The Cave*, a TV announcer makes a tremendous thing out of the fact that Jasper Harrick, who is lost in a cave, has begotten an illegitimate child; and a newspaper editor starts a huge campaign for contributions from the public for the support of this child. In *Poor No More*, Craig Price's mistress, Libby, insists that "I'd rather have a bastard brat by Craig Price than a whole litter of legal children by anybody else I know!"

In *Return to Peyton Place*, Elizabeth Standish finally tells her daughter about the daughter's being a bastard and says about the girl's father: "I've never been sorry. I loved him and he was good to me. And I got you. That's a lot more than most women ever have." In *Lady Chatterley's Lover*, Clifford tries to induce his wife, Connie, to take a lover and have a child by the lover, since he himself is incapable of fathering an heir.

Even in two highly religious novels, illegitimacy is accepted and approved. In *The Devil's Advocate*, both Nerone and Nina, his mistress, are delighted when she becomes illegitimately pregnant by him. In *The Thirteenth Apostle*, the hero and his beloved are not in the least abashed when she becomes pregnant before they are married. Later in the novel, Mona becomes impregnated illegitimately by the saint-like Crispian and, again, they are both delighted that she should return to her village to give life.

In the 1960's then, we still find that the inconsistencies which exist between one set and another of attitudes toward illegitimacy are enormous. But the trend is definitely toward less condemnatory and more accepting views of unwed parenthood. Progress in this direction is surely, if slowly, being made.

CHAPTER 10
Birth Control

While one public-opinion poll after another seems to indicate that birth control is heartily accepted—and even more heartily employed—by the majority of American people, a survey of our leading publications and dramatic productions gives the reverse indication.

In fact, almost the only references to birth control that could be found in our study of American mass media were quite negativistic. These references consisted largely of statements by Catholic spokesmen, who were not in the least bashful nor indecisive about damning contraception. Thus we are unhesitatingly told—

That a husband who uses a condom to protect his wife from catching any sex disease which he may have "would still commit a grave sin, for a good end does not justify the commission of an intrinsically evil act" (*American Ecclesiastical Review*, quoted in Paul Blanshard's *American Freedom and Catholic Power*).

That any artificial method of birth control is unforgivably wicked and sinful (F. J. Sheen, in *Peace of Soul*).

That even when "natural" means of contraception are employed, "planned parenthood" is iniquitous if it is resorted to merely for the happiness and "selfishness" of husbands and wives who wish to ease their life burdens by bearing fewer children (Aloysius McDonough, in *The Sign*).

That "birth control is nothing else than mutual masturbation or unnatural lust" (Father Dominic Pruemmer, quoted in *American Freedom and Catholic Power*).

That the so-called rhythm method of birth control is not proper except under certain special circumstances, such as extreme poverty of the parents employing it, and is "sometimes venial sin, sometimes mortal sin" (editorial comment in *Integrity*).

·Against all these indictments of birth control, only relatively mild protests could be found in the course of our survey, like those of Blanshard in his *American Freedom and Catholic Power* and of W. E. Garrison in his "The Problem of 'Catholic Power,' " published in the magazine *Religion in Life*. Both these writers are much more concerned with the power of the Catholic Church itself than with American attitudes on birth control, and they only incidentally favor more liberal attitudes toward contraception.

For the rest, American publicists, and particularly fiction writers, almost completely abjure taking any stand whatever on birth control. In all the millions of words which are written each month describing torrid love-making scenes, the question of whether or not contraceptives are employed by the participants, or if so what kind, is invariably blithely ignored. The implication is clear, however, that, in those cases where the fictional participants employ adequate contraceptive techniques, to say that they do would be entirely unromantic, unaesthetic, and unduly pornographic.

This implication is made more explicit by the single fictional reference to birth control we could find in the entire literature examined for this study. This reference is included in an anecdote from *Joke Parade*, which goes as follows:

"The little girl's mother sent her to the druggist to get something to stop palpitation. By the time the child had reached the pharmacy she had forgotten what she was sent for, and when the druggist asked her what she wanted, she thought for several minutes and then said, 'Mother needs something that will stop population.' "

It can be seen that the whole point of this joke is that it is entirely improper, nasty, and obscene for a little girl to purchase contraceptives for her mother. Why? Because, obviously, contraceptives themselves, even when employed by individuals who may heartily believe in their necessity and desirability, are never quite proper, clean, or publicly admissible.

Further proof of the American view that birth control devices are essentially indecent and vile is found in another significant omission in

96

our public prints: namely, advertisements of contraceptive techniques. Even "feminine hygiene" ads were conspicuously few among the thousands of advertisements surveyed for this study; while ads for specific contraceptive devices and accessories amounted to absolutely zero.

One further convincing bit of evidence—and again one of omission —which shows how underlyingly negative our attitudes toward contraception are can be found in the scores of stories, and especially "true" stories, which infest our newsstands every month. As we noted in our chapter on illegitimacy, many of these stories are concerned with a girl's horror of possible or actual pregnancy. But obviously these girls would not be so terrified if (a) they were aware of proper contraceptive techniques and (b) employed them effectively in their extramarital affairs. As one can easily see, however, the girls depicted in these stories have no such awareness nor make any effective employment of adequate birth control measures. Which shows, of course, that normal young girls in our culture are supposed to be so impressed with the undesirability of birth control that they never learn how to use it at all, or do so very sporadically and inefficiently.

From reading between as well as on the lines of modern fiction and nonfiction, therefore, we can see that birth control is stalwartly opposed by many Americans and that it is viewed in a shameful light by many who do not openly oppose it. As for its adherents, they seem to be publicly scarce or unvocal.

Now the question arises: How does the actual practice of birth control in America stack up to publicized theory? As is usual with tabooed sex acts, it seems to stack up, all right—but in an opposed direction. For indications are that contraceptives are very widely used in America—and frequently by those who are theoretically opposed to their use.

Blanshard, for example, tells us that polls by popular magazines, conducted by reputable public-opinion organizations, have conclusively shown that even the majority of Catholic women practice birth control. A writer in the letters column of *Harper's* magazine points out that in Connecticut and Massachusetts, which absolutely forbid the dissemination of birth control information even by physicians, the "birth rates in these two states are among the lowest in the entire country." And the World Almanac discloses that in recent years the birth rate in the United States has been about a million and a half births, or 10 per 1000 population. This, of course, is only a small fraction of what it would be if contraceptive techniques were not very widely employed.

Birth control, then, seems to represent one more aspect of sex behavior which, in our nation, is widely condemned in public representations, legally banned in various sections of the country, shame-facedly viewed by perhaps the majority of the people who theoretically accept it—and which, in practice, is exceptionally widespread. It would almost appear that one of the best ways to assure the popularity of any mode of sex behavior in America is to pan it and ban it—and thus most effectively fan it.

More seriously, however, the grim fact is that millions of our citizens seem to be in grave internal conflict with themselves because (a) they favor birth control and yet consider it shameful; or (b) they disfavor it and yet feel compelled to resort to it. If they either favored it and considered it thoroughly decent and unshameful, or if they disfavored it and were easily able to keep from resorting to it, their minds would probably be at rest in either of these eventualities. But since unanimity of opinion and action on birth control is publicly non-existent today, both the inter-individual and intra-individual conflicting views which are widely held concerning it tend to make American sexual peace of mind concomitantly non-existent.

Attitudes Toward Birth Control in the 1960's

In the 1950 study of sex attitudes in American mass media, it was found that there were very few references to birth control and that nearly all these were conservative. In the follow-up study of attitudes in the 1960's it has been discovered that there are fairly many references to birth control in the same kinds of public sources of communication and that the great majority of these are pro- rather than anti-contraception. This is a startling change.

A good deal of this change resulted from the fact that, during the period studied, there were many references to birth control in the newspapers, largely in connection with the controversy over the United States sending contraceptive information to some of the backward countries of the world which had requested this. But even eliminating these references, there still remained a distinct tendency for contraception to be discussed more openly and more favorably in public print than was evident a decade before.

On the anti-birth control side, several indications were found. According to the *New York Times*, an Orthodox Jewish rabbi declared that "population control by birth limitation was an 'absolute contradiction to the moral motif of modern faith' and 'anti-Godly' when practiced on a 'communal scale.' " In the *New York Journal American*, Bishop Fulton J. Sheen wrote an article on *The Peril of Birth Control* in which he stated that "the attitude of birth control is negative, failing to see beauty, truth, love, and life as a whole."

In the Catholic periodical, the *Sign*, we are told that "The use of contraceptive means is always gravely forbidden, for this is to abuse the nature of marriage." In the novel, *Poor No More*, Craig Price tells his wife, when she says she is in condition for having sex relations again after her accident, "I'll have to make a little sneaky trip to the drugstore tomorrow." And the magazine, *Twenty-One*, reprints the joke about the girl who goes to a doctor to ask for a method of birth control and is told to try orange juice. "Before or after?" she asks the doctor. "Instead of," he replies.

These were all the anti-contraception references that were found in the 1960 literature. Some of them, as can be seen, are hardly unequivocally disapproving; but all contain some measure of non-acceptance of birth control.

On the positive side, references were far more frequently discovered. In *Man's Conquest*, an enthusiastic note on a new practical birth control pill is published. *Scientific American* reports that "in the United States birth control for overpopulated countries has recently been advocated by two governmental advisory groups." In the *Saturday Review*, Dr. Warren S. Thompson writes a favorable review of the book, *The Population Explosion and Christian Responsibility*, and concludes that both Christians and non-Christians might well accept birth control measures and thus help "lead to a better world."

Realife Guide contains one of my own articles, "Psychological Aspects of Discouraging Contraception," in which the enormous psychological disadvantages of banning birth control information are pointed out. The same magazine also features a favorable statement on the new contraceptive pills.

The *New York Times*, during January 1960, features a whole series of news articles and editorial matter on contraception; and most of these items indicate that various church groups, including the Unitarian, Episcopal, and United Church of Christ groups, strongly favor birth control and harshly condemn officials, including President Eisenhower, who deny contraceptive information to densely populated countries, such as India. Other highly favorable comments on artifical means of curbing population growth are published in *Sexology*, *The Realist*, and the *New Republic*.

Even in Catholic publications, acceptance of the necessity for some form of birth control is considerably greater than it ever previously was. Thus, in an article in *The Catholic World*, Thomas K. Burch notes that "in the future, fertility or mortality or both must change and change significantly. One of two courses seems likely in this regard. Assuming peace and a rate of development sufficient to raise standards of living to reasonable levels the world over, mortality will stay low. But in response to rapid population growth most people will adopt deliberate measures to keep their families small."

Mixed attitudes toward contraception, encompassing both positive and negative views, are included in several of the mass media studied, including the *New York Times*, *The Realist*, and *Commentary*. The last-named publication has an excellent summary article by Kingsley Davis and Judith Blake on "Birth Control and Public Policy." In this article, the authors point out that "The Michigan-Scripps study of a national sample of wives aged eighteen to thirty-nine found that 85 per cent of the Protestant wives and 45 per cent of the Catholic wives capable of conceiving had used some means of birth control, and over half of them a method banned by the clergy. Statistical breakdowns of the clientele of various birth control clinics have also shown that a good proportion of the women are Catholics."

Here we have the epitome of modern attitudinal conflict about contraception. Catholics obviously feel quite uncomfortable about using artificial means of birth control—but not quite so uncomfortable as they would feel if they rigorously refrained from using them.

We may appropriately conclude this addendum with a joke, taken from the *Florida Orange Peel* and reprinted in *Campus Howl*, which nicely indicates how many Americans still are very favorably inclined toward the use of birth control techniques but still have guilt and anxiety in this connection. The joke is about a young man who purchases condoms at a drugstore and, when the druggist knowingly smiles, gives him a glowing description of the girl he is seeing that night. When he goes to see the girl, he first talks about the weather and similar topics but then insists that the girl and her parents accompany him to church. About half way through the service, the girl leans over to the young man and whispers, "I didn't know you were so religious." "No," he replies, "and I didn't know your old man was a druggist either."

CHAPTER 11

Abortion

This chapter shall be quite short—and grim. For abortion, about which the chapter concerns itself, is one of those things which publicists seem to feel should better be left unsaid, and that is precisely the way in which they usually leave it.

In all the material surveyed for this study, only five clear-cut references to abortion could be found. One was of a purely factual nature, and the other four were savagely negative. Indeed, although the four value judgments that were found on abortion were in radically different kinds of writings—one was in a play, the second in a non-fictional article, the third in a magazine story, and the fourth in a polemical book—they all used exactly the same word to describe abortion. That word was *murder*.

Thus in a *Redbook* story a woman asks her husband why their son's girl friend, who is about to have an illegitimate son by him, does not have an abortion performed, and he replies: "There are people who look on that as murder."

In an article in *Better Health* entitled "Abortion Kills More Than a Baby," the author tells of a girl who had an abortion performed and who then "began to condemn herself. Over and over again she told herself that she was a criminal. Not only a criminal, but a murderer. The worst kind of murderer. For she had killed her own child."

In Sidney Kingsley's play, *Detective Story*, McLeod, the hard-boiled detective hero of the play, learns that before he even met his wife she had become pregnant by another man and had had an abortion. We then have the following dialogue between McLeod and his wife:

MCLEOD: You carried his child awhile inside you... and then you killed it.
MARY: Yes. That's true.

In *American Freedom and Catholic Power* Paul Blanshard quotes several Catholic authorities who hold that abortions are nothing less than the murder of a human soul; that therapeutic abortions, even for the purpose of saving the life of the mother, are sinful; and that if a physician decides to perform an abortion on any patient in a Catholic hospital "and the authorities cannot shake the determination of the doctor or patient to procure abortion, the authorities must order the patient removed to another institution."

Abortion, then, is considered to be an exceptionally heinous offense in present-day America; and even when it is not punished legally, it presumably rests very hard on the conscience of both the abortionist and the woman having the abortion. Yet the article in *Better Health* which we previously quoted informs us that hundreds of thousands of abortions are performed annually in America; and, because of their being performed illegally and under poor medical conditions, "according to competent medical authority, at least 50,000 American women are made sterile every year as the result of such criminal abortions, and thousands of others either lose their lives or are permanently maimed during an abortion."

In other words, millions of American women loathe abortions and consider themselves murderesses when they have one—yet thousands upon thousands of these same women keep having abortions performed on themselves, even under the worst possible medical conditions. Obviously there must be something which these women find even more loathsome than abortion—and that is having unwanted, and especially illegitimate, children. That this is so is partly confirmed in an article by Dr. Lena Levine in *Today's Woman*, in which she points out that many women in our society rush for unnecessary abortions when their menstrual periods are a few days delayed and when they are not actually pregnant.

The fact is, then, that the average woman in our society seems to have ultra-ambivalent attitudes toward abortion. Consciously and/or unconsciously she looks upon it as a horrible crime and a dreadful sin, and at the very same time she views it as a relatively desirable operation which she must resort to in case of an unwanted or embarrassing pregnancy. Since in practice she so frequently does resort to abortion, she is liable to the most severe type of conflicting feelings concerning it. The result is the bearing of a frightful load of (conscious and unconscious) guilt by millions of American women.

The abortion problem is closely linked with two other sex attitudes which we have already examined in this study; namely, those toward birth control and illegitimacy. For abortions are mostly had by married women who, for one reason or another, do not wish more children, or by unmarried women who wish to avoid the stigma of illegitimacy. But if married women freely and fully accepted contraceptive techniques they would of course very rarely require abortions; and if unmarried women did not consider illegitimacy sinful, or if they employed adequate birth control methods, they, too, would have much less need for abortions.

Ironically enough, therefore, conventional sex attitudes toward birth control and illegitimacy often lead to the flouting of conservative attitudes toward abortion. Or, otherwise stated, rigid sex attitudes in one area frequently seem to cause sex problems in other areas and result in human conflicts and disturbances along a much broader range than would at first blush appear to exist.

In any event, the references to abortion in modern mass media make it quite clear that, on the one hand, the practice is widely condemned and, on the other hand, frequently resorted to. This is the kind of attitudinal-action situation that can only spell considerable human suffering, and it unquestionably does.

Attitudes Toward Abortion in the 1960's

In the 1950 study of attitudes toward abortion, it was found that there were very few references to this subject in the popular literature and that all these were strictly conservative. In the study of sex attitudes in the 1960's, a good many more references to abortion were found; and most of these were either liberal or permissive or at least a mixture of pro- and anti-abortion views. While beliefs concerning abortion had hardly changed completely during the ten-year period that elapsed between the original and the follow-up study, they had certainly become remarkably more tolerant.

On the strictly negative side, *Zest* magazine reviews a sex-filled movie and reports that the hero of the film is so incensed by his girl friend's threatening to have an abortion when he has got her pregnant before marriage that he threatens to expose her to her father, her friends, and to the whole town unless she has the child. In the *New York Times*, a routine news item is printed telling how five members of an abortion ring were trapped by the police and are being held for trial. These were the only two wholly anti-abortional attitudes that were found in the material surveyed.

A good many mixed attitudes toward abortion were also found, however. A letter in *Cosmopolitan* points out that abortion may not be such a bad thing, but that, if so, we should change our philosophy of government and law which now holds that it is. In a tale in *Intimate Story*, a girl's mother-in-law urges her to get an abortion when the girl becomes illegitimately pregnant; but her physician refuses even to consider the possibility of an abortion. The *Realist* quotes the view of the Catholic Union of Kansas that it would be tragic if "God-fearing persons were to accept murder in the form of abortion as the solution to the so-called overpopulation problem." But the publication then goes on to show how insane and immoral this view is.

In several contemporary best-selling novels, a most equivocal view toward abortion is taken. In *The Best of Everything*, April realizes with half her mind that she should be very grateful to those who are helping her get rid of her illegitimate pregnancy by the abortion route; but she is also quite shocked by the idea of having an abortion. In *Poor No More*, Jimmy Wilbur calmly tells Craig Price that he arranged a quiet abortion for Craig's daughter when she was just over sixteen; and then, ironically, Craig forgets his own promiscuous sex affairs long enough to become quite horrified about this idea.

In *Peyton Place*, Nurse Mary Kelley, a good Catholic, feels quite guilty about helping Dr. Swain perform an abortion on Selena Cross and about lying to back up the story that Selena is having an appendectomy; but she nevertheless forgets her Catholicism long enough to surrender to her humanitarian feelings in favor of Selena.

Even less equivocal and more favorable attitudes toward abortion are also prevalent in the literature of the 1960's. In Robert Penn Warren's novel, *The Cave*, Mr. Bingham, the town banker, has no hesitation whatever in arranging an abortion for his daughter when she becomes illegitimately pregnant. In discussing the girl's pregnancy and what will happen in regard to it, we find this edifying discourse between the Commissioner of Police and a police lieutenant on his force:

" 'Well,' the commissioner said, just suppose the chick does not lay the egg. Then what?'

" 'Listen, boss, are you playing dumb? That chick is the daughter of the local folding money. She is the legal and legitimate daughter of the guy who is the local mother of money. He brings it forth. There is going to be a lot of whitewashing. The egg will not be laid. I bet Baby-Girl is on her way this minute to Nashville's best abortionist. Who is it, by the way, since old Doc Pickerall had his trouble?'

" 'You in trouble, Lieutenant?'

" 'Naw,' Lieutenant Scrogg said, and grinned, 'but if you had to be, statutory and all, you could do worse than what that Jasper had for the condemned man's last toot. She is nookie-built. She is evermore built.' "

Even more remarkable, perhaps, than this nonchalant attitude toward abortion is the view taken by Dr. Alan F. Guttmacher, Director of the Department of Obstetrics and Gynecology at Mount Sinai Hospital, New York, in an article that first appeared in *Redbook* and that was reprinted in that ultra-conservative magazine, the *Reader's Digest*. "The number of illegal abortions performed each year in the United States," states Dr. Guttmacher in this article, "has been estimated at from 200,000 to 1,200,000." Since almost all these abortions are illegal, he urges the adoption of a modern law, patterned after those now existing in Norway, Sweden, and Denmark, which would "permit abortion for four general reasons. (1) Strict medical reasons—when an existing disease which would be adversely affected by pregnancy poses a threat to the life or health of the mother. (2) General health—including the matters of too many children, or children too close together. (3) Eugenic reasons—mental deficiency of parents or the probability of a congenital disease or malformation in the unborn infant. (4) Humanitarian reasons—pregnancy resulting from rape or incest or the impregnation of a girl less than 15 years old."

From the foregoing indications it would appear that more criminal abortions than ever are now being performed in the United States but that many of the people involved in them are considerably less anxious and guilty than they would have been under similar circumstances a decade or more earlier. American attitudes toward abortion are still messy and inconsistent; but not as much so, apparently, at least on the part of a good part of the populace, as they have previously been.

CHAPTER 12

Pregnancy

Directly expressed attitudes toward pregnancy in American mass media are relatively few, since for the most part pregnancy has only recently come to be a fairly acceptable, and hence rather neutral, phenomenon. American newspapers and magazines frequently advertise maternity dresses, and columnists vie with each other to announce the expectant motherhood and fatherhood of famous people. In these announcements there are sometimes overtones of salaciousness, but they are usually quite mild.

One notable point about these advertisements and announcements, however, is that they virtually never mention the word "pregnant," but instead use "expecting," "in the family way," and other euphemisms: thus displaying underlying puritanical viewpoints. Moreover, the maternity dresses which are so widely advertised are designed not primarily for comfort, but for looks—for *hiding* the appearance of pregnancy as long as possible.

Some elements of older and more rigid attitudes toward pregnancy also seem to hang on in present-day America and to find expression in our public prints. And these hang-over attitudes are almost uniformly negative or prissy. Thus a digest of her autobiography published in the *Catholic World*, Maria Augusta Trapp informs us that one of her pregnancies was quite embarrassing to many Americans with whom she came in contact, and that when she became quite swollen with her child "the newspapers mentioned the 'stately' mother, the 'majestic' figure, but that was all."

In *Cheaper by the Dozen* this embarrassment over pregnancy is even more acutely revealed in Mrs. Gilbreth's shame over her husband's frankly announcing her expectant motherhood; and, in addition, it is pointed out that Mother Gilbreth—a most efficient psychologist, industrial consultant, and what not—"just couldn't bring herself to explain" to her own children where babies came from.

Contemporary American attitudes toward pregnancy are further revealed in an article by Sallie Reed Hughes in *Your Psychology*. According to Miss Hughes, millions of our Southern white and Negro women still abjure having their babies in hospitals and swear by old midwives whose main function is to deliver the mother-to-be from evil spirits. Some of the charms and superstitions employed by these midwives are setting chicken feathers on hot coals under the pregnant woman; putting mustard seed on the doorstep; having the husband wear a black hat; crossing a knife and fork under the mother's pillow; giving her a big dose of gunpowder, snuff, or red pepper; or taking the wing of a jaybird, the jaw of a squirrel, and the fang of a rattlesnake and, after mixing them with the blood of a frizzly chicken, burning them to ashes on red-hot metal.

It may be noted that American attitudes regarding menstruation —which is a process closely allied to pregnancy—parallel those relating to childbirth. Thus while scores of ads for "sanitary napkins" and tampons fill our newspapers and magazines, they never directly mention the term "menstruation," but always euphemistically get around it. Secondly, menstrual functions are rarely mentioned in stories, plays, films, or even printed anecdotes, even though they presumably play an important part in the life and well-being of millions of American women. Thirdly, as Theodora M. Abel and Natalie F. Joffe point out in "Cultural Backgrounds of Female Puberty," published in the *American Journal of Psychotherapy*, superstitions, misinformation, and puritanical notions concerning menstruation are rife in modern America. These authors tell us, for example, that it is still widely believed in our country that menstruating women should not take permanent waves, that they should refer to themselves as "sick" or "unwell," that they should take hot drinks to relieve their pains, and that they should not get their teeth filled while menstruating.

From these illustrations it can be seen that in contemporary America a sizable part of our population still looks upon pregnancy as a shameful, evil process which has to be spoken about in muted or euphemistic tones, kept from the ears of children, and counteracted with spirit-killing charms and superstitions.

On the other hand, among the more sophisticated elements of our population pregnancy is looked upon as literally a joking matter—and the more salacious the jokes, the better. Here, for instance, is a sampling of anecdotes from current humorous periodicals:

From *Penn State Froth*: "And then there was the man on relief who was so accustomed to having things done for him that he went out and married a widow with three children."

From *Wet Hen*: "Young Ensign: Please, sir, I really must have a leave—my wife is expecting a baby. Commander: Listen, young man —remember that you are only necessary at the laying of the keel. For the launching you are entirely superfluous."

From *Laugh Book*: "So that she might post her letter and not miss her bus, an obviously pregnant girl hurriedly walked into a drugstore to buy a stamp. Breathlessly she approached the clerk. 'Could you give me a special delivery, please?' The clerk paled and stammered. 'I'm sorry, lady. I'm only a pharmacist, but I'll be glad to call an ambulance for you.'"

From *Wet Hen*: "Definition: Optimist—a man of seventy who gets married to a young woman of twenty and starts looking for a house near a school."

It should be evident that in relation to pregnancy American attitudes are still dichotomous. The old concepts of pregnancy as a shameful, impure business still partly hang on; and these very concepts lay the roots for the deliberate employment of pregnancy situations in lascivious, salacious terms.

Meanwhile, the average pregnant woman in America goes along feeling quite proud that she is bearing a child—and at the same time feeling ashamed about the cause of her pregnancy and about its semi-sexual effects. To the normal physical pains and inconveniences of childbearing she must, in our society, add some measure of psychological shame of and disgust with herself; which certainly does not benefit her at this fairly crucial period of her life. From a mental-hygiene standpoint, then, the best that can be said about contemporary attitudes toward pregnancy is that they are improving—but that they are still negative and conflicting enough to cause considerable needless fear and guilt among that portion of the population which is particularly in need of healthy attitudes—namely, expectant mothers.

Attitudes Toward Pregnancy in the 1960's

Whereas, in the study that was made of 1950 mass media for the first edition of this book, references to pregnancy were found to be few and to be preponderantly conservative, those found in the follow-up study in 1960 were discovered to be fairly many and to be preponderantly liberal. Even the women's magazines, which are traditionally quite sensitive in this connection, are now apparently much less vulnerable than they used to be and are publishing frank, detailed descriptions of menstruation, pregnancy, and other aspects of female reproduction that they would not have dared publish a decade or more before.

In the only out-and-out negative reference to pregnancy that was found in the 1960's, there is a passage in James Michener's *Hawaii* which describes the missionary, Abner's "shaking with embarrassment" as he attempted to deliver Sister Urania's baby when there was no physician around to help. But this scene is set in the early nineteenth century and is not supposed to be indicative of attitudes toward pregnancy today.

Some semi-negative attitudes toward pregnancy are still found in advertisements for menstrual pads and tampons in contemporary periodicals, since the language of these advertisements often tends to be, as was found in the 1950 study, quite equivocal and vague. But not always! A recent ad in *Cavalcade* boldly proclaims: "PERIOD

DELAYED . . . DON'T WORRY! Use Solfera Tablets: Be relieved of this worry! Your period delay may be functionally delayed menstruation as a result of secondary anemia due to iron deficiency, and Solfera Tablets may bring relief!" Another ad in *Screen Stories* is headlined: "NOW—TOTAL RELIEF FROM PERIODIC DISTRESS. NEW FEMICIN TABLETS." So the old-time prudery concerning the advertising of menstrual products seems to be definitely on the wane.

Frankly favorable attitudes toward pregnancy are evident, during the 1960's, in even the most respectable publications. The *Ladies' Home Journal* has an article entitled, "Our Baby Was Born at Home," which most candidly gives many of the details of the authoress's pregnancy, and includes quite revealing photographs of her actual labor. *Mademoiselle* magazine includes a story where the hero dreams of his wife's giving birth to their child—and again, all the gory details are included. *Family Circle* has an illustrated article on the chances of a woman's having twins. In the film, *Happy Anniversary*, Alice not only tells her husband, Chris, that she is pregnant again, but goes out of her way to tell him that she has taken a rabbit test as proof of her pregnancy. *True Story* has a most clinically detailed article on how a woman gave birth using the Lamaze method of painless childbirth.

Other widely different public sources also favorably and most specifically have stories and articles in regard to menstruation and pregnancy—including *My Love Secret*, *Cavalcade*, *Intimate Story*, *Revealing Romances*, *Realife Guide*, *Twenty-One*, *Sexology*, *Science News Letter*, *Inside Story*, and the *New York Times*. In the vastly popular book, *Baby and Child Care*, Dr. Benjamin Spock advises parents, when their children ask questions about pregnancy, even at inopportune moments when others are present, to "try to curb that impulse to shush the child."

Novel writers, in the 1960's, seem to go out of their way at times to mention previously unmentionable aspects of pregnancy and menstruation. In *Poor No More*, Craig says to his girl friend, Susan, "I can be in love with you on a rainy Sunday when you've got the curse and there's nothing on TV and lousy double features and the town closed tight." In *The War Lover*, we have this dialogue between the narrator and his beloved, Daphne: " 'Listen, Daph,' I said, 'is anything the matter?' 'No, darling,' she said, 'I just fell off the roof.' I sat up. '*You what?*' I was so used to assuming that people were crazy in those days that I really wasn't surprised or alarmed to find that Daph was, too. All that was happening, in truth, was that Daphne was talking to me in code, but I hadn't the key; my old fiancée, Janet, had been a secretive one. I pushed out a 'Hunh.' 'My period, she said. My headache vanished with one heartbeat; I felt gentle and unselfish.'"

For one of the best examples of the changing attitudes toward pregnancy that seem to be taking place in this country year by year, we have this joke from *Campus Howl* (quoted from the *Florida Orange Peel*): "A harassed father was trying to tell his son that there was to be an addition to the family. 'Son,' he said, 'someday soon the stork is going to swoop down over our house.' The son thought carefully, then said, 'Well, I hope he doesn't scare Mother. She's pregnant, you know.'"

The case for the increase in favorable American attitudes toward pregnancy and female reproductive functions rests.

CHAPTER 13

Nudity

From a story in *Collier's* magazine: "Then she stood up. 'I'm going to change clothes. What're you going to do?' I looked the other way while she put on a dress." The *I* in this instance happens to be the same man who, the day before, has not only seen our heroine in an extreme state of undress but has also done with her what a man and woman normally do when so accoutered.

From an article in *Better Health* magazine: "Only one out of twenty of the ladies sleeps naked. But mind you, three times that number say they would like to sleep *au naturel*! Either they are more inhibited or their husbands want them to be clothed."

From a scene in the novel, *The Woman of Rome*: "I may be stupid, I may be old-fashioned, anything you like, but I really can't swallow the fact that Adriana takes off all her clothes in front of these artists every day. . . . Because, in a word, it isn't moral." The speaker, in this instance, is Adriana's fiancé—who has seduced her with a promise of marriage when actually he is irrevocably married to another woman.

One might well be led to believe, from these illustrations, that nudity on the part of women is hardly *comme il faut* in modern America; which, in many respects, is putting it mildly.

Confirmatory evidence of the iniquity of nudity comes easily to hand as one surveys the public prints. We find therein, for example:

That for a lady to wear a black silk transparent nightdress, designed only for her husband's eyes, is "wicked, that's all" (Henry Green's *Loving*).

That for a woman to be caught naked in bed by her maid is most shameful (*Ibid.*).

That any boy who climbs a tree to spy on a girl getting undressed is fit to be burned alive (*Cheaper by the Dozen*).

That any advertiser who puts a full-page, full-breasted torso of a woman in a national magazine has to tint her black or make her look like a statue (*Art News Annual*).

That a man should be ashamed to be seen with a woman who is dressed in a scanty evening gown (*Adventures of Sam Spade*, broadcast by the National Broadcasting Company).

That a country fair which includes unclothed woman is "raw" and should be closed by the authorities (*The Farm Quarterly*).

That a girl who wears a scanty bathing suit is "indecent" (*Love Novels* magazine).

That it is horrible for a husband to be interested in the nakedness of night-club beauties (*Colgate Theatre*, telecast over National Broadcasting System).

That any man who rescues a girl from an automobile accident and undresses her himself in order to put her to bed is a low-down cad (*Gay Love Stories* magazine).

And so on.

To sum up the traditional American attitude toward nudity, we have this satirical poem from *Laugh Book*:

> *The naked hills lie wanton to the breeze,*
> *The fields are nude, the groves unfrocked;*
> *Bare are the shivering limbs of shameless trees;*
> *What wonder is it that the corn is shocked?*

And the actual result of these anti-nudity attitudes which are so clearly expressed in contemporary literature? Merely that American newspapers, magazines, billboards, and stage productions are so full of woman dressed in minus nothing that the only realistic defense against continual contact with nudity in our country would be total blindness.

By way of illustration, take American magazines. Newsstands are literally weighted down with periodicals like *Eyeful, Flirt, Night & Day, Pic, Sir!, Beauty Parade, Exotic,* and *Picture Show,* which specialize in what the well-undressed girl shall wear. A typical feature from one of these magazines, which purports to answer the question "Do Women Upset Office Routines?" consists of seven poses of a pretty girl supposedly imitating her boss. In all seven poses her expanse of leg is as high as the traffic will bear, and in five of them it is even higher. This theme, with endless variations, is repeated in virtually all the picture magazines seen.

The exploitation of nudity by American picture magazines is appropriately satirized in the musical show, *Texas Li'l Darlin'*, where a representative of a great national magazine, *Trend*, insists that he must get a *Trend-worthy* picture of the heroine of the show—and is not satisfied until she raises her dress until it is over her head.

Not to be outdone by the newspapers and magazines, American stage productions cater to the nudity market in an unabashed fashion. While burlesque has (theoretically) been banned in a few cities like New York, it flourishes so widely in the rest of the nation that *Billboard* devotes a weekly column to news of the strip-teasers and their associates, and *Variety's* anniversary issue features many greetings from the burlesque field, including a full-page ad for the greatest stripper of them all, Gypsy Rose Lee.

According to *Picture Show*, moreover, strip-teasing has now invaded Hollywood in a picture titled *Hollywood Burlesque*, which is "replete with strippers, low-down comedians, and a line of chorus girls of assorted sizes and shapes." And, *Picture Show* continues: "Now that burlesque has found its way on film, you may be seeing it on your living-room television set. After all, a lot of television is made up of things on films, and why should anyone discriminate?"

Where burlesque is not openly permitted, it goes blithely on under various assumed names, especially in American night clubs. As the New York *Times* reports: "Today Fifty-second Street is scarred with all the dubious accretions of a quarter century. These include ... burlesque, a form of entertainment theoretically banished from New York in 1942 by the late Fiorello H. La Guardia. ... Four of [the night clubs] presently are devoted to the strippers, who call themselves 'exotic dancers' and exponents of 'bacchanales' these days. They still take off most of their clothes, however, to the spirited accompaniment of trumpets, tom-toms, and heavy breathing, and their owners get into trouble with the authorities."

The legitimate theater and the ballet are other media in which nakedness finds the frankest kind of public expression, albeit in highly "artistic" forms.

Some points especially to be noted about American public displays of nudity are these: (1) Almost always it is the female, and not the male, whose undraped charms are pandered to the populace. (2) The display of feminine nudity, when it is open and public, is never quite complete. Girls are continually shown with next to nothing, but never with absolutely nothing on. Or, if they are, then they are obscured, shadowed, or screened in some manner, or else shown to be dark-skinned natives of some foreign country.

The fact that only female nudity is ordinarily emphasized in our country and that even then it is teasingly rather than—shall we say? —nakedly displayed shows how essentially attitudinal our concepts of nakedness are. Because we make little fuss over bare-chested men, few extra copies of picture magazines can be sold by thus exhibiting them.

And because we refuse to show women completely ungarbed, we create an ardent desire for them to be shown 98 per cent naked. If pictures of jock-strapped males were taboo, girls would probably rush to buy them under the counter; and if women strolled around the streets entirely in the nil, so, too, would be the interest of men in their epidermises.

American women, however, are never allowed to be shown to the public entirely bare-fronted or bare-bottomed—with one curious exception: the nudist magazines, such as *Modern Sunbathing*, which are the only publications permitted to show full views of truly naked white women. This is apparently allowed on the assumption that nudism is a religious cult whose deluded followers should be enabled to express themselves in curious ways, as long as it is clearly understood that they are cultists and are not typical Americans. Even here it is to be noted that the nudists virtually never publish a picture which is non-artistic or which includes a clear view of male genitalia—which shows that they, too, are limited in their public expression of nudity.

The editors of *Modern Sunbathing*, incidentally, make a serious commentary on American attitudes toward nudity when they point out that whenever reporters visit a nudist colony and write a story about it "you can be fairly sure of reading (a) an exaggerated and subtly salacious story, (b) a serious, restrained type of article in which the reporter is obviously as determined to be fair to our strong moral characters and high principles as he is to make it quite clear that naturism isn't for him, or (c) some cheap wisecracks."

As if publication and stage expressions of nudity are not enough, these public displays are multiplied many times over by the everyday divestiture of Miss and Mrs. America. For, compared with the number of American girls and women brashly exhibiting their charms on stage, screen, and photograph, the number routinely undressing for bathing beach, Main Street, and evening wear is infinitely larger. Thus, despite many shocked protests from traditionalists against scanty swim suits for women, these have become ubiquitously popular. Necklines in women's dresses have sunk almost to the navel, so as to require special Low-'N'-Behold brassieres. And the normal street attire of milady today would make some of the burlesque queens of a few years ago look prudishly overdressed.

Modern trends in women's clothing have led to an entire series of anecdotes on the same theme, a typical one of which, taken from *Wet Hen*, goes as follows: "After a tiring day at the studio, a star changed into a strapless evening gown and was ready to leave the house to attend a party. 'I am so exhausted that I really don't feel like going,' she told her husband. 'Okay,' said the co-operative husband, 'put on something and let's go to bed.'"

Even women's lingerie, never noted for its modesty, has recently become more revealing than ever. As reported by the San Diego *Union*: "NEW SHEER NIGHTGOWNS BECOME LINGERIE RAGE IN FASHION WORLD.... It used to take big money and small inhibitions to buy a see-through garment. But not now. Transparent nightwear has been lifted out of the scandalous black lace category by smart designers who are giving it demureness."

Which means—what? Apparently that, in regard to nudity, the more enjoined, the more enjoyed. The nudists, in their publications, keep contending that, once people get used to going naked, the aphrodisiacal qualities of nudeness are diminished to the vanishing point. However that may be, modern anti-nudist views certainly seem to support the converse hypothesis: namely, that when people are not allowed to get used to nudity, they tend to see it as one of the most desirable, sex-appealing, ravishing, alluring evils imaginable.

That Americans, and notably American males, do find inestimable joy and delight in female nudity is shown by the great popularity of the publications and productions featuring nakedness, as well as by various attitudes more directly expressed in some of these mass media. Thus in *Mister Roberts* the sailors almost go insane with joy when they are able to look through binoculars to see American nurses taking showers on a nearby island. In a cartoon in *1,000 Jokes* a hunter says to his guide as they spy upon a woman bathing naked in a stream that he's got to hand it to the guide—who sure knows these woods. In a story in *Private Detective* the hero and one of the girls he meets have no end of fun going bathing in the nude. And both *True* and *Cosmopolitan* magazines print the story of the two attendants in a mental hospital who are hotly pursuing a beautiful naked female patient, followed by another attendant carrying a large pail of sand. "What's that pail of sand for?" an onlooker asks one of the first two attendants. "Oh," he replies, "that's his handicap. He caught her the last time."

The inescapable conclusion would seem to be that nudity in America is prohibited—and exhibited; execrated—and consecrated; iniquitous—and ubiquitous. In which respect it would appear to have, along with a great many other interdicted modes of sex expression, considerable company.

Attitudes Toward Nudity in the 1960's

It was found, in the course of the study that was made for the original edition of this book, that relatively many references to nudity were included in the mass media in the early 1950's and that most of these references were liberal or permissive. In the follow-up study that has been made of communicative outlets in the 1960's, it is clear that the number of references to nudity have considerably increased and that an even greater percentage of these are distinctly in favor of nakedness—particularly that of a beautiful female.

113

The men's magazines, which previously were quite enthusiastic about the charms of an undressed female, have now gone virtually wild in their espousal of feminine bareness. Whereas in the early 1950's they frequently featured women in states of semi-undress, in the 1960's they are featuring, and literally by the hundreds, completely unclothed beauties, with their breasts and their rear ends unashamedly showing, and very frequently the photographs that they display are in full color and are huge double-page spreads. The open depiction of pubic hair is still tabu; but practically everything else goes. The humor magazines are also frequently pro-nudity in their attitudes; and none of the important classes of publications are especially anti-nudity.

On the conservative side of the fence, clearcut disapproval of nakedness or even states of semi-undress still exist. In Paul Gallico's novel, *Too Many Ghosts*, Susan is horrified to have her room turned upside down by a burglar, and to have the guests in the house in which she is staying see it in this state, with her clothes and underthings strewn around. "I just can't bear having anyone looking at my things any more," she tells her boy friend. "Now everybody knows what I've got on underneath."

In Grace Metalious' *Return to Peyton Place*, we are told that "Jenifer Burbank Carter was 22 years old and never once, in the six months of her marriage, had she undressed in front of her husband. 'It's not nice,' she had told him with finality." In Ruark's *Poor No More*, Craig Price, one of the greatest whoremasters in the city of New York, is shocked at the swarm of nearly-naked brown bodies in his own swimming pool, especially by that of a girl who had just come wet from the pool, "and her pubic hair was frankly shadowed beneath her sketchy loincloth."

We also learn that an ex-king posed in the nude with two pretty lasses and they "assumed a half-dozen different disgraceful positions" (*National Enquirer*); that everyone was shocked when a curvaceous French starlet posed in the nude at the Cannes Film Festival (*Vue*); that it is soul-searing and horrible for a woman to pose with her lover for "blue movies," even though she wears a mask when doing so (*Esquire*); that it is utterly indecent for a young girl to wear tight-fitting, low-cut dresses (*True Confessions*); that several Catholic girls have had to withdraw from bathing beauty contests because their Archbishops threatened that they and their families "would be deprived of the sacrament of communion" if they paraded in bathing suits (*New York Mirror*); that children are often not allowed to see Brigitte Bardot's films because of her tendency to appear undressed or half-dressed in these films (*New York Herald Tribune*); that a Broadway actress's name "wouldn't be worth a candle" if old pictures

114

of her posing in the nude were ever republished (film: *The Gazebo*); and that it is shameful for a woman to acknowledge that her mother was a stripper in a burlesque show (film: *Seven Thieves*).

In today's mass media, material that favors nudity is almost endless. In *Frolic* magazine, for example, there are 135 photographs of nude or semi-nude females accompanying the articles and 69 additional nude representations in the advertisements. All told, in a 70-page issue of this periodical, there are 204 nudes. In *Follies* magazine, there are 141 nude illustrations for the articles and 73 additional nudes in the ads, for a total of 213 nudes—again in a 70-page issue of the magazine. Similar numbers of nude photographs and drawings are to be found in such magazines as *Tab, Vue, Candid, Revels, Bare, Gala, Pose, Hit Show, Stare, Rapture, Ace, Harem,* and *Scamp.* Literally scores of other magazines of this nature now exist.

As usual, completely muddled and contradictory attitudes toward nudity are often expressed in the same story, paragraph, or line of many contemporary writings on the subject. *Starlife* features an article by starlet Marianne Gaba on why she posed semi-nude for *Playboy* magazine and highlights how dangerous this posing was for her career and her friendships—and how advantageous and approved it also was. *Vue* has an article which reports that "the typical housewife goes into her favorite store, catches sight of one of the ultra-revealing (bathing) suits, and takes it home with her." Then "her conscience begins to get bothersome. She wonders what the Old Man will say if he sees her strutting her stuff before the admiring eyes of the beachjockies. After much soul-searching, into the bottom drawer goes the bikini."

In Kerouac's novel, *On the Road*, the narrator, who doesn't bat an eyelash when he and his friends fornicate all over the place, gives us this equivocal passage on nudity: "And he went over and kissed her several times. On the wall was a nude drawing of Dean, enormous dangle and all, done by Camille. I was amazed. Everything was so crazy." In *Campus Howl*, quoting from the *Cornell Widow*, we have this definition: "Plunging neckline—Something you can approve of and look down on at the same time."

Summing up: although the popular literature of the 1960's is far more liberal concerning nudity than that of the early 1950's, a considerable amount of equivocation is still present. Nudity is still disfavored—and savored. Attitudes toward it continue to show that in present day America we may justifiably say: "Inconsistency, thy name is sex."

CHAPTER 14

Sex Organs

It would appear at first blush that American writers are whole-heartedly in favor of the full and frank display of human—and particularly female—sex organs. For a cursory reading of American publications and attendance at stage and screen performances would make it seem that the paramount desire of American men is to view women's breasts, rumps, loins, legs, and other sexual appurtenances, and that the main object of American females is to let them.

By way of illustration, take the matter of the female mammary appendages. The modern male's passion for large-breasted women is monotonously played up in hundreds of magazine and newspaper advertisements for brassieres, falsies, sweaters, bust creams, books, exercisers, and scores of other apparatuses and techniques for developing small bustlines into bouncing beauties. "For," a typical ad tells us, "it is the woman with a beautiful, alluring bust contour who wins the admiration, popularity, and affection every woman desires. And there can be no *complete* feminine beauty without a warmly rounded, lovely bust contour, symbol of woman eternal."

Other asseverations of the desirability of women's breastworks are prevalent wherever one turns. In the motion-picture realm, for instance, we find three clear-cut examples: (1) in *All the King's Men* one character asks another: "Was she pretty?" Answer: "How do I know? I wasn't looking at her face!" (2) In *Battleground* a soldier is scandalized when a girl cuts a loaf of bread by holding it up to her chest. He is obviously thinking of the tragedy that would occur if her knife slipped, and the audience knows just what he means. (3) In *Sands of Iwo Jima* one of the marines says: "I want to get in and see some of those Wellington babes. I hear they were built when bricks were cheap."

Popular jokes would lose one of their best and most overworked subjects if women's mammae suddenly lost their power to move American males. Thus *Reader's Digest* quotes Margaret Lindsley: "The best camouflage for a woman's bowlegs is a low neckline." *Laugh Book* avers that the husband of a famous movie actress doesn't allow her to do any cooking "because he doesn't want me to lean over the stove and endanger my career." The *Mercury* has a doctor advising a nurse that if she wants to stop the patient's pulse increasing every time she bends over him she should button her collar. *Sir!* shows us a pretty girl riding on a bicycle behind a man and holding him around the chest to retain her balance. Says he eagerly: "Let's change places—so you can learn to drive." *Cartoon Humor* depicts a young girl purchasing a tight sweater and telling the salesgirl that this is her last chance to hook a guy—since she's already tried perfume, flattery, and home cooking.

Women's legs are also most favorably viewed in the public presses and productions. In the film *Battleground*, there is a shot of a soldier's Christmas tree with a shapely female leg hanging from it. Peter Arno, in his *Sizzling Platter*, shows us two men in an orchestra seat viewing only a sea of legs of the chorus girls. Says one: "That little lady third from the end isn't bad." *Hello Buddies* depicts a night-club producer scolding a luscious singer: "Next time wear a short skirt. Your voice sounds better when your legs are showing." *Wet Hen* gives us this gag: "Woman Driver: Didn't you see me stick out my hand? Man: No, I didn't, miss. W.D.: If it had been my leg you'd have seen it."

The New York *Journal American* prints an Associated Press item: "Hollywood. The very first scene in Betty Grable's new picture, *My Blue Heaven*, will be a shot of the famous Grable legs. The publicity boys call this, appropriately enough, putting the studio's best foot forward." *True* magazine tells us that the police of a Texas town, giving a description of a woman suspected of passing bogus checks, stated that she wore a low-cut dress with a short skirt, making it very hard to gain a description of her facial features.

Nor are other parts of the female anatomy entirely neglected by approving publicists. *Laugh Book* portrays a husband eagerly gazing at the rump of a young girl he and his wife have hired to mind their baby and remarking: "What a beautiful sitter!" A girl in the film, *On the Town*, tells us that when her sailor boy wanted to see the beautiful sights of the beautiful city of New York—well, she showed him plenty. In the play, *Clutterbuck*, one man says to another in regard to a girl who has been their mutual mistress, "Oh, she had beautiful feet!" Replies the other: "Yes—as well!" The Amarillo *Sunday News-Globe* prints this United Press dispatch: "ADVISES AGAINST GIRDLES. Girdles and short hair-dos take away a girl's sex appeal, a beauty expert said today. Joyce Slone, advisor to Broadway's beauteous Wally Wanger show girls, said women should 'show a natural curve' if they expect to 'attract and hold their men'. . . . She said girdles and other supports made the figure 'too confined. . . . A show girl's face and figure are her fortune. Few wear girdles.'"

In all the voluminous material that fills our newsstands, bookstands, and entertainment halls, it is difficult to find a single unfavorable reference to human sex organs. Apparently those publicists who do not feel that nothing is more aesthetically satisfying than certain parts of the female anatomy do not often break into print or speech in contemporary America; or, if they do, they write and talk about other things.

What one does consistently find, if one looks closely enough at public references to sex organs, is that the same thing applies to them as we have seen applying to so many other sex acts and attributes; namely, that even when they are considered desirable and enjoyable they are also considered to be distinctly shameful and off-color. Thus it is not even proper to mention certain sex organs by name in many segments of our society—as this satirical limerick from *Laugh Book* makes clear:

> There was a young girl named De Map
> Who liked winter's sparkle and snap,
> But alack and alas
> She sat down in the grass
> And frost-bit the back of her lap.

Again, we have the ironic scene in *Born Yesterday*, where the ruthless, crooked, sensuous junk tycoon, Brock, is being told by a politician that he is grateful for Brock's support. "Don't mention it," says Brock. "Just tit for tat." He suddenly stops, realizing that the politician's wife is present, and exclaims: "Excuse *me*!"

Another indication of American prudishness concerning sex organs is shown in the *1,000 Jokes* cartoon of a housewife asking a group of small girls, who have been having a party in her home and who now are engrossed in watching a cat suckle several of its kittens, if they don't have to go home for supper or something.

One of the best examples of American ambivalence toward sex organs which shows how, at the same time, we prize female mammae very highly and yet are ashamed of so doing is Peter Arno's cartoon in his *Sizzling Platter* showing a man surreptitiously trying to look down the breasts of a woman on his television set, while his wife unknowingly reads a newspaper.

Perhaps the best illustration of all of contemporary American prudery in regard to sex organs is one of omission rather than commission. For in the literally hundreds of stories and articles, books and dramatic productions, songs and news items analyzed for this study, the great majority of which made some pointed references to sex and love, only a single direct allusion could be found to sex organs other than those which are clearly revealed, at least in outline, to the public eye. The one exception to this rule was the magazine *Sexology*, which mentioned sex organs like the vagina and the penis, and even gave pictorial illustrations of them. As far as the other publications and productions were concerned, however, men and women have breasts, backsides, hips, and legs—but no genital sex organs.

Even the sex-book ads only vaguely hint that women may have vulvas, vaginas, and internal sex organs, and never mention these specifically. In all the literature perused for this study, only three indirect references to genitalia could be found: (1) A poem in the little magazine, *Wake*, contained the lines: "Christ, I have walked around your erection, The Cross, that begot, upon a sky of prayer, A billion men, devoted in humility." (2) *Touchstone* included this anecdote: "A woman was shopping for a pair of pants for her little boy. 'Do you want knickers with a zipper?' asked the clerk. 'No, Johnnie has a sweater with a zipper and he's always getting his tie caught in it' was the reply." (3) John O'Hara has one of his characters in *A Rage to Live* tell this joke to three other characters: "And she had a third [drink of liquor], and he had a third, and when he finished the third, he said to her, 'Say, if I have another one of these, I'm gonna feel it.' And she said, 'Say, if I have another, I'm gonna *let* you.'"

Aside from these symbolic, humorous, and quite indirect references to genitalia, the American publicists whose works were surveyed in this study apparently got along very nicely with no mention of them at all.

Characteristically, whenever there is a clash between Americans' feeling, on the one hand, that something sexual is good and their feeling, at the same time, that there is something shameful about it, one thing happens: that sexual act or thing is continually thrown at and up to the American public in a most lascivious manner in all forms of popular writings and performances. And sex organs, apparently, are no exception to this rule, since an overemphasis on them is displayed in innumerable popular writings and public performances.

The net result of all the material found on sex organs in our culture seems to be a now-you-see-it-now-you-don't effect which we have found so typical of many other aspects of our sexual attitudes. On the face of things, sex organs are enthusiastically accepted in our society as good, pleasure-giving human appendages. Underlyingly, however, they are only partially and, in fact, very prudishly accepted. Then, precisely because they are hypocritically approved on the one hand and rejected on the other, they take on an exaggerated value in the (male) public's eye and they are lasciviously overemphasized in every way imaginable.

This means that, consciously, most of us believe that sex organs are both good and bad—e.g., that woman's breasts are beautiful, but that to show them unreservedly or to be caught looking at them openly is naughty and immoral. Unconsciously, nearly all of us have even more conflicting views about sex organs—since, if we happen to be males, for instance, we may unconsciously worship breasts as milk- and life-

119

giving founts, loathe them as remembrances of incestuous wishes toward our mother, idealize them as a symbol of mothering, be afraid of the homosexual trends they may arouse in us, have mixed aesthetic-sexual feelings toward them, et cetera.

Even aside from these unconscious conflicts which may rack us because of ambivalent attitudes toward sex organs, our conscious, almost entirely culturally imbibed, conflicts concerning them are bound to be so deep-seated and so consistent that no matter what we do in regard to sex organs—whether we frankly enjoy them or stay strictly away from all thought and contact with them—we are almost certain to feel guilty and/or deprived. This is the usual human fate when the individual is confronted with alternatives that are culturally good and bad and whose essential morality is unclear and confused. An inconsistent sex attitude normally leads to a consistent (conscious or unconscious) sex conflict.

Attitudes Toward Sex Organs in the 1960's

Between the start of the 1950's and the start of the 1960's there seems to have been relatively little change in American attitudes toward sex organs as these attitudes are expressed and implied in our mass media. In both decades relatively many references to sex organs were discovered in the literature and these references were preponderantly liberal. In the latter decade, however, there was at least a moderate tendency toward more frank and open references to sex organs in the literature—particularly in best-selling novels. Moreover, whereas the earlier literature concentrated on breasts, buttocks, and thighs as organs of sexuality, the current literature tends to be more specifically oriented toward penises and vulvas, and in this sense is considerably more directly sexual.

On the negative side, only a few references could be discovered where there were out and out statements indicating that human sex appendages are distinctly bad or shameful. In the novel, *The Cave*, Jo-Lea walks down the hall of her school, holding "her left forearm across her breasts as though, in shame, to press them back, conceal them, protect them." In a *Personal Romances* story, the female narrator is medically examined to see if she has been raped, and in spite of the doctor giving her a pill to quiet her down, she relates that "that examination was the most humiliating thing I've ever experienced."

In three different cartoons, negative attitudes toward sex organs are also displayed. In a cartoon in *Swank*, a girl sunbathing on the beach has a book over her face to keep off the sun; but when several men stop to stare at her bathing-suit covered breasts, she puts another book over them. In a *Jest* cartoon, a girl who is bathing slaps a man who has obviously touched her rump swimming, saying to him: "That's not what I meant when I said 'let's see who can touch bottom first!' " In a cartoon in *Twenty-One* magazine, a girl who has apparently been sexually attacked is viewing a group of suspects who have taken their pants down and are standing in their shorts. Says the attending police officer to her: "We can only go so far, Miss. Does that help any?"

Much more favorable attitudes toward sex organs are considerably more common in the mass media of the early 1960's—particularly, as noted above, in the best-selling novels. In Robert Penn Warrens *The Cave*, there are about a dozen references to sex organs. On page 11, Monty Harrick thinks of Jo-Lea and the "soft, suffocating weight of her own breasts." On page 41, we learn that Nick the Greek had "a scrotum like two doorknobs stuck in a chamois bag." On page 110, concerning Isaac Sumpter and Rachel Goldstein: "...she was to adjust herself and, with gentle decisiveness, lay her right hand on his readied member and conduct it to its proper path." On page 112, Goldie says to Isaac: " 'I would just always be holding your head in my hands. I would just'—and she ran over to him—'I would just hold your beautiful head between my big soft white pneumatic blisses and run my fingers over your head ...' " On page 263, Jebb Holloway says to Isaac Sumpter: "You know what, we found that-air Jo-Lea's drawers in front of the cave. Hit's a fack. Bet he give her the meat before he crawled in." Responds Isaac: "Yes. She has sure got the biscuits. She has got the self-rising biscuits." And so on and so forth, throughout the entire novel.

In Robert Ruark's *Poor No More*, Crane says to Wilbur: "There ought to be a few town gals around tonight. There's one.... *No.* I want her for me. I got seniority on that one. She's got the biggest pair of ..." Crane sketched two halves of watermelons with his hands. "Like they were cut in two and pasted on." Later on in the novel, Craig Price wakes up in bed with Susan and we learn that "her trim buttocks looked, Craig thought amusedly, as he crawled out of bed, like two jolly searchlights peering outward from a dark-gold night."

In D. H. Lawrence's *Lady Chatterley's Lover*, finally a best-selling novel after many years of suppression, we have this description of Connie asking to see Mellors' penis: " 'Let me see you!' He dropped the shirt and stood still, looking towards her. The sun through the low window sent a beam that lit up his thighs and slim belly, and the erect phallus rising darkish and hot-looking from the little cloud of vivid gold-red hair. She was startled and afraid. 'How strange,' she said slowly. 'How strange he stands there! So big! and so dark and cock-sure! Is he like that?' The man looked down the front of his slender white body, and laughed. Between the slim breasts the hair was dark, almost black. But at the root of the belly, where the phallus rose thick and arching, it was gold-red, vivid in a little cloud. 'So proud!' she murmured, uneasy. 'And so lordly! Now I know why men are so overbearing. But he's lovely, *really*, Like another being! A bit terrifying! But lovely really! And he comes to *me!*' "

Later in the same book Mellors returns the compliment to Connie: "He stroked her tail with his hand, long and subtle taking in the curves and the globefulness. 'Tha's got such a nice tail on thee,' he said, in the throaty caressive dialect. 'Tha's got the nicest arse of anybody. It's the nicest, nicest woman's arse as is!' "

In Grace Metalious' *Peyton Place* there are also several passages dealing openly and favorably with male and female sex organs. When Rodney goes driving with Helen, she "unbuttoned her blouse and showed him one perfect breast. 'Look at that,' she said, cupping the breast with her hand, 'no bra. I've got the hardest breasts you ever played with.' Rodney raced the car motor violently in his eagerness to be gone from the drive-in's parking lot. Helen did not rebutton her blouse, but leaned back in the seat leaving her breast exposed." In the same novel, Rodney also has an automobile encounter with Betty, who "writhed on the seat until she was lying down, with only her legs and feet not touching him, and Rodney lifted his body to her without taking his mouth from hers. 'Is it up, Rod?' she panted, undulating her body under his. 'Is it up good and hard?' 'Oh, yes,' he whispered, almost unable to speak."

In almost all the other best-selling novels perused in the present follow-up study of sex attitudes in the 1960's male or female sex organs are similarly mentioned. In *The War Lover*, the hero-narrator tells about wanting to touch his beloved "with my life force stirring and swelling." In *The Darkness and the Dawn*, one of Attila's wives twits him on his once not being able to see enough of her rump. In *Lolita*, Humbert gives his nymphet "to hold in her awkward fist the sceptor of my passion." In *Advise and Consent*, Crystal Danta dares her Uncle Bob, Senator Munson, to spank her bottom, as he did when she was a child. In *Wake Up, Stupid*, Mark Harris cites the tale told of Samuel Johnson: "Said a lady to him: 'Sir, your penis is sticking out.' Said Johnson in reply: 'Madame, do not flatter yourself; it is *hanging* out.' "
In the *Devil's Advocate*, Monsignor Meredith investigates the phallic worship of the peasants and finds that "the marble block was stained and discolored, but the phallus was white and polished as if by frequent contact. Did the women come here, as they used to in old times, for an assurance against barrenness? Did the males still worship the symbol of their dominance?" In *Anatomy of a Murder*, there are long passages describing the sex organs and the sex act, such as the one where a doctor testifies in court that vaginal pains and disorders could follow a woman's being raped. "Ordinarily," he says, "when a woman intends to have sexual relations there is a secretion of fluid, a

122

natural lubrication. When the act is taken against her will there is no preliminary secretion and consequently more friction and subsequent inflammation and pain."

Descriptions of sex organs, such as those just cited, are so frequent in modern novels that one wonders whether they have become requisite for sending a work of fiction into the best-selling lists. Since the old, mild depictions of intercourse have seemingly lost their ability to excite, and even sex deviations have now become commonplace in modern fiction, the current logical step seems to be detailed descriptions of the sex organs themselves. It is difficult to imagine what the next step in salaciousness will be.

The pleasurable and favorable depiction of sex organs hardly begins and ends in contemporary popular novels. In a story in *The Dude*, a girl pointedly tells her boy friend that since he has begun to make love to her her breast measurements have grown. An article in *Candid* is entitled "Who Is Our New Bosom Queen" and begins: "Bigger—bigger-BIGGER! The cry goes out and we don't mean just cars, salaries and bar bills, for in this space spacious age even women are going all out for inflation—and it's all in their chests!"

In a *Man's Magazine* article about Reverend Clarence Richeson, who seems to have been quite a lover in his day, we are told that when he looked over the maid of honor of a young bride whom he married, "he felt an old, familiar stiffening—but not in his conscience. . . . Avis simply had it where it should be, and in just the right amounts. The only thing she lacked was experience, and Richeson began to figure how he could fill in that provocative gap."

In an article in *Revels*, men are advised to go horseback riding with girls and to "repair to the edge of a stream for a bit of relaxation and gentle caressing of each others saddle sores."

In the field of humor, more jokes than ever were found which made direct or veiled references to sex organs and which treated them in a highly liberal and favorable manner. Here are some samples:

From *Pageant*: "Female weather forecasters on TV should not wear plunging necklines because it's confusing when they talk about cold fronts."

From *Twenty-One*: "A woman brought an infant to a doctor who asked whether he was breast-fed or bottle-fed. 'Breast-fed,' she replied. The doctor asked her to strip to the waist and examined her. He pressed each breast, squeezed and pulled the nipples. 'No wonder this baby is suffering from malnutrition,' he exclaimed, 'You don't have any milk.' 'Naturally,' she replied. 'I'm his aunt. But I'm glad I came.' "

From *Cavalcade*: "Joe: How was your date last night? Charlie: She was neither slow nor fast. She was half-fast."

From *Snappy*: " 'Well,' said the college girl showing her new outfits to her roommate, 'by next fall I'll have outgrown this sweater and then it will fit better!' "

From *Pageant*: "The way to a man's heart may be through his stomach, but a pretty girl can always find a detour."

Finally, to show that in the area of sex organs, as in the areas of virtually all other aspects of human sexuality, hot and cold, pro and con attitudes are prevalent in one and the same squib, we quote the anecdote from *Rapture* about the young man who went out on a date with a flat-chested girl. He started making some passes at her and she stiffened indignantly. "Here, here!" she exclaimed. "Where, where?" he replied.

Thus American attitudes toward the public mention of sex organs seems to be becoming more liberal than ever. But enough inconsistencies remain in these attitudes to make for philosophic and behavioral confusion among our males and females. Sexual mix-up leads to emotional mix-up. What else could one logically expect?

CHAPTER 15

Scatology

> SCATOLOGY—Study of excrement . . . by extension, study of
> or interest in things filthy or obscene, esp. in literature.
> —*Webster's International Dictionary*.

What, officially, the American public's attitude is toward scatology can hardly be doubted: it is agin it. Dramatization of this official anti-scatological attitude comes in the controversy which has raged about the Italian-made film, *Bicycle Thief*, which was acclaimed by almost all prize-awarding groups as the best foreign picture of its year, and by the National Board of Review as the best foreign or domestic picture.

In spite of these accolades for the uncut version of *Bicycle Thief*, several American pressure groups lobbied against two of its episodes and, in consequence, the Production Code Authority of the Motion Picture Association of America banned the film, without the deletion of these two episodes, from being shown in any theater associated with the MPAA. One of the banned episodes concerns an Italian workman and his son who are pursuing a thief who has stolen the workman's bicycle. As Bosley Crowther of the New York *Times* describes this episode: "Breathless, distressed, and exhausted, the lad tarries momentarily, by the side of a Roman building, apparently to heed nature's call. But even before it is evident exactly what he intends, his father has compelled him to keep running. It is as brief, slight, and innocent as that." This innocence was not convincing enough, however, to prevent the board of directors of the MPAA from stoutly upholding the dictum of its Production Code Authority to the effect that the morals of American audiences would seriously be impaired by the retention of this scene in the film.

It may finally be noted, in this connection, that the ruling of the MPAA was thereupon neatly avoided by a considerable number of motion-picture exhibitors, and that the uncut version of the *Bicycle Thief* proved to be quite a box-office bonanza for these saboteurs of public morality. Which would seem to indicate that the great American public, after officially insisting on having itself protected from demoralizing scatological influence, can unofficially enjoy itself to the hilt.

Enjoy, apparently, is exactly the word of choice here. For the curious fact seems to be that human excremental processes, which are theoretically so disgusting, repulsive, and publicly anathema to twentieth-century mankind, are almost exclusively employed, in contemporary public communications, in outright humorous or ironically shocking ways.

Take, for example, the question of the human buttocks which, for obvious anatomical reasons, have been so often endowed with a scatological implication. To find serious, straight-faced mention of this honorable appendage in American literature of the century is quite difficult. But tongue-in-cheek, double-entendre references to the great American backside are common.

Thus in the film, *Sands of Iwo Jima*, one of the American soldiers gets a bullet in his buttocks, and the usual humorous attitude is taken toward his wound which would under no circumstances be taken if he had been hit in almost any other part of his body. In Peter Arno's best-selling book of cartoons one picture shows a group of night-club chorines, whose costumes clearly reveal their backsides, one of whom is saying to a steady customer of the club: "Valerie won't be around for several days. She backed into a sizzling platter." This joke about Valerie's painful injury—which would of course be meaningless if she had burned, let us say, her foot, side, shoulder, or head—is considered so funny as to give the cartoon book its title; namely, *Sizzling Platter*.

Again in the American version of Giraudoux's play, *The Madwoman of Chaillot*, the Ragpicker, satirically representing a wealthy capitalist, speaks up: "I am the law. When I speak, that is the law. When I present my backside, it is etiquette to smile and to apply the lips respectfully. It is more than etiquette—it is a cherished national privilege, guaranteed by the Constitution." In Nelson Algren's *The Man with the Golden Arm*, great fun is made of the cuckolded Polish husband, who runs out of his bed in the middle of the night when his wife brings home her lover. And, points out Mr. Algren, "the fact that the right-hand button of the underwear's trap had now loosened didn't in the least detract from the dignity of the old man's exit." Even in William E. Wilson's novel, *Abe Lincoln of Pigeon Creek*, there are several scenes such as the one where Tom Lincoln shouts to the future Great Emancipator: "Abe! You get your skinny butt down outen the air now and go on with your chores."

H. Allen Smith, in *We Went Thataway*, informs us that every year more than seventy-five thousand post cards are sold showing a man pulling a stubborn mule over the border line from Texas to Arkansas. The caption on the post card is: "MAN IN ARKANSAS AND HIS ASS IN TEXAS."

Obviously, the human rump, in the so-called "modern times" of the twentieth century, is considered to be (a) indecent, (b) shocking, (c) uproariously funny, and (d) exceptionally interesting and exciting. To be thought of as being merely one ordinary, neutral, unglamorous part of the human anatomy—that, most certainly, it is not.

So much for the seat of man's scatological attitudes. If we would try to become more pointed and inquire into his feelings in regard to those more central portions of his excremental organs which include the anus and the intestinal tract, we find very little material to work on: since our writers manage rarely to touch, even in the most oblique ways, on these vital human centers. One notable exception, however, may be found in the novel, *The Egyptian*, where the author not only goes out of his way to tell how one of his characters concealed a sacred scarab "in a part of my body that it is an indignity for a god to inhabit," but also goes on to say that this character showed the scarab to the hero of the novel and that it "was still foul from its unpleasing hiding place." Here, obviously, the novelist is using anal allusions in a deliberately shocking, unpleasant, but titillating way.

For the rest, though, anal allusions in contemporary literature seem to be painstakingly indirect and humorous, and largely center around the quaint custom of "goosing." Two illustrations should suffice here. *Laugh Book* prints the current joke: "Two geese in a farmyard— one of them screamed, 'Ooooh—I've been peopled.' " Also from *Laugh Book* comes the story of the five-year-old girl who, holding up her wilted dress, came into the room where her mother was entertaining the Ladies' Aid. "What has happened, dear?" asked her mother. "Plenty," replied the child indignantly. "Somebody left the lid up, and I darned near drowned."

Going still further than this, American publications keep using the process of excretion itself about which to weave one bit of humor after another. From one of the humor magazines, for example, we note: "Two sweet old ladies were comparing notes. 'And so you are troubled with constipation, too,' said one, 'and what do you take?' 'O,' replied the other, 'I just usually takes me knitting!'" From the *Ladies' Home Journal*: "Boy writes urgent letter from camp where there are no 'conveniences,' 'Dear Mother: Send me a flashlight at once. I need it at night to——Mother, there is something I have to tell you mouth to mouth.'" In the popular film, *Battleground*, the audiences are reduced to screaming maniacs as one of the American soldiers in the film pointedly picks up some German propaganda leaflets and ambles off into the woods to use them for you know what.

Again, in the musical comedy, *Texas Li'l Darlin'*, much is made of a magazine owner giving a key to the executive toilet to his hireling, Brewster, when Brewster has done a fine promotional job for him. Says the boss to Brewster: "I want you to feel free to use it!" In the *Harvard Lampoon* a cartoon depicts a Radcliffe girl dashing madly past doors marked MOLLUSCA, PISCES, AMPHIBIA, et cetera, to one conspicuously marked WOMEN. In the musical show, *Kiss Me, Kate*, one character naively asks another what he does, in Washington, D.C., about the pigeons. "Duck, my dear, just duck," he replies. In *Gentlemen Prefer Blondes* a healthy, athletic male sings how he owes all his prowess "to roughage, rough rough roughage." In *Touchstone* we are told that a farmer mistakenly gave a pint of castor oil to a sick cat, instead of giving it to a sick calf. "Well, what did he do?" asks a veterinarian. "Last time I seen him," said the farmer, "he was going over the hill with five other cats. Two were digging; two were covering up; and one was scouting new territory."

So much for humorous references to excrementary processes. Even more significant, however, are probably the more serious, albeit indirect, employments of scatological references in contemporary realistic plays and novels. Thus in Kingley's *Detective Story* a photographer and a newspaperman are talking about Park Avenue. "Spell it backward," says the newspaperman. "K-r-a-p," spells the photographer. "You got it," snaps the other. In *Born Yesterday* the junk tycoon makes himself very clear: "Lemme give you some advice, sonny boy. Never crap a crapper. I can sling it with the best of 'em." And in the stage version of *Mister Roberts* people and things that are especially disliked are continually referred to as "cruds" or "cruddy."

In all this joking and serious referring to excremental things just a little reading between the lines makes it perfectly clear that, in the twentieth century, Americans by the millions believe that (a) defecation is an evil, ugly, immoral business; (b) direct, favorable mention of it in public print and statement is unforgivable; (c) indirect, tongue-in-cheek reference to it is cute, naughty, and most enjoyable; and (d) frank acceptance of it, in a sufficiently toned-down format,

127

is the mark of one's being a non-sissified, real man.

Everything that can be said about present-day attitudes toward defecation can be repeated, with ample illustrative material, about our attitudes toward urination. Thus we have the polite horror of and euphemistic attitude toward it shown in the fabulously selling book (and, later, movie), *Cheaper by the Dozen*: wherein, we are told, "For family delicacy, Dad coined two synonyms for going to the bathroom in the woods. One was 'visiting Mrs. Murphy.' The other was 'examining the rear tire.' They meant the same thing."

Again we have the naughty but titillating attitude expressed between the lines of Ardyth Kennelly's novel, *The Peaceable Kingdom*, " 'But first I got to go tinkle,' Gertrude announced, 'wait till I get back, before you tell, Mamma.' 'No, you don't got to go tinkle,' Mama said. 'The least little thing, you get all excited and right away have to tinkle. You sit quiet there for a minute.' "

Touchstone supplies us with this humorous note regarding urination: "Little Audrey nailed the bathroom door shut and then laughed and laughed because she knew that her father was having a beer party that night."

Finally we have the same subject treated by John O'Hara, who has a minor character in *A Rage to Live* apotheosize urination in this wise: " 'I like the toilet downstairs,' said the Governor. 'It saves climbing upstairs for just taking a little pea. . . . Often-times at home my bladder says, "Dunkelberger, run up and take a little pea." But I know better. Too many times was I fooled by that. I got up to take a little pea, I stand there five minutes, ten minutes, the water in the spigot I turn on, I make in my mind pictures of the Niagara Falls, Atlantic City, but no pea. I give up and come down, and my bladder says, "NOW Dunkelberger, now!" So what I do, I go out in the flower garden, and if the neighbors have objections turn their faces the other way. That's all this is good for any more. Ah, a pea is good.' "

Notice, particularly, in this passage from O'Hara's novel, how the next to the last sentence quoted cleverly links up the act of urination with the act of sex itself. This linkage is, of course, implied, though much less obviously, in virtually every twentieth-century statement about and attitude toward scatological things: since the main reason why such things *are* considered to be intrinsically wicked, laugh-provoking, and exciting is patently their underlying sexual content. True, urinary and fecal matters are to some extent esthetically and odoriferously obnoxious in themselves; but little of the highly emotionalized disgust which modern Americans feel about toilet matters seems to be specifically traceable to this type of obnoxiousness alone, and much more of it seems to be related to their sexual connotations.

A similar illustration of this may perhaps be found in Mary Lass-well's novel, *One on the House*. This volume is largely concerned with three old women who have plenty of *joie de vivre* but who also have exceptionally puritanical notions of sex behavior. Aside from an incidental affair between two subsidiary characters, it contains few boy-meets-girl themes like those rampant in most other best-selling novels of today.

But this novel does contain numerous humorous references (a) to urination (e.g., Mrs. Feeley's crying out that she is going to shed a tear for Garfield as she races off to a door marked LADIES); (b) to the human buttocks (e.g., Mrs. F.'s telling the moving man to put the bed "under me dimpled butt, boy! Under me dimpled butt."); (c) to the genito-urinary apparatus (e.g., Smiley's inspiration that they ought to advertise the fine boiled crabs they serve at their bar by a huge sign saying: "You get Crabs at Timmy's."); (d) to gastrointestinal out-bursts (e.g., when Mr. Flink downs his mug of beer "he emitted an eructation that had everything in it but kettledrums"); and (e) to other excremental matter (e.g., "Mrs. Feeley closed her gums over a short sibilant word. 'Of all the . . .' 'Scatological skunks!' Miss Tink-ham finished indignantly").

Not apparently satisfied with their ambivalently shameful attitudes toward direct scatological things and appendages, American citizens tend to carry these over as well into less direct excremental channels. We find, for example, that human flatus, belching, vomiting, men-struation, pubic hair, men's drawers, and women's lingerie—these and various other excremental processes, or organs allied to them, or clothes associated with these organs—may be found incessantly joked about, made the target of trite innuendo, and continually flaunted but never really faced in public writings and utterances. We shall refer merely to one more example.

We find that women's menstrual processes are considered to be so shameful that a leading manufacturer of sanitary napkins blatantly, and in all seriousness, displays large advertisements in many leading magazines which show a picture of an ordinary wrapped box. The copy reads:

NOW . . . MODESS IN THE WONDERFUL NEW-SHAPE BOX!

A pretty secretary was asked, "What's in this wrapped box?" "I just can't guess," she said, ". . . it looks like so many things!"

The wrapped box in the picture above *does* look like so many things! It might contain stationery . . . facial tissues . . . a jewel box. But . . .

It contains Modess! For now Modess comes in a *new*-shape, *dif-*

129

ferent-shape box. So discreet ... keeps your secret so nicely.

Imagine the shame of a modern twentieth-century miss whose neighbors discover, from the shape of the box she is carting home, that she has regular menstrual periods! How *would* she ever live it down?

Contemporary attitudes toward human excremental processes may perhaps best be summarized by this satirical passage from a story, "Pure Phoebe," published in one of the little magazines, *Wake*:

"Phoebe was pure. Never had she allowed an intrusion within the orifices which her body possessed in common with those of other women, save for the unavoidable necessities that must be tolerated in the degrading business of animal existence....

"With what mortification and disgust Phoebe submitted to the primordial curse of womankind! ...

"Only slightly less revolting were those other eliminative functions —and, in fact, through arduous training she had habituated herself to limiting their performance to a minimal twice a day. And nowhere were the tissues so copiously consumed as in Phoebe's toilet! ...

"No soiled handkerchief profaned the handbag of Phoebe....

"And with revulsion she beheld all the other indelicate malfeasances of her body—the waxy secretions of her ears ... the growth of down upon her legs, the gas escaping from her bowels—though never be it said that Phoebe farted!"

From all of which we may conclude—what? Well:

That although, officially, the American people are opposed to scatological references, their everyday conversation and writings overflow with such references.

That precisely because scatology is theoretically taboo, it acquires emotionally and sexually stimulating qualities that make it immensely popular.

That because it is banned in polite society, scatology takes on an aspect of strength and character that makes its use and enjoyment a mark of distinction for those who would be considered strong, unsissified individuals.

That scatological outlets frequently serve as a normal mode of expression for those elements of the populace who permit themselves relatively few direct or indirect sexual outlets, and that scatological humor sometimes serves as a substitute for more deeply repressed sex expression.

That the great majority of twentieth-century Americans seem to consider scatology to be, at one and the same time, (a) dirty, filthy, wicked, and unclean and (b) gay, titillating, clever, and exhilarating.

That, in consequence, American attitudes, feelings, thoughts, and actions in relation to scatology are incredibly chaotic, childish, and confused.

As we have just seen, there were extremely few expressed and implied attitudes toward scatology in the American mass media of the early 1950's; and those references that were found were all on the conservative side. In the early 1960's, the trends ran in exactly the same direction, at least as far as the disapproval of scatological things was concerned. There were, however, considerably more lascivious references to scatological processes, especially in contemporary fiction.

That references to human excrement and urine should be largely or exclusively negative is, of course, to be expected, since excremental functions are hardly the most esthetic or pleasant, even when objectively viewed. It hardly comes as a surprise, then, when we read such negatively toned descriptions as this one in *Lolita*: "Clumsily playing my part, I stomped to the bathroom to check if they had taken my English toilet water; they had not; but I noticed with a spasm of fierce disgust that the former counselor of the Tsar, after thoroughly easing his bladder, had not flushed the toilet. That solemn pool of alien urine with a soggy, tawny cigarette butt disintegrating in it struck me as a crowning insult, and I wildly looked around for a weapon."

In less serious vein, several jokes were found in the magazines of the 1960's that showed conservative attitudes toward scatology, and yet by their very existence also showed a kind of lewd acceptance of excremental and urinary functions. For example:

From *Twenty-One*: "A finely dressed woman entered a taxi with her dog and during the trip the dog urinated on the seat of the cab. When the driver noticed what had happened he glared at his passenger. 'Don't you dare say a word,' she haughtily insisted. '*I* did it.' "

From *Campus Howl*, quoting from the *Florida Orange Peel*: "The alien craft landed in a field and several small, green men disembarked. Marching single file up to a nearby farmhouse, they knocked solemnly on the door. When the door was answered, one of the extraterrestials said haltingly but in perfect English, 'Take ... us ... to ... your ... bathroom.' "

The one unequivocally approving attitude toward scatological functions that was found in the literature of the early 1960's was this passage from D. H. Lawrence's *Lady Chatterley's Lover*: "All the while he spoke he exquisitely stroked the rounded tail, till it seemed as if a slippery sort of fire came from it into his hands. And his finger-tips touched the two secret openings to her body, time after time, with a soft little brush of fire. 'An if tha shits an' if tha pisses, I'm glad. I don't want a woman as couldna shit nor piss.' "

Scatological references of a fairly objective kind are amazingly common in modern best-selling novels and are almost certainly included, in most instances, to add some kind of left-handed salacious interest to the work. Here are some typical illustrations:

From *The Devil's Advocate*: " 'Why do you always look at me like that?' Black smiled calmly and said: 'You are beautiful, Paolino. Like the Young David whom Michelangelo carved out of a piece of marble. I am an artist—a lover of beauty. So, I like to look at you.' 'I want to piss,' said the boy, grinning. He leapt up and walked to the edge of the plateau and stood straddle-legged, easing himself in full view of Nicholas Black, who saw the mockery in it but made no protest."

From *The War Lover*: "Marrow had understood at once what the trouble was: that in rarefied upper airs a man may be unable to belch or break wind. Prien's stomach was already famous among us, for he stored immense amounts of gas in it, and sometimes he emitted *flatus per rectum* for what seemed like minutes on end. And indeed, that was all there was to it. At twelve thousand Prien took his oxygen mask off and got relief, via both exits. In a big way, I mean, it was remarkable. Right away he was himself again."

From *The Cave*: Rachel Goldstein to Isaac Sumpter: "I just love to make A's. I make plenty of 'em, too. I was at Radcliffe two years, and I made plenty of A's. I made a few F's too. When something bores me it's just to hell with it. Sometimes I get bored crapless, then I crave the F—I just crave it—it sort of keeps you clean inside to get that F when you know that even if you are bored crapless you could make an A if you were that kind of a bloody little sharp-kneed case of walking constipation with that kind of a myopic dandruff-trap on your shoulders."

From *Wake Up, Stupid*:

'Why do you pass,' Harry was asked,
'Gas through your mouth?
'Are you perverse?'
'No, just reverse,' Harry replied, genially chuckling
'Which is to say,'
Harry added, warily meditating,
'That the gases where my mouth is
'Seeped up from where the South is,
'While the brain displaced by gases
'Dropped to where an ass's
'Brains are said to be.'

From *Hawaii*: "So the dreadfully constipated missionaries took ipecac and rhubarb and calomel and castor oil. But mostly they

132

walked. . . . And the day was half spent with no time allocated for emergency cases on the part of those who in extreme desperation had taken a master dose of ipecac, rhubarb, calomel, and castor oil. It therefore became necessary for Brother Whipple, with Captain Janders' amused consent and with able help from Keoki Kanakoa, to rig an unclosed improvised privy aft of the stern. At stated intervals all females would go below decks, and one minister after another would test his good fortune on the open seat, his hands wrapped desperately about the timbers Keoki had hammered into place, his pallid white bottom winking at the whales."

From *On the Road*: "By and by we came to a town, slowed down, and Montana Slim said, 'Ah, pisscall,' but the Minnesotans didn't stop and went right on through. 'Damn, I gotto go,' said Slim. 'Go over the side,' said somebody. 'Well, I *will*,' he said, and slowly, as we all watched, he inched to the back of the platform on his haunch, holding on as best he could, till his legs dangled over. Somebody knocked on the window of the cab to bring this to the attention of the brothers. Their great smiles broke as they turned. And just as Slim was ready to proceed, precarious as it was already, they began zigzagging the truck at 70 miles an hour. He fell back a moment; we saw a whale's spout in the air; he struggled back to a sitting position. They swung the truck. Wham, over he went on his side, watering all over himself."

All in all, these contemporary novels, as well as various other forms of popular literature, seem to be asking one supremely important question, over and over: "Defecation and urination, anyone?"

Scatological sentiments in modern mass media, which are far more salacious than either liberal or conservative in their content, may be nicely summed up by the following sample of several jokes and cartoons that were found in surveying the literature of the 1960's:

From *Cavalier*: "Here's a riddle you can use to shock your stuffy friends:

What is it that a man does standing up?

A woman does sitting down?

A dog does on three legs?

(When there has been an appropriate pause, you can reply, 'Shake hands.')"

From *Playboy*: Caption to a still from an old movie showing a group of men and women looking up at the sky in terror: "Here come those damn pigeons again!"

From *Rapture*: "Two elderly matrons were using adjoining booths in the ladies' room of a swank night club when one of them, a little hesitatingly, knocked on the neighboring booth and said: Pardon me, but do you have some extra paper in there? Sorry, came the reply, but

I've barely enough for myself. Any newspaper lying around? No, sorry. I don't see any. Well, er, do you happen to have an old envelope in your pocketbook or anything else like that? No, terribly sorry. Well, then—could you let me have two fives for a ten?"

Apparently, to the bolder writers and editors of today, as distinct from the more squeamish ones of a decade or more ago, excretion is the better part of valor.

CHAPTER 16

"Obscenity"

That mode of sex behavior which probably has the distinction of being, at one and the same time, the most widely condemned and condoned American sex practice is the employment of "obscenity." It may well be said that the great majority of Americans consciously and verbally deplore the use of improper sex representations—and then just as consciously and verbally participate in that fabulously popular modern pastime, the telling of "dirty" jokes.

As a matter of fact, it is virtually impossible to tell or to laugh at any sex anecdote without simultaneously accepting and applauding "obscenity." For the fact of telling or listening to such jokes is certainly a (direct or backhanded) acceptance of them; and, since the whole point of these stories *is* their sexual content, the very chuckle or guffaw with which one responds to them proves that one *does* consider them "dirty" and "obscene."

Public disapproval of alleged obscenity is unusually widespread in contemporary America and is officially promulgated by several organized groups which immediately condemn any off-color inclusions in magazines, books, films, plays, et cetera. Thus the Legion of Decency, with literally millions of sworn supporters, each week publishes lists of "indecent" writings and performances which are printed in hundreds of leading periodicals. Activities of the Legion and of numerous local Watch and Ward and Vice Suppression societies (such as the well-known ones in Boston and New York) result not only in unofficial boycotts of "obscene" plays, films, and publications, but in many police actions directed against such representations.

In contemporary mass media themselves we find multiple vociferations against alleged obscenity. In the popular magazines, for example, we may note the *Family Circle* movie critic lamenting that a very popular team of comedians has become in recent years "so risque they were unbearable." Dr. Winfield S. Pugh, in the ordinarily liberal magazine, *Sexology*, writes as follows: "This process is usually called

intercourse, marital relations, sexual congress, or *sexual communion.*
There are, of course, many undignified terms applied to it by ignorant
persons. *Nice people never use such gutter language.*" Falk Johnson,
in an article on obscenity in the *American Mercury*, tells us that because American strip-teasers objected to the "unfortunate con-
notation" of the term *strip-teasing* they induced H. L. Mencken to
coin a new designation, *ecdysiast*, for them.

Contemporary newspapers follow the magazines in giving us illustrations of anti-"obscenity" attitudes. Thus a New York *Enquirer*
columnist suggests that "those who speak 'straight from the shoulder'
should manage to speak from a little higher up." And a New York
Herald Tribune cartoonist satirically lampoons the girl-filled shows of
Billy Rose, the risque song lyrics of Cole Porter, and the "unclean"
language of the play, *Mister Roberts.*

American fiction also contains a good many anti-"obscenity" attitudes. In the novel, *Earth Abides,* the hero becomes quite incensed
at another character's telling indelicate stories. In *Abe Lincoln of
Pigeon Creek* much is made of honest Abe's refusing to tell certain
anecdotes because "there's ladies present." In a story in *Private
Detective* a girl allows herself to be blackmailed rather than to have
"a slightly off-color record" that she has made become generally
known. In *The Man with the Golden Arm* one character is sent to jail
"for unbecoming words to a lady," and another character, a night-club
chorine, apologizes and blushes to her paramour when she explains
some of the gestures she employs in the course of her nightly routine.

The epitome of anti-"obscenity" attitudes is reached, perhaps, in
this quotation from Falk Johnson's "The Ups and Downs of 'Dirty'
Words," published in the *American Mercury*: "Vance Randolph, an
authority on the customs of the Ozarks, has found many examples . . .
In a study made some years ago of 'Verbal Modesty in the Ozarks,' he
tells of a 'grown-up mountain woman, the mother of several children,
who blushed scarlet when she heard *physics* mentioned as a part of
the high-school curriculum.' And he reports that the local experts with
the shotgun do not 'cock' it. Instead they 'pull back both roosters.'
Randolph reports, too, that other people refer to 'cock and bull'
stories as 'rooster and ox' stories. Likewise, when Professor J. M.
Steadman, Jr., made a study of verbal modesty at Emory University in
Georgia, one student wrote: 'I avoid *circumscribe* because I am afraid
that I will say *circumcise* by mistake.' Other students indicated that
they avoided such words as *butt, Butte, rumpus,* and *elicit.*"

From all this material it should be painfully clear that "obscenity"
in America is not merely theoretically opposed by large portions of
our populace, but that the opposition to it is often of a highly ver-
balized and widely publicized nature. In the light of this quite specific

and overt condemnation of "obscenity," one would not expect to find anyone coming out frankly and strongly in its favor. Yet in at least a mild sort of way that is what we do sometimes find.

In *Queen New Orleans*, for example, a character, Bernard de Marigny, teaches his own children "broad" songs, in spite of the furious opposition of his wife. Over the Mutual Broadcasting System network, a commentator blithely tells us that a certain movie actress loves to shock her friends with risque stories. And a New York *Journal American* columnist actually names, in her accolades of the year, a socially prominent woman as the "BEST RISQUE STORY-TELLER ... [who] looks the most respectable, straightlaced grande dame, but in the right company she unleashes her wit, jokes, and bon mots that panic any party."

Humorous acceptances of the goodness of "obscene" representations are also not uncommon in our culture. *Wet Hen*, for instance, quotes this anecdote: "Young Wife: How was the stag party last night? Husband: Revolting, repulsive, disgusting! I ought to know, I was in the front row." And another humor magazine gives us this exchange. "Are you troubled with improper thoughts?" "No, I rather enjoy them."

To make matters infinitely more confusing, at the very same time when "obscene" writings, performances, and conversations are, on the one hand, excoriated and on the other hand approved, it must also be clear to anyone who even slightly uses his normal faculties that sexual indelicacies are most publicly employed in our nation and that, in fact, their utilization is so frank and widespread as to constitute veritable public sanction.

Take, for instance, the advertisements in American publications. Hundreds of these ads appear every month which are as sex-provoking as they could possibly be; and a good many of these, as is only to be expected, border on the "obscene." Thus one of the widely published ads in the magazines shows a man peeking through a keyhole and exclaiming: "OH! WHAT FUN!" And, it goes on to say, if you send one dollar for twenty booklets and three hundred cartoons, "you'll get a carload of fun and laffs to amuse you! All you can stand—and then some. . . . All shipped prepaid in plain sealed wrapper."

Another typical magazine advertisement says: "BLUSHFUL! DARING! Famous Dwight Fiske and Nan Blackstone Party Records. Now available by prepaid, insured mail."

Curiously enough, some of the sexiest advertising even slips into the shopping-guide columns of family magazines. One such release, for example, shows a photograph of a woman dressed in a "Bloomer Girl" apron, this announcement stated: "For a touch of well timed ribaldry, guaranteed to set a party off in high spirits, a duck apron comes in the curvaceous shape of a bloomer girl for you or your husband. Marked with such provocative truisms as 'Let's Get Tight,' 'Stop Ribbing,' etc. $1.95 postpaid. Shocking, yes, but riotous, too!"

One step behind—or, sometimes, ahead of—the advertisements in the employment of off-color language and behavior are the modern stage plays. Thus in *South Pacific* much humor is derived from the United States Marines' deliberately teaching Bloody Mary to express herself in impolite terms:

MARY: Stingy bastard! (She turns back toward the marine for approval.) That good?

MARINE: That's great, Mary! You're learning fast.

MARY: Stingy bastard! ... I learn fast. ... Pretty soon I talk English good as any crummy marine. Stingy bastard!

In *Detective Story* the talk is again free and loose, as when Callahan remarks: "I ain't no friggen barber-college detective with pleats in my pants."

In *Mister Roberts* one of the characters collects pillowcases on which are embroidered such handy sayings as: "Tonight or never ... Compliments of Allis-Chalmers, Farm Equipment .... We plow deep while others sleep."

Following direct suit, modern novelists also liberally employ descriptions and scenes which, with little stretch of the imagination, can be seen to border on the "pornographic." In *The Egyptian* we are introduced to "a big Negress, whose breasts hung down on her belly like black cooking pots. [She] had undressed so as to be the first to receive Kaptah, and she cried, 'Give me my beloved that I may press him to my bosom! Give me my elephant that he may wind his trunk about me!' "

In *Divine Mistress* a scene is described where four hypnotized people imitate a Black Mass performance in this wise: "Gradually the pantomine of lust became no longer a pantomine. Indecent gestures led to repulsively carnal acts, and youthful bodies, locked in lustful embrace, rolled upon the floor. Over it all was the highpitched wailing sound of the music."

In *The Man with the Golden Arm* beautifully realistic portrayals of the normal human use of "obscenity" are given, as when a prisoner who is soon to be electrocuted derisively shouts to two other prisoners: "Hey! You the guys gonna split my pants 'n shave my little pointy head?" Nelson Algren, in the same novel, also gives us this inimitable picture of Vi: "She wasn't going to live with old Stash another day, she told the house. 'Or any other of you goddamned hairy-ass morphodyke booze bums who think a girl got to be grateful

137

when her old man brings home bargains from Nostriewicz's Hi-Klass Bakery.... Stash is too old for a zipper anyhow, it's just for young guys in a big hurry.' "

Humorous uses of "obscenity" are fairly easy to find, as may be witnessed by this verse quoted in *The Old Line*:

> *Mary had a little plane,*
> *And through the air she'd frisk.*
> *Now wasn't she a silly girl*
> *Her little **

Even popular songs frequently have a double-entendre, ribald appeal, as witness the hit tune, "I've Got a Lovely Bunch of Cocoanuts," which, without saying anything that is directly sexual, manages to convey a throughly off-color impression: which impression, of course, adds immeasurably to its popularity.

Back on the factual side of the ledger, we find that "obscenity" is apparently most liberally employed in everyday American conversation and action. As Wolcott Gibbs, writing in *Cosmopolitan*, puts it: "The facts ... are that ... all gentlemen and most ladies acquainted with, and under stress habitually employ, all nine of the famous Anglo-Saxon monosyllables." The movie reviewer for *Family Circle* tells us that whenever a sex picture is shown in American theaters there often are many "mugs in the audience, waiting to let loose with nasty yaks." And, confirming this, a New York *Herald Tribune* writer informs us that when a capsule presentation of Jean-Paul Sartre's play, *The Respectful Prostitute*, was shown in a Times Square movie house, "movie indoctrination was apparent in the whooping delight with which the uninhibited language of the trollop-heroine, Lizzie, was received. Comments from patrons were frequently heard; and the reaction to the plain talk about matters of sex was not unlike that encountered at an Elks' smoker."

A final illustration of the American public's propensity for "obscene" representations may be seen in this excerpt from *Pace* magazine's account of the trial of Brenda Allen, famed Los Angeles madam: "August 8: 2,141 pages of testimony heard by the Grand Jury were released today and revealed, among other things, some lurid and exotic details of life in a brothel. According to Brenda Allen's testimony, 'sexual circuses' were staged whenever enough customers wanted to perform. 'For instance, there would be three or four men from the studios,' said Brenda. 'I won't mention names because they are very nice professional people, you know. The way it was done, these circuses, I mean, the lights are blue light and very low. You just have all the chairs and couches back against the walls and you spread a sheet or blanket out on the floor. Then everyone does what he wants to.' 'In full view of the spectators?' she was asked. 'Yes, sir. They are all nude. The girls and the men, and spectators can watch from the room or behind drapes.' 'Do these spectators pay for the privilege of watching?' 'Yes, unless he was a police officer.' "

On this elegant, self-explanatory note, perhaps, we should tactfully leave our discussion of "obscenity." We cannot, however, forego one more quotation (from *Joke Parade*) which, with charming finesse, sums up the common American overt and covert attitude regarding "obscenity." "Mother: Mary, where did you get that dreadful book? Mary: Why, it was in the bookcase in your room, Mother. Don't you remember it?"

Attitudes Toward "Obscenity" in the 1960's

In the study of attitudes toward "obscenity" that was made of mass media in the 1950's, it was found that relatively few references existed in the literature at that time and that these were mainly conservative. In the follow-up study of attitudes in the 1960's it has been found that a good many more references to "obscenity" exist and that these are preponderantly on the permissive side.

As usual, let us first take a look at some of the anti-"obscenity" views that commonly appear in contemporary sources of public communication. In Rona Jaffe's novel, *The Best of Everything*, April is shown a photograph by the change-maker at a subway booth and we learn that "She looked at him curiously and picked it up. At first she didn't realize what it was, it seemed like two people in a strained and unaccustomed posture, wrestlers perhaps. Then she saw it was a man and a woman, and when she discovered what they were doing to each other she felt her face redden and her hand began to shake so hard she could scarely push the picture back through the slot. She turned to flee."

In an article in *Scamp* on "Is It Pornography or Is it Art?" we are told that you won't find on the shelves of your public library the hilarious treatise by Benjamin Franklin on *How to Convert the Offensive Odors of Flatulence into Sweet-smelling Aromas by the Addition of Chemical Powders to Food*, nor will you be able to locate easily Mark Twain's *1601—Conversation as it was by the Social Fire-place in the Time of the Tudors*. Both of these works are con-sidered to be, at least by librarians, highly "obscene."

In Faulkner's novel, *The Mansion*, Gavin Stevens blushes furiously when Linda Snopes asks him in the vernacular to copulate with her; and in the printed version of the novel, the word she uses is indicated by a blank.

In a story in *My Love Secret*, the female narrator tells her readers that "A truckdriver picked me up. I've never forgotten that—his leering face and the terrible things he said to me." In another story in the same magazine, we are told that "there followed a string of curses that even made my ears burn—some I'd never even heard, but they were vile."

In a *Redbook* story, when the heroine thinks to herself that "she would get the hell out of there," the word *hell* is not printed but is replaced by a dash.

In the *New York Daily News*, a news item shows that a pornography probe in Brooklyn led to the arrest of "one of the largest pornography rings" in the borough. "A man who made a cocktail hour appointment to purchase 200 reels of pornographic film at $7 a reel last evening turned out to be a detective, and as soon as he got the film, he placed the two alleged salesmen under arrest."

In an article in the *American Mercury*, the recent liberalization of the United States censorship laws, particularly in regard to the novel, *Lady Chatterley's Lover*, is rabidly inveighed against. The article begins: "When Postmaster General Arthur Summerfield lost the right in court to ban *Lady Chatterley's Lover* from the mails, the decent and law-abiding citizenry of this country suffered a defeat so far-reaching that its impact can scarcely be comprehended. . . . How did the present disgraceful situation come about?"

In the film, *Can-Can*, Simone loses half her audience of "respectable people" because she becomes a little tipsy and executes a bawdy dance and a risque song. The *New York Times* carries this significant item showing how afraid of profanity American public figures are: "PRESIDENT SETS RECORD STRAIGHT ON 'DAM' SLIP. President Eisenhower wanted it clearly understood today that he was not to be accused of profanity after a slip of the tongue led to a mention of 'that dam business.' He was telling his news conference about United States participation, through the World Bank, in the financing of the Aswan Dam in Egypt when his inadvertent remark filled the conference room with laughter. Quickly recovering from his split-second, blushing embarrassment, the President went on to say: 'I don't want to be accused of profanity around here.'"

On the humorous side, "obscenity" and profanity are also frowned upon in several examples. Thus, in *Campus Howl*, quoting from the *Florida Orange Peel*, we read: "Did you hear about the deaf mute who said so many dirty words that his mother had to wash his hands?" And in the *Reader's Digest* we have the anecdote about the husband who found his wife distraught, when he arrived home one evening, because of her terrible day. "First the baby cut his first tooth," she said, "then he fell down and cut his lip on the tooth." "What happened next?"

her husband asked "Then," she added in a shocked voice, "he said his first word!"

Obviously, as the foregoing examples show, "obscenity" is still disapproved of in many of the references that may be found in today's mass media. But, at the same time, it is also tacitly or openly approved. By way of illustration, in many contemporary novels "obscene" words are freely employed by the characters; and in some instances, such as Hersey's *The War Lover*, the books are literally full of this kind of language. A typical passage (one of very many) from the Hersey novel reads: "Soupie actually put in to be shifted to another ground crew because he said it was a f . . . ing bore to take care of *The Body*, it was like being a f . . . ing gas-pump winder at a service station; but the powers-that-be wouldn't transfer him. 'What a way to fight a God-damn war,' Soupie said one day. 'In my opinion I avoid all pigs that there's no risk of the clap if you put it to 'em. Life's short. S . . .! You got to gamble.' "

In Robert Penn Warren's *The Cave*, we have another steady round of "obscenity," with several passages along this typical line: "He saw the red traffic light ahead. 'Fuck the light,' he said, and giggled with delicious gaiety, and barrelled right through." In D. H. Lawrence's *Lady Chatterley's Lover*, there are also many such "obscene" uses of words, some of which have been quoted in previous chapters of this book. Yet, in a courageous and highly important decision, Judge Frederick Van Pelt Bryan ruled that "a book is not to be judged by excerpts of individual passages but must be judged as a whole. . . . Judged by these standards *Lady Chatterley's Lover* is not obscene. The decision of the Postmaster General that it is obscene and therefore non-mailable is contrary to law and clearly erroneous."

Not only the main sex organs, but the auxiliary ones, particularly the buttocks and anus, are frequently referred to in an "obscene" way in modern literature. In Michener's *Hawaii*, Whip tells a visitor who threatens to come into his plantation, "If you try it, you'll be thrown out on your inalienable ass." In Warren's *The Cave*, Isaac Sumpter needs a telephone line strung to the vicinity of the cave he is working in and tells one of his helpers "to kick out of the asses of whoever is putting the line up whatever is in their asses." In Kerouac's *On the Road*, one of the minor characters says over and over again: "Them goddamn cops can't put no flies on *my* ass!" In *Exodus*, Ari tells Dov Landau: "You're not going to get to Palestine by sitting here on your arse and doing nothing." Etcetera, etcetera.

Aside from modern novels, permissive uses or advocacies of "obscenity" are to be found in many other mass media sources. *Tab* magazine has an article showing that the frankest kind of sex depictions

141

are now becoming prevalent in films and concludes that "If the present trend continues unchecked, perhaps before long you will be able to plunk down the price of admission at your neighborhood cinema and view a Cinemascope, Technicolor, Stereophonic version of Henry Miller's *Tropic of Cancer*—or similar fare once considered too lewd and lascivious for the U.S. movie going public!"

In the serialization of Errol Flynn's autobiography in *True* magazine, Flynn tells about two horrible flops he made in the films; and then says: "Ah, screw 'em all, I said. Let 'em chase me around the world." *Scamp* enthusiastically welcomes the republication of *Lady Chatterley's Lover* and other works previously held to be "obscene." *The Ladder* reports a talk by Dr. Eberhard Kronhausen in which he claimed that pornographic literature may well act as a sexual stimulant but does not normally lead to behavior that is antisocial, harmful, or maladjusted.

Rolland Howard, in an article on pornography in the *Mattachine Review*, refers to women who curl up their noses and look properly disgusted when they view examples of pornography as "frustrated old biddies, most of whom must be sexually 'unemployed' widows, divorcees or spinsters." Neill D. Summers, reviewing Allen Edwardes' book, *The Jewel in the Lotus*, in *One* magazine, writes: "The naughty atmosphere of Boccaccio's fictional *Decameron* with actual seasonings from (the unexpurgated) *Arabian Nights* provides frankly told entertainment well worth the book's price. The breezy fetching style of telling adheres to everyday speech but broadens the vocabulary at times. Do you wonder where we get our vulgar use of 'prick'? Male effeminates and dancing girls sing: My coynte have I subjected, without shame, to the prickles of more than I can name."

To end this follow-up survey of attitudes to "obscenity" in the literature of the 1960's, we quote this anecdote which appeared in both *Jest* and *Comedy* magazine: "Artist, as he and his friend gaze at a modernistic painting: It's obscene, I tell you! Friend: I wish I could see it your way."

The excoriation and suppression of "obscenity," then, is still very much with us. But much of what appears in today's mass media, and by its very appearance is tacitly presented as *not* being considered any longer "obscene," would certainly have been banned and made grounds for criminal action only a decade or so ago. Previous "obscenities" are apparently joining, on today's calendar, the snows of yesteryear.

CHAPTER 17

Lasciviousness

Among present-day writers in our culture there appears to be a dichotomous unanimity of opinion concerning sexual lust and lasciviousness. The religious writers—Monsignor Sheen, Fulton Oursler, Thomas Merton, Norman Vincent Peale et al.—consider unabashed sex desire as just about the most dreadful thing in the world; a good many other publicists consider it just about the best.

Typical of the modern religionist attitude toward lasciviousness is Norman Vincent Peale's estimation: "Men allow their minds to become shackled in many ways—by self-pity, by anxiety, by self-interest, by lust, by greed."

Typical of the non-religious writer's attitude toward and employment of glaring sensuality is—well, where in the world can we possibly begin? So many examples favoring or employing lasciviousness were found in our study of American mass media that to quote all of them would require an entire volume rather than a single chapter. A small sampling will be now be examined.

Periodicals of the *Life-Look-See* variety continually publish revealing pictures of lovely girls who are not merely as naked as the censors will allow and as high-breasted and lean-limbed as to be almost unbelievable, but their writers strive for some kind of "angle" or "gimmick" which will make these girls appear to be unusually seductive and easily beddable. Thus in a typical feature article on press agents and their publicity stunts, *Man to Man* gives us four pictures of unclothed beauties—three of them with their bosoms literally bursting through meager coverings, and the fourth clothed largely in a wooden stock which makes her look much more nude than she actually is. All of these girls have come-hither looks designed to make the average American male water at the mouth and curse the day he met his wife or girl friend.

In less pictorial vein an article in *True Experiences* on natural childbirth has a mother reporting, "I was so submerged in my job that, while I knew what was happening . . . the only thing of real importance, the only thing that could reach me, was my obstetrician's saying, 'Now I can see a spot as big as a fifty-cent piece of your baby's head—with black hair!' " And a *Variety* columnist, in commenting on television tubes and screens, notes that "today a person is known by the size of his tube. Now I say this is wrong! The size of the screen means nothing, it's what you see on the screen that counts. For instance, the other day a friend of mine presented me with a key ring with a miniature telescope attached. Now this telescope had only a ⅛-inch lens. But . . . when you looked into it . . . WOW!"

So much for magazine nonfiction. Modern fiction, both in periodicals and in best-selling novels, tends to be even hotter. Typical of much magazine fiction is this description from a *Private Detective* story: "She wore a thin dress so tight on her body that she must have used a shoehorn to get inside. The neckline was low. What was inside looked interesting. She pulled herself erect, leaned against me. Her hair smelled of—of damp violets. 'I've been waiting,' she murmured. 'Why?' 'I could go for you in a big way, big boy.' 'Jackie?' Her face stared up at me, lips parted. She took a slow, deep breath to tighten the upper part of the dress, and my eyes almost popped out. She was built, that girl. I have an eye for beauty, even when I'm busy."

If a somewhat higher literary level is wanted, here is a piece of exposition from a story in *Partisan Review*: "The high-breasted maid moved smoothly and majestically. She had an excellent figure, was nearsighted and rather haughty. In her open gray eyes one saw a petrified lewdness."

Modern novels, in particular, make good and continual use of lascivious passages, as these illustrations from best-sellers will convincingly show:

From John O'Hara's *A Rage to Live*: "The moment he touched her the rage began. 'Do everything! Kiss me? Kiss me here? Let me—no. Go in me. Quickly, Sidney, please. I'm going. I'm going. Don't do anything else, go in me. Oh, you're in me and I'm all around you, just in time, time, time.' "

From Edison Marshall's *Gypsy Sixpence*: "She was sitting very still, speaking in a low voice, but when I moved my arms a little in invitation or entreaty, she clung to them, her breast pressed hard as a child's against mine. Her quick, countless kisses covering my face seemed to tell me that she was frightened; they became fiercely hungry, my lips between her teeth felt exquisite pain. . . . She touched the blanket. 'It's awfully rough.' 'That fits too, doesn't it?' Horse blankets on the stone in the moonlight. 'Yes, it's a wonderful fit. Hurry, Rom, because I'm so cold and empty.' "

From Mary Lasswell's *One on the House*: " 'You're in like [Errol] Flynn!' Mrs. Feeley laughed. 'Mrs. Feeley!' Miss Tinkham raised her lorgnette. 'Are you sure you read all the details of that case?' "

From Alberto Moravia's *The Woman of Rome*: "She would lie at her companion's back with her chin resting on his shoulder, her legs entwined in his, her arm around his waist, her hand on his groin and her fingers feeling languidly across his belly—like roots seeking for nourishment in the deepest earth."

From Dorothy C. Wilson's *Prince of Egypt*: "In the shelter of a cluster of feathery acacias Moses took her again in his arms, not gently this time, with the deference due to royalty, but urgently, almost roughly. They were no longer prince and princess; their love had become something simple and honest and elemental, like the fragrance of fresh earth still clinging to their fingers. Her breasts, unencumbered by linen or jewels, were soft and warm against his flesh. The red lips crushed beneath his own were unsweetened by any more subtle perfumes than youth and health and sunshine."

From Nelson Algren's *The Man with the Golden Arm*: "Making no particular effort to keep from waking him, she crawled over him, teasing the hairs sticking out of his nostrils with the nipple of her breast just for the hell of it. . . . Her G-string was upheld by court plaster and a gilded cardboard crescent swung for some reason from her navel while she went into a convulsive series of bumps; like some dark Diamond Lil just fed on Spanish fly. . . . with the G-string bounce-bounce-bouncing."

From Mika Waltari's *The Egyptian*: "And there I met a lovely woman whose robe was of linen so transparent that her breasts and loins might be seen through it. She was straight and slender, her lips, cheeks, and eyebrows were colored, and she looked at me in unabashed curiosity. . . . 'But it is not true! My body does not burn at all like fire; indeed, it is said to be desirable. Feel for yourself!' She took my limp hand and carried it to her belly. I felt her beauty through the thin stuff so that I began to quake, and my cheeks burned. 'You still do not believe me,' she said with feigned disappointment. 'My dress is in the way, but stay—I will draw it aside.' She pulled away her robe and held my hand to her bare breast. It was soft and cool beneath my hand."

From Walter Havighurst's *Signature of Time*: "Her hands cupped his smooth cheek, freshly shaven. They pressed his deerskin jacket. They crept under his jacket and under his linen shirt. . . . His fingers shook as he fumbled at her waist. Then her dress parted and his hands pressed her flesh. 'I found a little fox,' he whispered, 'in a den. It was not so soft as you.' He lifted her in his arms and cradled her. He carried her back and forth across the room and laid her on the bed. She reached up her hands to draw him. 'M'sieu is strong,' she said, and then there was only her warm tremulous breathing, and loneliness ran away and away, further and further. She crept from his bed before daylight. It was a dreamlike leaving—her soft lips, her whisper. 'M'sieu come back to Buffalo,' she murmured. 'Marie make him not lonely again.' "

A summary comment on the lasciviousness of modern fiction may be found in Peter Marshall's *Mr. Jones, Meet the Master*. Notes Mr. Marshall: "Authors of recent best-sellers have vied with each other in their lurid descriptions of sexual orgies, until millions of readers have filed in the libraries of their imagination pictures that dance obscenely in the half-light of desire and passion."

Lest it be thought that this use of lasciviousness by modern novelists has no relation to the sales appeal of their books, we may note that Bennett Cerf, in his *Saturday Review of Literature* column, comments on Moravia's *The Woman of Rome*: "Sales are over the hill—the Fanny Hill, should we say?—and going away."

Plays like *Mister Roberts*, *Detective Story*, and *Born Yesterday* get most of their laughs from highly sexed-up situations in which the males are continually thinking of the girls in one specific way—and we don't mean as possible marriage partners. Musical shows like *South Pacific*, *Texas Li'l Darlin'*, *Where's Charley?*, *Gentlemen Prefer Blondes*, and *Kiss Me, Kate* are, if possible, even more lust-ridden than the non-musicals.

We may mention, in this connection, the recent revival of Mae West's *Diamond Lil*. As Bernard Sobel points out in a feature story of Miss West in *Variety*: "Instead of saying, 'Thou shalt not!' Mae said: 'C'm up and see me sometime.' And this intimate admonition soon became the American sin-onym for sin, with a dash of laughter. Proof of Miss West's importance as a reformer came with the recent revival of *Diamond Lil*. For lines and situations which had shocked audiences of twenty years ago were accepted this time as realistic, matter-of-fact, and humorous side lights on the fascinating, perennial battle between the male and the female."

As for the movies, they seem to follow as closely to the stage pattern as the censor will allow. War pictures like *Battleground* and *Sands of Iwo Jima* include precisely the same attitude toward sex as their stage counterparts, *Mister Roberts* and *South Pacific*. In both stage and screen productions the members of the armed forces are continually thinking and talking about the same thing—and it isn't chow. Thus in *Battleground* a young Frenchwoman with ample breasts innocently asks some American soldiers, on a frosty morning, if they'd like to come into her house and warm up. Whereupon they, with unmistakable meaning, reply: "Oh brother!"

The film musicals, like *On the Town*, are essentially the same as the musical plays on Broadway and, as in this case, are often closely adapted from them. They are, when they can get away with it, not a whit less lusty and lascivious than their Broadway counterparts. The film, *On the Town*, in fact, is not only entirely preoccupied with males lusting after women, but also with the reverse. Its frank sensuality would be difficult to match in any other mass medium.

An excellent example of Hollywood's lust for lust is shown in Cecil B. De Mille's *Samson and Delilah*, which critic after critic went out

146

of his way to point out was a typical De Mille cocktail of religion and sex, bearing suspiciously little resemblance, in many succinct details, to the biblical version of the story. As the *American Legion* magazine reviewer wrote: "Hedy Lamarr's trim figure and pretty face, showed off to advantage in low necks, midriffs, and split skirts, provides the sex."

Another revealing comment on the movies' deliberate use of sex may be found in *Variety's* review of the film *South Sea Sinner*, which begins in this fashion: "Including some spicy dialogue and a very patent attempt to prove that sin does not pay, *South Sea Sinner* is good melodrama. It presents Shelley Winters as a vivid water-front café singer-dancer, but the torrid moments have been carefully adulterated by the Motion Picture Association codemakers. With enough sex ballyhoo to help the ambitious exhibitor, it should do generally nice business."

A more concrete example may be noted in this scene from the shooting script of the film, *Prince of Foxes*: "As the camera pulls back we see Orsini standing before Alfonso, who is rather lecherously admiring the portrait [of Lucrezia].... ORSINI: Lucrezia, like the fire in Your Grace's foundry, needs only your breath to make her burn white-hot."

Besides Broadway and Hollywood productions, other kinds of shows also make lavish use of lasciviousness. Night-club acts, for instance, are notoriously sexier than almost any other kind of performance. Beauty pageants, county fairs, business exhibitions, circuses, and numerous other kinds of shows also make excellent use of lasciviously displayed feminine charms and racy humor. *Picture Show*, illustratively, contains an article entitled "Should the New World's Fair Sell Sex?" This article frankly tells how the last World's Fair at New York was so sparsely populated during its first year that "it was almost possible to shoot deer and bear on the grounds, so scarce were humans. Then somebody had an inspiration for the second year, a brain storm that acted like adrenalin on worried bondholders: put in girls, and invite Broadway producers like Mike Todd, George Jessel, and famed Billy Rose to do their stuff. From then on, things hummed at the box office as Gypsy Rose Lee, Rosita Royce, the natating and extremely beautiful Eleanor Holm did their stuff for the suddenly interested crowds."

In addition we have the never-ending herculean labors of American advertisers to sell everything from chewing gum to sex books with the most inviting palaver and pictures imaginable. If the average American male never read a story, saw a play or a movie, nor listened to a radio or television show, he would still be so overwhelmed by sexiness in newspaper, magazine, transportation, billboard, and other ads that his daily sex temperature would still tend to rise many degrees every time he viewed a good copywriter's handiwork.

Perhaps the fullest flavor of lascivious American advertisements may be gained from reviewing the contents of three picture magazines, *Beauty Parade, Flirt,* and *Eyeful.* These magazines, which all have similar formats and which seem to feature the same kind of advertisements, were found to contain, respectively, 80, 85, and 96 lascivious ads, including hawkings of (1) sex books, (2) sexy salt and pepper shakers, (3) honeymoon love drops, (4) lonely hearts clubs, (5) strip-tease photos, (6) sex pamphlets, (7) photos of "artists' models," (8) sex comic books, (9) sex films, (10) sex jokes, (11) bust creams, (12) sexy perfumes, (13) sex cartoons, (14) telescope for watching bathing beauties, (15) courses in how to achieve masculinity, (16) sex puzzles, and (17) various other objects, from penknives to drinking glasses, embossed with sexy pictures.

We may note, finally, that American gag writers and cartoonists are most unbashful in their employment of sex, as these sample products of their pen will quickly show:

From *Man to Man*: " 'In some parts of the world they are so afraid of being buried alive that they have a most peculiar custom. When a man dies they bury him, and after sixty days he is dug up and placed on a cold slab. Twenty beautiful dancing girls are then brought in and dance around him for several hours.' 'What good does that do?' 'Well, if he doesn't get up they know he's really dead.' "

From *True Police Cases*: Cartoon of a man taking a lie-detector test. On the graph, instead of the usual lines, pictures of luscious, naked women show up.

From the *Mercury*: "ADVENTURES IN CLICHE-LAND. Fictitious Reviews. A Satire on conventional contemporary literature by Gerald Gross. I—THE HISTORICAL ROMANCE. *The Cover*: The cover inevitably shows a sensuous, lovely half-breed girl in a transparent lisle negligee, against the brawny, tawny, excessively manly chest of the hero. *The Blurb*: Here in *Passion's Progress*, the whole turbulent, dynamic story of the settlement of southeast Mozambique in the ninth century A.D. is told against the seething heat of the love affair between Lance Dreck and the fiery half-breed Carillon D'Desire. Thomas L. Mundane thrills you again as he did in *The Pale Pansy*, and *Lapidus, Lord of the Lapidaries . . .*"

From *Hello Buddies*: One businessman to another, as they note a series of sharp declines in the production chart of their firm: "We finally found the trouble—it happens when your secretary walks through the shop!"

From *Joke Parade*: "Jill: What are you dreaming about, Jerry? Jerry: Same things as you, darling. Jill: How dare you!"

From *Wet Hen*: "Associate Editor: Let's not have any more jokes about sex, drinking, or profanity. Editor: Okay, I'm tired of putting out this magazine too."

Having sufficiently belabored the point that examples of lasciviousness are rampant in American fiction, nonfiction, movies, plays, advertisements, and humor, what may we conclude? Clearly that the diatribes against lust, lewdness, and lasciviousness which heavily stud the religious writings of today are having little or no overt effect on the sensuous attitudes and actions of millions upon millions of American citizens. Inwardly, it may well be imagined, these anti-lascivious attitudes of a highly vocal minority are having an appreciable effect: since the fact that our countrymen are so *overly* eager to participate in lusty enjoyments of all types raises the suspicion that they find special adventure and excitement in them which are born of their forbidden-fruit nature.

That is to say, if moralists did not fret and fume about directly expressed sex desire and participation, it is doubtful if the sexuality indirectly expressed in the widespread patronizing of pin-up photos, risque stories, sex-tinged gadgets, et cetera, would be a fraction as popular as it obviously is today. Sexual lasciviousness seems to be at least partly a function of sexual anti-lasciviousness, and most normal men who carry the seeds of the latter concomitantly reap the crops of the former. Which seems to account for and leave us at precisely the same impasse with which we entered this chapter.

Attitudes Toward Lasciviousness in the 1960's

In the 1950 study that was made of sex attitudes and expressions, it was found that very few references contained clear-cut positive or negative attitudes toward lasciviousness; and these were fairly evenly divided between liberal and conservative views. In the follow-up study it has been found that a considerable number of attitudes toward lasciviousness are now being presented in our mass media and that the overwhelming proportion of these are favorable.

While scores of advertisements for sexy products, especially for books, photographs, film strips, and motion pictures, were found in the 1950 periodicals, literally hundreds of such ads are prevalent in each month's issue of new periodicals in the 1960's. And the copy for these ads, including the illustrations often used in them, have become infinitely more daring and inviting. Here are a few current examples:

From *Scamp*: "STORIES FOR MEN. MANY WITH ARTIST ILLUSTRATIONS. FABULOUS PHOTOS YOU'LL NEVER FORGET! A book of the most fantastic stories, photos and illustrations you've ever seen; at least not since you used to pass them along on typewritten pages back in the 'good old days.' Straight from the originals, every detail intact and vivid."

149

From *Frolic*: "S-H-H! My girl friends and I enjoyed posing for these shots, and as you'll see, we had a ball ... especially me. So send just $5.00 for your own PRIVATE SET."

From *Zest*: "FROM PRIVATE FILES. BREATHTAKING GIANT COLLECTION OF 500 TANTALIZING BIG GLOSSY UNCENSORED PHOTOS. You'll thrill to these exciting, revealing and unretouched poses. Every imaginable picture of Hollywood's most uninhibited! Featuring BUSTY BROWN. DARING AND REVEALING!"

From *Ace*: "JUST IMAGINE. THE FOR MEN ONLY KIND. Over 100 poses and positions. Over 100 girls. From private studio files a portfolio collection of over 100 lovely young beauties of Hollywood, completely uncensored, daring, intimate, printed from originals in breath-taking detail!"

Such ads as these almost literally go on forever. *Gala* magazine, for instance, carries 72 of them in a 70-page issue; *Pose!* has 69; *Hit Show*, 60; *Follies*, 72; *Frolic*, 75; many other magazines, similar numbers. Most of the advertisers, moreover, use a good many publications each month for the same ad and keep using some of the magazines month after month. So there is every reason to believe that these advertisements keep pulling in the intended customers.

Leaving such ads for awhile, and going on to consider more editorial matter, we find that numerous modern periodicals favorably and salaciously make use of items featuring sexual lust. Here are some typical examples:

From a story in *Tan*: "In one single motion he had gathered me up in his arms and his lips came down hard against mine. They were slightly moist, and soft, and warm, yet firm and determined—experienced in the art of accomplishing what they desired. I could feel myself yielding to his touch, tingling to his embrace. I wanted to pull away, to brake the surge of emotions that swept over me, but the tide was too great. The more I pushed against his steel-like arms, the more I could feel myself weakening, enraptured with the sheer intoxication of bliss, quickened with the passionate desire of a yearning love that had gone too long unattended and unfulfilled."

From a tale in *Fantastic Universe*: "The Doll was fascinated. Then I made the mistake of taking a close look at her again and fainted. It was purely practical; not just emotional or anything. She was just too much; even imagining it laid me out. I came-to sitting upright but in the Doll's arms. I went out again."

From a *Mystery Digest* story: "Now, I'm a stripper—or, as they say in the business, an exotic dancer. The public in the joints where I work never change. Most of the customers who come to the show are badly in need of a veterinarian-psychiatrist. Their conversation is always Sex. On the stage curtain was painted the Venus de Milo. Once, two guys in the audience were speculating how she lost her arms and what she was doing with them at the time."

From an article in *Revels*: "A SEXRETARY ON EVERY LAP. Secretaries admittedly have become an integral part of the modern day business world. The problem is that too many of them look as though they have already had the business! We suggest that the regular secretary be put on a four-day—Monday through Thursday—work week, and that new blood be introduced into the staff. Friday becomes SEXRETARY DAY, with a delectable young thing replacing the frustrated efficiency expert who normally takes your calls."

From a feature in *Candid*: "One day, not long ago, a distributor left 100 copies of a new issue of a girlie magazine on a Hollywood newsstand. Thirty minutes later every single copy of the racy magazine had been sold! 'It was absolutely amazing,' said the newsstand owner. 'I've never seen a magazine sell so fast in the 30 years I've been selling magazines. No sooner had the distributor left the bundle of magazines when a crowd of men suddenly converged on them, took one look at the cover, and began grabbing copies like mad. It was as though a school of piranha had smelled fresh meat. I didn't even have a chance to put any copies on the racks.' The foregoing incident is by no means unique nowadays. Newsdealers all over the country are experiencing the same big demand for girlie magazines."

From an article in *Cavalcade*: "Aboard the vessels, the orgies went on unabated. Infected by the excitement, men and women abandoned themselves to ever wilder excesses. Drunks swarmed and roiled along the passage-ways and through the salons. Some couples didn't even bother to go into the staterooms for their lovemaking. They flopped onto settees or into corners."

From another article in *Cavalcade*: "The dancing continued, becoming more and more frenzied with each beat. More and more people were joining in as they got high on the home-grown marijuana and 'chica,' quickly seeming to enter a trance-like state, legs wide apart, bending backwards to the breaking-point, mouths agape, their eyes rolling in their sockets. A young girl screamed 'Ojala!' and tore off her clothes in a frenzy and the crowd pressed in, clapping. Two men now carried forward a life-size image of Ojala. Tall and muscular, with the head of an eagle, its straddled legs were those of a goat, but the monstrous caricature of the male organ between them was definitely human. The girl made a strange moaning sound and pressed herself against the statue, kissing it. Then she suddenly embraced it, enfolding its limbs with her arms and legs. The crowd's handclaps beat faster and faster as she writhed seductively, then stopped abruptly as she sank limp and exhausted to the ground. 'Ojala!' they screamed. . . . It went on all night like this, one wild ceremony following another with almost monotonous regularity."

Not to be outdone by today's periodicals, the best-selling novels of the day also contain their share of highly lascivious passages. Witness:

From *Peyton Place*: Constance MacKenzie to Michael Rossi: " 'I suppose you were being driven by this tremendous basic urge at the age of 15 or 16.' 'Fourteen,' said Mike, and laughed at the look on her face. 'Fourteen, I was. She was a kid who lived in the tenement on the same floor as I, and I caught her in the toilet at the end of the hall. I took her standing up, with the stink of potatoes boiled too long in too much water, and filth and urine all around us, and I loved it. I may even say that I wallowed in it, and I couldn't wait to get back for more.' "

From *On the Road*: "I went to the cold-water flat with the boys and Dean came to the door in his shorts. Marylou was jumping off the couch; Dean had dispatched the occupant of the apartment to the kitchen, probably to make coffee, while he proceeded with his love problems, for to him sex was the one and only holy and important thing in life, although he had to sweat and curse to make a living and so on."

From *Lolita*: "How marvelous were my fancied adventures as I sat on a hard park bench pretending to be immersed in a trembling book. Around the quiet scholar, nymphets played freely, as if he were a familiar statue or part of an old tree's shadow and sheen. Once a perfect little beauty in a tartan frock, with a clatter put her heavily armed foot near me upon the bench to dip her slim bare arms into me and tighten the strap of her roller skate, and I dissolved in the sun, with my book for fig leaf, as her auburn ringlets fell all over her skinned knee, and the shadow of leaves I shared pulsated and melted on her radiant limb next to my chameleonic cheek. Another time a red-haired school girl hung over me in the metro, and a revelation of axillary russet I obtained remained in my blood for weeks. . ."

From *The Cave*: "He was about to utter something, to ask what she had said, for the words had been lost in his surprise, when he caught a full whiff of her perfume, and the words simply wouldn't come. He found himself swallowing hard, trying to pull back from her. He did manage to pull back, a little, and then was sick with desire."

For some final examples of the positive power of lascivious thinking, we may quote a few of the jokes and cartoon gag lines appearing in today's publications:

From *Swank*: One female Roman citizen to another, while they are in the midst of a highly orgiastic party: I love these orgies—there's something doing every minute."

From *Cavalcade*: "The doctor knocked on the door of his patient, a very attractive brunette. He came over to her bed, rolled back the covers and told her to take off her night gown. 'Must I, Doctor?' inquired the gal. 'Certainly!' replied the doctor. 'I'm going to give you a thorough physical examination.' This he did. He examined her from top to bottom. Front and back. He didn't overlook anything. When he was through, the girl said: 'Doctor, there is one thing I am curious about. Could I ask you one question?' The doctor told her she could. 'Why did you bother to knock?' "

From *Snappy*: "Psychoanalyst, lustfully leering at his beautiful female patient who is lying in a state of semi-undress on the sofa: Would you mind going back and repeating the part beginning where your boy friend took the back seat out of the car!"

As many of the foregoing illustrations indicate, the quality of the lascivious passages now being widely published is far more detailed and revealing than similar passages published a decade or more ago. Because, as indicated in the first section of this chapter, American mores still *theoretically* oppose highly sexualized presentations, the examples that *actually* get into print tend to be far more suggestive and exciting than they otherwise would be. Just as individuals who are emotionally disturbed and whose overt behavior is abnormal or bizarre (as I have pointed out in several recent publications on rational psychotherapy) must ordinarily have underlying *ideas* or *philosophies* which are driving them to their peculiar feelings and actions, so must the exceptionally lascivious individual have ideas or philosophies which are motivating his behavior. And these ideas, ironically enough, largely consist of the notion that just because sex desires are "bad" and forbidden, they are inordinately "good" and exciting. To ban or discourage a sex act is usually to give it the most favorable kind of publicity.

CHAPTER 18

Sexual Intercourse

This shall be a relatively lighthearted chapter. For the question it is concerned with is: What do the American people think of sexual intercourse when it occurs in legal marriage? And the majority answer seems to be: They like it.

Sexual copulation, in, of, by, and for itself, is not—as we have seen in several of our previous chapters—very enthusiastically accepted in modern America. Indeed, one quickly gains the impression, in reading the public prints and in witnessing movie, stage, radio, and television performances, that the very last thing for which Americans accept sexual congress is its own sake. Decent-minded citizens, presumably, copulate for love, for marital happiness, for child-begetting, for duty, and for a thousand other reasons—but never, apparently, for the mere fun of copulation.

Once, however, a man and woman have been legally coupled, it is widely believed that sexual congress is a good thing for them and that more of it would quite probably be a better thing. Thus our magazines frequently run ads on some device or technique purporting to enable men to increase their virility and prolong their capacity for coition. "ARE YOU LOSING YOUR ADAM POWER?" demands one of these ads in *New Physical Culture* magazine. If so, write for details of the nonpareil Virility Course. "VITALITY!" screams another ad. "*Thousands* take pills—pore over books—consult 'quacks' to gain the priceless possession of strong, virile manhood. Yet the real means are right within *anyone's* grasp—easily and economically."

Another warm acceptance of sexual coitus is found in—of all places—Hollywood movies. Thus in the film, *On the Town*, one of the girls tells one of the boys, with unmistakable gestures and tone of voice, that if they were on an island together she would be all he would need. In the picture, *Prince of Foxes*, Cesare Borgia notes with a hearty chuckle that "Alfonso is a blacksmith. He needs a lusty woman, not one of those frail French birds." In *Adam's Rib* a scene is shown where the hero and heroine (who are married, of course) are about to go to bed, whereupon they revive the old gag about there being only a small difference between men and women—but *vive le différence!*

Modern novels also laud the pleasures of sexual intercourse, as when the hero-narrator of *The Egyptian* tells how his Syrian wife "dogged my footsteps in a continual desire to take pleasure with me." He finally gets rid of this spouse by giving her to a Syrian who desires her, saying to him: "I will give her to you without payment, and I beg you to accept of her and do with her all that the wildcat within you desires—for if I do not deceive myself, her heart is inclined toward you, and she will be content, for in her body also lurks many wildcats." In George Stewart's *Earth Abides*, the hero, after a great disaster has struck the earth and killed almost everyone finally meets a man and a woman. " 'Yes,' the man went on, 'yes, we're doing fine. Plenty to eat, plenty to drink, and lots of——' He made an obscene gesture, and grinned at the woman. She giggled again. . . ."

In modern magazines the frank approval of sexual intercourse in marriage is much the same. In *Your Marriage* we learn that "twin beds are a major menace to matrimony. . . . For marriage is primarily biological while twin beds are strictly a product of the machine age."

In a story in *Woman's Day* one of the characters says: "You're a mighty handsome man, P'fessor. You better be careful. Miss Em has been a widder four years now—and that's about as long as a woman can do without a man when she's used to one."

In *New Physical Culture* almost half the magazine seems to be devoted to featuring the relationship of Bernarr Macfadden ("vital and virile at 80") and his new wife, Jennie Lee Macfadden (lovely and beautiful at 44), and to hinting that if everyone lives the way *they* do, life will begin after 40 in more ways than one.

Finally, we may note that the humorous magazines also have much to say in favor of intercourse. Thus *Laugh Book* approvingly quotes this verse purportedly found in a hotel guest book:

> *Room Seventeen—breezes galore.*
> *Wonderful beds—rice on the floor.*
> *A paradise of secrets, all to be kept.*
> *We played around while the rest all slept!*
>   (P.S. Know what I mean?)

Also from *Laugh Book* we have the story of the widow who told her new husband that the first thing she did every morning was to go to the window, open it, and say, speaking to the spirit of her first husband, "Good morning, Charles darling." Her new husband didn't object, so they prepared to retire, and she went to the window, opened it, and said softly: "Good night, Charles darling, I hope you will understand." Then they cuddled up in bed and so forth far into the night. The next morning, happy and weary, she crawled out of bed, slowly pushed the window open, and said, "Good morning, Charles. Phooey to you!"

In more ways than one, then, it would seem that contemporary American publications and productions freely accept sexual intercourse—in marriage—and look upon it as a good thing. Not, however, without reservations.

In the first place, marital coitus is virtually never publicly referred to as copulation, sex congress, or even sexual intercourse. In nonfictional sex books or articles it may be so designated, but in fiction, advertisements, films, plays, and other media it is almost always referred to in an indirect, euphemistic way. Thus the sex-virility ads talk of "Adam power," "vitality," "strength," and "vigor," when they obviously mean copulative ability.

Secondly, the fact that Americans consider sexual intercourse, even among married couples, somewhat shameful is shown by the continual notation, in advertisements for devices and books concerning coition, and all material *will be sent in a plain wrapper* or *very confidentially*.

Thirdly, the very plethora of sex books blatantly advertising techniques of copulation shows that we neglect any systematic teaching of coital methods in our regular institutions of learning—obviously because we cannot directly face sexual intercourse, and believe that there is something nasty or wicked about it.

Fourthly, we find that husbands and wives, when they do accept sexual intercourse, seem to sanction only limited, "normal" forms of it and are afraid of any "abnormal" manifestations. Thus an article in *Your Psychology* tells us that "in most cases marital relations should cease altogether during the last two months before the birth." The obvious assumption here is that "marital relations" are synonymous with copulation and that other types of sex relations between husbands and wives are not even thinkable. In John O'Hara's *A Rage to Live*, we find Sarita, a prostitute, saying to one of her customers: "I don't know what you're like. A little fancy, I'll bet. Not too fancy, I hope though. Some things I won't do." And that, sexologists tell us, is precisely why married men patronize prostitutes today; because there are some things relating to sexual intercourse that they *will* do but that the wives of these men won't.

Fifthly, millions of twentieth-century Americans seem to find sexual intercourse so essentially tainted that they cannot tolerate the fact that Mary might have had other children after she gave birth, supposedly immaculately, to Jesus. While Sholem Asch, in *Mary*, specifically mentions three other of her sons, Fulton Oursler, in *The Greatest Story Ever Told*, denies this version of the New Testament. The *Catholic World* also contains a caustic review of Asch's book which makes it clear that Mary could not possibly have had sex relations with her legal spouse, Joseph, at any time at all during her life.

Sixthly, we find that marital coitus is frequently treated in a smutty, joking manner, as if there were something not quite nice and decent about it. Thus in the film, *Adam's Rib*, a homemade film within a film is shown in which a husband's and wife's going into a barn together is treated as if it were the dirtiest joke imaginable. And in *We Went Thataway* H. Allen Smith tells us that "the moment they arrived on board they identified themselves as newlyweds. In so doing they immediately acquired the status of public property and were subjected to almost constant sniggering."

In many respects, therefore, American publicists look upon sexual intercourse as a dubiously proper mode of human behavior; and, while they normally accept it under limited marital circumstances, they still manage to get across the idea that there is something not wholly clean and decent about it.

At the same time, these same publicists make the most lascivious use

156

of coitus possible in their stories, advertisements, and anecdotes, and thus clearly reveal that the American public—precisely, no doubt, *because* it believes that copulation is not an entirely nice activity—also believes that it is an exceptionally exciting one.

Examples of the lascivious employment of coitus are particularly rife in modern novels. In *The Egyptian* the King of Babylon says to the hero: "I am also curious to see how an Egyptian lies with a woman, for every nation has its own customs. If I were to tell you the ways of those wives who come from distant lands, you would not believe us and would be greatly astonished."

In *Earth Abides* the hero tells the heroine, in a land where all the physicians have been killed off by a great disaster, that he'll read a book on childbirth so that they can have a child together. Where-upon, we read: " 'You know,' she said, 'I might need a little more help than that!' Her body was close and warm against him."

In *The Man with the Golden Arm* we have one scene after another showing how Violet and Sparrow make good use of their bedroom. For example: "The bedposts had taken to leaning together with a faintly disapproving air. They'd seen them come and they'd seen them go: this one wouldn't last as long as some of the others, they calculated, the reckless way he was going about things. A cooler head was what was needed; a cooler head, an older hand, a bit more restraint, and snatches of sleep between rounds."

In *Divine Mistress* we have a portrait of Doña Catherine's going through, under hypnosis, a re-enactment of an obvious prior event in her life: "She writhed in an abandonment of motion which could have only one significance: the reliving of a seduction in which she had played an active and, from all appearance, a willing part. Cries of animal passion came from her lips, and the voluptuous movement of her limbs grew so wild that she thrashed about in the bed in an ecstasy of remembered passion, panting with the efforts, her mouth slack. . . . Then suddenly Doña Catherine was quiet. She lay panting, mouth slack, a look of deep and utter contentment on her face."

Films and plays of our era are also not backward in making lascivious use of references to sexual intercourse. The film, *Devil in the Flesh*, by way of illustration, symbolizes the violent sex relations of its hero and heroine by a prolonged shot of a raging fire, first burning higher and higher, and then gradually dying down. The motion picture, *Tight Little Island*, opens with an announcer's voice telling the audience that the people of the island in question are "a hearty people with few and simple pleasures"—whereupon follows a shot of a seemingly endless file of children coming out of the house of one of the natives. In the musical play, *Gentlemen Prefer Blondes*, one of the girls remarks about a lackadaisical lover who is a health enthusiast: "How can that guy eat so many carrots and be so unlike a rabbit?" And in the Cole Porter musical, *Kiss Me, Kate*, there are salacious references to intercourse in no less than four of the songs. (1) In "Always True to You (In My Fashion)" the girl tells how, when the bore falls on the floor, she lets him *lay*. (2) In another song we are told that when your baby is pining for pleasure you should let her sample *measure for measure*. (3) In "Too Darn Hot" much is made of the fact that the singer will be a flop with his baby tonight and that there'll be no repeat with his baby tonight, since it's too darn hot. (4) In "I've Come to Wive It Wealthily in Padua" we are distinctly told that in the dark all women are the same.

Finally, we may note that modern humor is literally overflowing with lascivious references to sexual intercourse. Witness:

From a college magazine: " 'Bring in one of the ladies of the harem!' 'Very good, Sultan.' 'Not necessarily.' "

From *Touchstone*: "Sign in a nudist colony: 'Gentlemen playing leapfrog, please complete your leap.' "

From *Wet Hen*: Cartoon of an old maid going upstairs with a candle in one hand and a box under her arm on which there are large letters reading: "DUZ does everything."

From *Touchstone*: "Old Lady to a Taxidermist: I would like these two dead monkeys stuffed. Taxidermist: Would you like them mounted? Old Lady: Oh no! Just holding hands."

From *Penn State Froth*: "Newspaper item: Mrs. Lottie Prim was granted a divorce after claiming that her husband had spoken to her only three times since their marriage. She was awarded the custody of their three children."

From *Touchstone*: Cartoon showing a tent in which a newly married couple are reposing and an elephant is sticking his trunk into the darkness of the tent. A scream is coming from the tent: "YE GODS—FRANK!"

The points of virtually all these anecdotes would probably be missed in societies where intercourse is taken for granted as a wholly good act. The thing that makes them humorous in our culture is the fact that the readers of these jokes all believe in their hearts that there is something essentially wrong—and yet damnably enjoyable—about sexual coition. And that, precisely, seems to be the underlying, semiconscious attitude which nearly all contemporary Americans take concerning copulation: that it is a good enough act, all right, but let's, by remaining aware of its essential smuttiness, keep it clean!

Attitudes Toward Sexual Intercourse in the 1960's

In the 1950 study of American sex attitudes, it was found that there were relatively many references to sexual intercourse in our mass media and that these were preponderantly on the liberal or permissive side. In the follow-up study of attitudes in the 1960's, it may be noted that there are a great many more references to intercourse than in the previous decade and that again the overwhelming majority of these are favorable.

Not only, as would be expected, do contemporary men's magazines feature highly salacious, specific, and approving attitudes to intercourse, but they are slightly outweighed, in the present investigation, by the number and quality of the allusions found in fiction best-sellers. In fact, each novel seems to be in stiff competition (no pun intended!) with other contemporary novels to describe the details of coitus as many times as it can get away with between a single set of book covers. Without even half trying to discover all the instances in point in best-selling works of fiction in the 1960's, it was found that *Peyton Place* has at least five highly specific accounts of copulation; *The War Lover*, five; *Poor No More*, six; *Lady Chatterley's Lover*, seven; and *Hawaii*, five. Other popular novels fall somewhat behind this average. Some of the typical passages describing the copulative facts of life are these:

From *Peyton Place*: " 'You are truly beautiful,' he said. 'You have the long aristocratic legs and the exquisite breasts of a statue.' She let out her long-held breath with a sigh that made her quiver and her heart beat hard under her breasts. He placed his lips against the pulsating spot, while he pressed gently at her abdomen with his hand. He continued to kiss her and stroke her until her whole body trembled under his lips and hands. When he kissed the softness of her thighs, she began to make moaning, animal sounds, and even then he continued his sensual touching and stroking and waited until she began the undulating movements of intercourse with her hips. She was lying with her arms bent and raised over her head, and he held her pinned to the bed with his hands on her wrists. 'Don't,' he commanded, when he tried to twist away from him at the first thrust of pain. 'Help me,' he said. 'Don't pull away.' 'I can't,' she cried. 'I can't.' 'Yes, you can. Press your heels against the mattress and raise your hips. Help me. Quickly!' In the last moment a bright drop of blood appeared on her mouth, where she had bitten into her lip, and then she had cried out the odd, mingled cry of pain and pleasure."

From *The Cave*: "Once in that darkening shop, long ago, as a spring evening fell, she had moved to him so soundlessly that he had not heard her foot on the earth floor, and had stood right behind him, and when he turned, not knowing she was there, she had put her hands up to his black-smudged face, pulling his face down to her, kissing him hard in the way he had taught her, not letting him go, getting her bare arms up around his dirty neck, thinking of her fresh- .

starched yellow dress getting all dirty against him, and thinking: *I'm glad of it, I'm glad of it*, suddenly thinking of herself, the dress gone, herself white, bare, distorted in the act of being possessed, there on the dirty floor, in all the dirt, with maybe some scrap of metal, a bolt or nut or some old discarded something, cutting into her intolerably, but perfectly and indispensably, from the dirt of the floor."

From *Poor No More*: "And suddenly her body was printed on his —not *on*, *in*—and it all started over again, the slow ascent, step by careful step, the tiny spasms that rocked her as they achieved a fresh height, the spastic quivering that made her body one long limpid tremolo, the head flung back, the eyes rolled back, a rising, rising moan, then a soft wail of almost painful satisfaction, and finally the wrenching breathless shock as they reached the top of the long climb, paused, and then hurled themselves over the abyss, locked together into a violent death in the darkness below."

From *Lady Chatterley's Lover*: "The quiver was going through the man's body, as the stream of consciousness again changed its direction, turning downwards. And he was helpless, as the penis in slow soft un-dulations filled and surged and rose up, and grew hard, standing there hard and overweening, in its curious towering fashion. The woman too trembled a little as she watched. 'There! Take him then! He's thine,' said the man. And she quivered, and her own mind melted out. Sharp soft waves of unspeakable pleasure washed over her as he entered her, and started the curious molten thrilling that spread and spread till she was carried away with the last, blind flush of ex-tremity."

From *Hawaii*: "Now when I get hold of a fat one and a skinny one, ma'am, I look to lock the door for about two days and I undress com-pletely—that's why you find me only in pants; I was interrupted and had to kill a man—and when I'm undressed I like to throw myself back on the bed and say to the girls, 'All right, the first one of you who can ... make me get hard can climb aboard, and when she does the other one has to blow on me!'"

From *Return to Peyton Place*: "He kissed her softly with his lips together in dry, unhurried kisses, and all the while he stroked her as if she were a frightened kitten he was trying to calm. He undressed her slowly, almost lazily, and when he put her on the bed it was as if she were that same kitten, quieted now, but who might, at any moment, jump up and run away in terror. He made her look at him but did not speak as his hands caressed her thighs and pressed gently against her abdomen. He watched her eyes grow dark and heavy and still he continued to stroke her, and when he kissed her the next time it was Selena who opened her lips, who probed against his teeth with her tongue. Only then did his fingertips seek her breasts, caressing and

160

stroking until she responded to him. 'Open your eyes,' he said. 'Selena, open your eyes.' He loved her slowly and watched, exultant, as the wildness grew in her eyes, as her mouth opened to cry out. It was as if a dam had burst within her, as if she were fighting a tidal wave of feeling. Until, finally, she let go and gave in to the strength that claimed her, that took everything from her in one shuddering, screaming, ecstatic moment."

From *The Mansion*: "Where right away Virgil showed himself the owner of a really exceptional talent—a capacity to take care of two girls in succession to their satisfaction or at least until they hollered quit, that was enough for two dollars, in his youthful enthusiasm and innocence not only doing it for pleasure but even paying for the chance until Clarence discovered him and put him into the money."

From *On the Road*: "That night Terry and I went to bed in the sweet night air beneath our dewy tent. I was just getting ready to go to sleep when she said, 'You want to love me now?' I said, 'What about Johnny [her young son]?' 'He don't mind. He's asleep.' But Johnny wasn't asleep and he said nothing."

From reading these excerpts from contemporary best-selling novels, it should not be concluded that *all* depictions of intercourse in these novels represent it in an entirely glorious, favorable light. Negative attitudes toward copulation are also present in many of the same works. In *Poor No More*, we are told: "Almost to a woman, bar the few nymphomaniacs, the child-bearing wives had never experienced an orgasm. After the first sweaty excesses of legalized fornication had dulled to formal routines—Sunday afternoon after a big dinner of chicken and dumplings and strawberry shortcake, or an infrequent recurrence of ancient lust at 2 a.m. after the Saturday dancing—intercourse meant only children and throwing-up in the morning and three's enough for any family, don't you think, honey?"

In *The Cave*, we are told, about the sex relations of Nick Pappy and his wife: "It was all right, for the moment. It was found, however, to occur to her that his having rumpled her or made her late to the main feature would scarcely account for all the grieffull goings on. This puzzlement increased with time, fed by his practice of leaping from ambush, his bursts of unspecified contrition, or whatever they were, and his habit, which she remarked more and more with the passing months, of keeping his eyes squinched tight while she was in business. Even when she couldn't see his face, and when, in fact, his face wasn't what she should have been concerned with, she was darned sure he had his eyes squinched tight, the crud. She couldn't get her mind off the fact, and it sort of got in the way of whole-hearted effort."

Negative attitudes toward intercourse are likewise evident in other forms of public communication. In a *Revealing Romances* story, a daughter cannot stand the knowledge that her father and stepmother are having sex relations: "I found myself listening for Dad's footsteps. How would I be able to stand that? It was too awful, just disgusting, that's what it was. I put the pillow over my head and muttered, 'I hate him, too.'"

Puritanical, bored, or squeamish attitudes toward copulation are also shown in a good many contemporary jokes. Here are some examples:

From *Candid*: "'That louse,' said the bride, 'doublecrossed me. He told me he'd saved up for fifty years—and I thought he was talking about money!'"

From *Cavalcade*: "It was two o'clock in the morning and two men were leaving for home after the poker party. One said, 'This is what I hate most. When I come home late as this, I have to coast into the the garage with my motor off. Then I take off my shoes and tiptoe into the house. I am as quiet as possible. But every damn time I crawl into bed my wife sits up and starts giving me hell.' The other man said, 'You're doing it all wrong. I never have any trouble. I zoom into the garage, slam the door, stomp into the house, and make a hell of a racket. I crash into the bedroom, slap my wife on her behind and say, "How about it, Kid." She always pretends she's asleep.'"

From *Comedy*: "'Well, Gracie, how do you like marriage?' 'Oh, it's an awful lot of fun, I guess; but so monotonous!'"

From *Campus Howl*, quoting from the *Florida Orange Peel*: "They were seated on adjoining stools in a dimly lighted cocktail lounge. 'Honey,' he said, 'what about forgetting your inhibitions and spending a quiet weekend with me at Kansas City?' 'See here,' she answered, 'after an exhaustive perusal of the corpus of documented evidence garnered by research on heterosexuality as applied to contemporary sociological mores, and in view of the innate predisposition to the more exotic manifestations of concupiscence evident in your demeanor, a categorical negative is my answer.' 'But honey,' he said, 'I just don't get it!' 'That's what I mean,' she answered."

Returning to the more positive side of the fence, there are scores of stories, articles, advertisements, cartoons, jokes, and other items in contemporary periodicals that most unsubtly indicate that coitus is a great, delightful pastime and that anyone who does not engage in it regularly had better have his or her head examined. To illustrate:

From *Cavalcade*: "Now! Whether you are newly married or long married this new book will show you HOW TO TASTE THE TRUE DELIGHTS OF IDEAL SEXUAL UNION. Yes! Sex is an art! There are variations in the ability to perform the sex act. Just as a master violinst, for example, can draw from the strings and wood of a violin, tones and songs of heavenly beauty, far different from the fiddle scraper—so can the sensitive, considerate and accomplished lover make of the sex act a thing of beauty, harmony and consummate joy."

From *True Police Stories*: "They petted a bit. And one thing led to another.... He parked the car in the shadows near the road and they repeated their love-making. At last, satiated with sex, he sighed and leaned back against the seat. But the woman, love-starved, was still amorous. She taunted him, gave him the 'so you think you're a man' routine."

From *Ace*: "NEW NON-PRESCRIPTION 'INVIGORATOR PILL' FOR MEN, WOMEN, DEVELOPED BY LAB.... It gives a distinct increase in the rapidity and accuracy of performance."

From *Men's Digest*: "New aid to virility! Now Perry Lakin, renowned dietician and trainer of two Mr. Americas, tells us that he has discovered two sure foods which will greatly increase virility. Wheat germ and soy bean oil are the magic dishes! ... Of course, we recommend one other thing even more strongly to you, if you would improve your virility. What's that? A beautiful woman, natch."

From *Cavalier*: "SEX HARMONY. Written by a well-known physician, this educational booklet frankly reveals true facts about Sex Harmony. Contains interesting information on marriage relations, love zones and the technique of making love. Explains why it is important that husband and wife reach the climax of relations together at the same time. Discloses an easy way to overcome man's early climax. Shows you how to achieve perfect mutual satisfaction."

From *Hi-Life*: "She danced Love without the throbbing belly-rhythm. Then, as quickly as she'd started to dance, Vivian came whirling back to me ... into my arms. Her arms clasped around my waist. Her head dropped back. 'Now!' It was a breath, not a word. Sticky with the salt rime, but not caring, we staggered off balance and fell, together, on the hard packed sand. When we finally fell apart, Vivian crept back to me, crouched and laid her cheek against my chest, over my heart. She let out a long, shuddering sigh."

From *True*: Errol Flynn tells of his bout with opium and the beauteous Chinese-Irish creature, Ting Ling O'Conner: "I was quite in charge of my limbs. As a matter of fact I seemed to have the strength of four men, let alone two. When I took Ting Ling to another room, I had never known I was capable of such feats. Today I'm told that the effects of opiates remove sexual desire in the man in adverse ratio to the female who becomes more excited. Dr. Flynn can tell you that such is not the case."

From *Rapture*: "He placed his hand on her stomach and drew it up to the base of her breast. She quivered and then reached and embraced him. Then they began to make love with all the passion and fury that they had gathered over the long agonizing months together. Systematically, and with deliberate violence, Eddie made love to her as if he were fighting a terrible battle that he had to win. His affection was perfunctory. He kissed her lightly now and then and stroked her in a watchful, absent way. And when his strength returned, he roused her, delicately at first, then more insistently and finally he united with her so forcibly and, at the same time, so unrestrainedly that she could no longer control her own response. Time after time he returned, until, from her trance of pleasure that was almost pain, she moaned, 'Darling, darling, what are you doing to me? Please, please, no more. Oh, oh, yes, yes, yes. . . . oh, my God!' "

From *Swank*: "I was exhausted, but my last thought before going to sleep was that I'd never be the same again. In the hours that had passed like moments, I'd learned things about love that I'd never dreamed existed! Moira—the daughter of an English Earl turned courtesan—had shown me subtleties and nuances that defy description. She had initiated me into sensations and sensory delights bizarre and voluptuous to the point of being almost incredible. Even the memory is enough to make the blood pound in my veins. . . ."

From *Sexology*: "Contrary to biblical injunction, informed medical opinion of today holds that, except for esthetic reasons, there is no objection to sexual intercourse during menstruation unless the flow is excessive in amount."

From *Real Confessions*: "There was a difference in my love-making now, and Chris knew it. He let me out of the car. We lay on the cool soft ground of the woods. Our moist, hungry mouths burned like wet fire, and our pulses raced. Our joy in one another raced toward a joy not yet reached, like strong, living cars, not of steel and gasoline but flesh and blood, straining toward the finish line. We raced to it and when I reached it I cried out. My cry was not only a cry of happiness but a protest that such sweetness was beyond bearing. . . ."

Obviously, passages such as these, and many more like them in contemporary literature, leave little to the imagination about coitus and its joys. Sexual anecdotes and cartoons, though a little less explicit in this regard, also frequently manage to convey the idea that copulation is the greatest good of life and the more of it an individual can engage in, the better and livelier his existence is. To illustrate:

From *Jest*: "When Mamie Jane told her mother that she was going out with Bill to stare at science things for hours, her mother asked: Stare at *what*? Well, Ma, we sort of stare and study together. I look up at the stars and things in the sky and he stares at the bugs on the ground; and you'd be surprised to know how much science we find out!"

From *Campus Howl*, quoting the *Florida Orange Peel*: "An old lady who was sitting knitting in her rocking chair, with her Persian cat reclining at her feet, suddenly saw a fairy who gave her a wish and she wished to be a beautiful young woman again. The fairy obliged; and then asked if she wanted a second wish. She said she would like a handsome young man. Turning to the cat, the fairy waved her wand and in its place rose a fine looking youth. He looked sadly at the girl and sighed, 'Now aren't you sorry you took me to the vet?' "

From *Scamp*: "At a recent beauty contest, the first girl smiled at the judge. Contestant number two winked at him. Number three kissed him and number four hugged him. Naturally, number ten won."

From *Modern Man*: "Eager male to friend who has brought him a life-size female mechanical doll: Everything? She does everything?"

From *The Dude*: "Sign at the site of a notorious lover's lane, where a disheveled male and female are returning to their car: RELAX! Next Time Try The Surf Motel."

From *Man's Magazine*: "Doctor to beautiful young patient who has got undressed: Hop up on the table, Miss Hollis—I'll be right with you."

From *Jest*: "Young bride to husband as they are waiting to go up to their room in a hotel: Let the bell boy carry our bags, dear—every man has his own job to do tonight in this hotel!"

In addition to the swarm of favorable references and the much smaller bevy of disapproving allusions to intercourse that are to be found in the literature of the 1960's, there are the usual two-faced references, where coitus is alluded to in both positive and negative ways at the same time. We quote two brief humorous examples from the same magazine, *Cavalcade*. Joke No. 1: "A beautiful moon shone down on the parked car. 'Goodness!' gasped the girl. "It's three o'clock. I should have been in hours ago!' 'So should I,' he murmered disgustedly." Joke No. 2: "The newlyweds wanted to fly United, but the hostess objected."

Summing up: Ten years after the early 1950's, which brought Americans, via their mass media, a most contradictory and muddled view of sexual intercourse, the scene has significantly shifted and the view is distinctly less conflicting. Coitus is apparently more freely and widely accepted as a good thing, among both the married and the unmarried, and milder overtones and undertones of puritan disapproval remain. The coital coast is hardly entirely clear; but the fog definitely seems to be lifting.

CHAPTER 19

Sex Crimes

Ask the average American what his attitude is toward sex crimes and his answer will be prompt and to the point; he is unalterably and violently opposed to them. So he thinks. Actually, he rarely seems to know what a sex crime is and frequently takes a much more lenient attitude toward many sex offenses than he imagines he does.

The reason for this seeming paradox lies in the fact that, while the average American citizen thinks of sex crime in terms of a violent and often fatal attack by a man on a woman or a child, most of the serious sex crimes on the statute books are of a radically different character, and the majority of offenders arrested under these statutes are rather harmless, mild-mannered individuals who would no more think of violently assaulting a woman or child than would the average pickpocket or confidence man think of being a trigger man for a mob of gangsters. Thus a large percentage of sex offenders are arrested for acts like exhibitionism, public indecency, obscenity, pimping, and statutory rape, while only a small percentage are apprehended for violent, unprovoked sex assaults.

Moreover, if the American laws against sex crimes were actually enforced against every offender, more than 90 per cent of American males (as Kinsey and others have pointed out) would be jailed at some time or other: since, in most of the states of our Union, sex acts like adultery, fornication, seduction, and public petting are felonies or misdemeanors punishable by fairly severe penalties. Consequently, while the average American looks with horror on assaultative rape or on a man's sexually abusing a young child, he frequently takes a more lenient attitude toward the violators of many of our other sex statutes. Especially when the violator is himself!

Concerning violent sex crimes, the American public has not merely a negative, but a virtually paranoid and trigger-happy attitude. Left to its own devices, it would probably arrange for the castration, death, or life-sentencing of all rapists, pedophiliacs, and perhaps even homosexuals—without at all taking into account that many or most of such offenders are mentally ill individuals who should be treated rather than punished. Thus, while admitting that violent sex criminals are generally "criminally insane," *Redbook* intimates that they should all be jailed for life—presumably without any psychiatric treatment. It also advocates instilling children and women with a deep-seated fear of sexual attack that will serve to keep them perpetually worried about

166

a contingency which may very likely never arise in their lives. *Quick* magazine likewise approvingly quotes a slogan (originated by labor leader Harry Bridges) for inoculating all school children against the supposedly grave danger of sex offenders: "Don't Stop to Talk—Just Run or Walk."

A graphic illustration of modern man's horror of sex crime is shown in the report in *True Police Cases* on the murderer, Joe Blaine. When arrested for fatally assaulting Lois Collins, Blaine freely admitted brutally killing her by hitting her over the head with a piggy bank and then stealing her jewelry. But despite the fact that an autopsy conclusively showed that she had been sexually assaulted after being killed, Blaine refused to admit the sex attack at all. Even murderers, apparently, have strong sex consciences.

Another excellent example of rapophobia of the American public is shown in the case of Shirley Ann Simmons, a fifteen-year-old girl who, according to an Associated Press account published in the New York *Herald Tribune*, accused three boys of repeatedly raping her in an automobile. States this news story: "The girl first told police she was abducted Sunday night on her way to church and that she was repeatedly attacked while they drove around. Her mother then refused to permit her to speak further, saying it would bring shame to the family."

As George Gardner states in a paper published in *Mental Hygiene*, "there is no type of delinquency that leads to such violent community reactions as delinquencies of this [sex] type—however minor; and even in the case of the youngest of our juvenile offenders, the community is willing to set aside their individualized and specialized treatment if sexual expression is a part of the offense. And every new offense calls for more stringent regulations, more committees, commissions, and investigations, and more legislative proposals for new laws to punish this class of criminal."

To cater to this public fear of sex crimes, an enterprising commercial firm advertises in several of the popular magazines: "AMAZING FOUNTAIN-PEN GUN. SHOOTS TEAR GAS 15 FEET. Fits pocket or purse ... guaranteed to stop man or beast." The illustration with this advertisement makes it clear that any woman who does not purchase one of these tear-gas guns and who walks unescorted on the street is simply inviting a violent sex attack.

According, then, to our popular newspapers and magazines, the American public seems to feel that violent sex crimes are exceedingly common, that sex offenders should all be electrocuted or jailed for life; and that a girl who is the victim of a sex crime may seriously damage her reputation by recounting the details of the offense. It may be parenthetically noted that in one of our large Eastern states, when all convicted sex offenders were psychiatrically and psychologically examined, it was found that there were less than a hundred in an entire year who committed serious offenses like sexual assault, rape, and carnal abuse of minors, that less than a dozen of these cases involved any amount of real violence on the part of the offender; and that there were no serious beatings or deaths at all.

The universal condemnation and exaggeration of the dangers of sex crimes in America do not in the least deter publicists from making salacious use of them. Quite the contrary. One would think, in reading the numerous true-detective-story magazines that overburden newsstands today, that every other crime committed in America consists of a murderous sex assault, for accounts of such assaults are omnipresent in story after story in these periodicals.

Where violent sex crimes cannot be found to fill the pages of true-detective magazines, the editors are not at all loath to suggest or invent them. Thus a caption on a picture in *Inside Detective* reads: "A lone policewoman was cornered by an armed criminal in this cabin. But the officer was able to escape unharmed." The fact is—if one reads the accompanying story carefully—that this "armed criminal," at the time he was in the cabin with the policewoman, had no idea of her identity, was not at all interested in her sexually, and was in fact interested in another woman who was his willing paramour. But the caption of the picture strongly hints at quite a different state of affairs.

An even better example of the lengths to which popular magazines will go to embellish a sex crime may be found in the story, "Carnage at the Cottage," in *Crime Detective*. On page 40 of this story, after an old woman has been found garroted, we read about Chief of Police Moore's exclaiming: "This fiendish crime is unspeakable! ... It's the most brutal thing this section of the country has ever experienced. Heaven help the man who did it if Portageville people ever get to him before we do. He not only murdered Aunt Mable Hendrix! He violated her body as she lay dying!" We also read, two paragraphs later: "What happened after that was too gruesome for words, but it was plain enough to all three officers. Changed into a beast, it was clear that the slayer had carried the unconscious woman to the bed, strangled her with the cord cut from the Venetian blind, and then assaulted her before robbing her purse."

From these passages it is crystal-clear that the murderer first killed his victim and then raped her—which, if true, would constitute a macabre and rather rare kind of sex crime. But on page 67, when the murderer is finally caught and confesses his deed, we are told: "When she turned her back, he had picked up the knife sharpener and slugged her, he admitted, then carried her back to the bed and assaulted her wice *before* strangling her and robbing her purse" (italics added). This is quite a different version; and one wonders why, when knowing exactly how this sex crime was actually committed, the magazine writer had to embellish it so gruesomely in the first part of his story.

Similarly sensationalized sex murders were found, in the course of his study, in *True Police Cases, Uncensored Detective, Inside Detective*, and several other magazines. Virtually all these stories over-emphasized the sex, rather than the murder, angle. In this respect, these magazines merely follow the lead of modern newspapers, which are notoriously filled with long, detailed stories of sex crimes which are entirely out of proportion to the incidence or the true horror of such crimes. Thus the Tacoma *News Tribune* frankly acknowledges that the third biggest story printed by it during the year was that of a mass statutory rape trial in which ten men were convicted for having sex relations with very willing teenage girls.

In more fictional fields we find sex crimes, or the possibility of them, being used for titillating effects even in sober novels like William E. Wilson's *Abe Lincoln of Pigeon Creek* and George Stewart's *Earth Abides*. In Wilson's novel we learn that "from time to time, as the boats passed in the night, Abe heard the women's screams carried by the wind across the river, and the next morning there would be another of them ashore in tattered, river-soaked finery, seeking shelter in the cluster of shanties and abandoned flatboat wrecking that formed a kind of settlement a mile or so below Anderson's Creek." And Stewart tells us, after a teen-age girl has run away from his hero, who is one of the few men left in a post-disaster world: "Perhaps she had experiences already, and knew that in such times the only safety for a young girl was in quick and final flight."

The only lighthearted and non-sinister references to sex crimes that could be found in the literature examined for this study were two cartoons, one in *College Humor* and the other in *College Fun*. The first cartoon depicts an elevator boy saying to a Young Thing who is about to step out of his car that this is the penthouse, and that if she needs any help she just has to scream. The second cartoon shows one old maid, returning from an out-of-town trip, being greeted effusively by her old-maid sister, who has a young baby in her arms. The sister tells the returned voyager that she certainly should have been home during the crime wave!

Aside from a few humorous references like these, sex crime in America appears to be viewed in a deadly earnest manner that brooks no cavil or quip.

In spite of the almost universal abhorrence of sex crimes in our country, the World Almanac indicates that there are some twenty seven thousand males arrested each year for sex offenses. This means of course, that several times that number commit chargeable se crimes and do not get caught, or else are booked on non-sexua charges, such as assault and battery or being a public nuisance. Ob viously, universal condemnation of sex crimes is not too effective deterrent to their perpetration.

Examination of many sex offenders, indeed, shows that they ar by no means sexually impulsive and promiscuous individuals, as th public seems to imagine, but that they are frequently quite constricted inhibited persons who are led to their offenses because they ar ashamed to utilize normal sexual outlets. Thus a study by William E Watterburg, published in *Sociology and Social Research*, reveals tha sex offenses in adolescent boys are relatively high where the father i reported dead and the boy goes to church regularly. The officer collecting the data used by Watterburg say that in many of these cases the boy was really born out of wedlock and the mothe camouflaged the fact by reporting that she had a husband who died Such mothers, presumably, are exceptionally guilty about their il legitimate births, bring their sons up most strictly, see that they go to church regularly, and also see that these sons acquire puritanical se views. These sex views, most ironically, then easily predispose the son to committing sex offenses.

In other words: having rigid attitudes on sex offenses not only does not eradicate sex crimes, but may actually stimulate them. Fo overimpulsive or compulsive acts, as psychologists and psychiatrist have long known, stem not usually from overpermissiveness, but fa more readily from underpermissiveness and overrestraint. Push normal sex urge down here, and it more readily—and often abnormally —flies up there.

Sex crimes, it may be hypothesized, are only in a limited sense com mitted by sex criminals. In a broader and truer sense, the real sex-law breakers are sex-law makers: who, by making normal sex conduc impossible for men and boys to achieve in a guiltless, healthy manner force many of them into abnormal and often mentally aberrated out lets. It is these outlets which are then officially designated as sex crimes

Otherwise stated: our own society, in fostering our existing con fused and muddled sex attitudes, makes it mandatory (a) that we wil have many unrealistic and unworkable sex laws which almost no normal person could help breaking, and (b) that we will produce confused, muddled, and mentally aberrated individuals who will in evitably commit many more serious sex crimes than would otherwise be perpetrated. Societal sexual confusion, in this way, produces more artificial *and* real sex crimes than would otherwise exist.

In the early 1950's, according to the study made for the original edition of this book, very few attitudinal references to sex crimes were found in American mass media; and these were preponderantly conservative. In the follow-up study of attitudes in the 1960's, a good many more references were found; but again, as might be expected, these were preponderantly on the conservative side.

A large slice of the negative references to sex crimes appears in today's newspapers, especially the tabloids, which in almost every issue have one or more accounts of rapes and sex murders, and which usually take a highly moralistic tone in connection with them, or else objectively report the condemnatory attitudes of the public or its officials toward sex crimes. Thus, the *New York Times* reports the lynching of a Negro by seven white men in Poplarville, Mississippi, two days before he was to have stood trial for the alleged rape of a young, white mother who was pregnant. And the *New York Journal American* notes that in Trenton, New Jersey, a man who attempted to rape two young girls was sent to prison for 40-52 years, even though no actual sex crime was committed. In sentencing this man, Mercer County Judge Clifton C. Bennett said: "I think this is the most horrifying example of crime I have faced during my experience on the bench."

Second to the newspapers in their moralistic attitudes toward sex crimes are the women's magazines. In a *Real Secrets* story, a woman's young daughter is afflicted with a "nameless, faceless terror that was worse than any terror a child could know" because one of her mother's male friends tries to force her, against her will, to have sex relations with him. In a *True Story* tale, a man's whole life is almost wrecked because a woman falsely accuses him of attempting to rape her. In a *Teen Secrets* story, a father and mother are forced to leave town because their teenage daughter has almost been raped; and she, the victim of the attack, pleads with them: "Please, Dad, don't make me go back to school. I can't face the other kids after those headlines." Again, in a *True Confessions* narrative, a girl feels that she is "awfully lucky to be in a new place where nobody knows what happened to me," after she has almost been raped by two young hoodlums.

Even in the men's magazines we find a similar theme: including the idea that it is horribly shameful for the victim of a rape attempt to have suffered such a humiliating experience. In two stories in *Off Beat Detective Stories*, a magazine that does not hesitate to feature sex violence for the edification of its male readers, a girl weeps "softly to herself, her whole body shaking in its shame," and another woman remarks that "I'm so ashamed. So terribly, terribly ashamed," when in both instances each has been the victim of a rapist. Other highly moralistic attitudes toward sex offenses are taken in such periodicals as *True Detective Stories*, *Master Detective Stories*, and *Confidential Tattler*—all of which publications are not in the least squeamish about giving all the gory details of the very sex crimes they excoriate.

At the same time, unusually permissive and tolerant attitudes toward sex offenses are also fairly frequently taken in American mass media. In an *Off Beat Detective Stories* tale a beautiful girl is disappointed because a drug addict who holds her up wants only her money and does not want to rape her; and she revengefully threatens, instead, to rape him. In an article in the *Mattachine Review*, a plea for the understanding of sex offenders and a toning down of laws against sex offenses is published. In *True* magazine, Errol Flynn tells how he had to persuade one of his friends to go to Hong Kong. Writes Flynn: "I had to talk him into it: 'Come on, sport, let's go to old Cathay! What do we have to lose? Nothing! What can we gain? Everything, old boy! Loot, rape, plunder.' It seemed to stir him. Especially the rape part of it." *Twenty-One* magazine carries a news item showing that sex offenders are not violent maniacs but, rather, quiet, conscience-stricken, religiously inclined individuals, who should not be severely punished for their crimes.

In modern novels, tolerant attitudes toward sex offenses are also included from time to time. In Kerouac's *On the Road*, Dean zestfully tells how, when he first met Marylou, "Oh, man, she was only fifteen and wearing jeans and just waiting for someone to pick her up." Three days and three nights in the Ace Hotel he spent with this luscious bit of jailbait; and his wholly unremorseful comment is: "She was so sweet then, so *young*, hmm, ahh!"

In Grace Metalious's best-selling novel, *Peyton Place*, Lucas is not at all abashed or ashamed at tying up and raping his young stepdaughter, Selena. We read: " 'She's pretty, Selena is,' Lucas continued dreamily. 'She's got the prettiest pair of tits I ever seen, and the little ends was always all brown and puckered up. I tied her up the first time, but I didn't have to, 'cause Christ, that cherry of hers was in there so tight I was sore for two weeks after. Couldn't hardly work I was so sore.' "

In a number of other modern popular works—including the novels, *Anatomy of a Murder*, *Hawaii*, and *Poor No More*—incidents of rape are salaciously employed; and although there is little indication that the act itself is a good thing, or that it should not be condemned and punished, there are heavy overtones of it's really not being such a heinous offense after all. Thus, we have this excerpt from *Poor No More₁*

"It was a town in which during a bastardy trial the Judge inquired of a young, but unmarried, mother: 'Is it true you had an illegitimate child for the Reverend King.' 'Yassuh, Judge, but I is only 16 years old.' Her mama, large and sweating and righteous, popped up indignantly. 'Yas, Judge, and she was fas' asleep, and he weighted over 300 pounds and wore a size 20 collar.' 'Guilty!' the Judge roared, 'of assault to kill!' "

As in the early 1950's, then, attitudes toward sex crimes are still mixed, with chillingly condemnatory views alternating with fairly permissive ones. But the tendency, as seems to be true in the case of so many other aspects of sex behavior, is in the liberal direction. Although laws against sex offenses have not been appreciably changed during the last ten years, the interpretation of these laws seems to have eased somewhat, and public condemnation of sex offenders, though still prevalent, is less dogmatic and absolute.

CHAPTER 20

Incest

What the American public thinks of incest is apparently so well known that it is hardly considered worth mentioning in modern mass media. Only four references to incest could be found in the entire literature surveyed for this study; and these, as might well be expected, were against it.

The first of the references to incest that were found was in Taylor Caldwell's novel, *Let Love Come Last*. In this story Oliver is in love with his foster sister, Barbie, and he has some reason to suspect that she may be his real sister. He is duly horrified at this possibility and goes to great lengths to track down his real ancestry. It is made clear that if he does discover they are blood relations he cannot possibly marry her.

In the second reference to incest that was found, Charles S. Braden, in commenting on Robinson Jeffers's poetry in the magazine, *Religion in Life*, pointedly notes that, like fornication, adultery, and homosexuality, incest is the worst type of "sex misadventure."

The third reference to incest that we found was in the Catholic publication, *The Sign*, where, in answer to the question whether it is possible for Catholic first cousins to be married, the authoritative point is made that "according to the Church's Code of Canon Law, 'in the collateral line, marriage is invalid to the third degree inclusively . . .' (Canon 1076). Thereby, marriage is prohibited between first cousins and between second cousins."

Finally, we have a feature article in *True Experiences* magazine entitled "I Almost Married My Brother." In this autobiographical

173

story Eileen Tully tells how her love for a boy "became both a bitter and tender experience" when she discovered that he was really her brother. The outcome, of course, was that she and he had to give up their plans for marriage and to rearrange their relationship on the basis of friendship alone.

These four unanimously oriented references to incest exemplify a fact of which there can be no doubt whatever in our modern culture; namely, that incest is presently viewed as a horrible, shudderful, unforgivable offense, and that a writer of our times would no more portray an incestuous union in favorable terms than he would deify a murderer. Indeed, while a good many murderers are, in our mystery stories and novels, made to seem like fairly jovial, benign, if somewhat misguided, persons, the unmitigated iniquity of deliberate participants in incestuous unions is virtually never similarly propitiated.

In addition to the unanimous condemnation of incest that is found in our literature, there is conspicuously lacking any humorous or lascivious employment of it comparable to that found in relation to other banned sex acts. Occasionally a story may appear in which, usually in a toned-down fashion, incestuous themes are used for the purposes of sex titillation (though none such was found in the wide selection of stories sampled for this study); but, in many hundreds of sex jokes perused in our survey, not a single flippant reference to incest was discovered.

The rationalization for anti-incestuous attitudes which is most frequently given is that the offspring of incestuous unions are poor eugenic risks. The scientific fact is, of course, that incest among normal (though not physically abnormal) couples is no more or less eugenically risky than are unions between non-related individuals. The fact also is, obviously, that if couples voluntarily wish to have incestuous relations they may easily do so today without having any progeny whatever. These facts, however, are completely ignored by the American public, which, in its emotionalized attitudes toward incest, patently carries on biblically based tenets and primitively originated taboos.

What the facts on the incidence of contemporary incest are, no one clearly seems to know, and doubtless even Dr. Kinsey would have difficulty discovering: since only a fraction of those individuals practicing incest at some time during their lives may ever be expected to admit so doing. Court records, which are quite fragmentary in this respect, would lead us to believe that incest is, in fact, relatively infrequent in this country and is surpassed in infrequency only by very few other sex offenses (such as necrophilia or sexual assault with intent to kill). Moreover, the great majority of incest cases which seem to occur involve a father's taking advantage of his daughter (frequently against her will), while relatively few involve mother-son or brother-sister relations.

It would appear, then, that, in the light of (a) the universal condemnation of incest in modern America, (b) the almost complete lack of lascivious or humorous use of incestuous themes, and (c) the relatively low incidence of actual consanguineous sex unions, incest is one sex act regarding which there is a virtual unanimous—negative—attitude. The American public, officially and unofficially, indubitably considers it a thoroughly heinous mode of sex behavior—and is so genuinely horrified at the thought of incest that the members of this public, for once, co-operate with their own views and rarely participate in incestuous congress.

Is there, then, an absence of self-conflict in the overwhelming majority of Americans who theoretically and actually abhor incest? Unfortunately not; for, as the last half century of psychoanalytic investigation has shown, many (perhaps most) normal individuals who consciously abhor incest unconsciously have quite strong incestuous desires at various times in their lives. While the universality of Oedipus conflicts, as posited by Freud and his orthodox followers, may well be doubted, few psychologists or psychiatrists today refuse to acknowledge the enormous (largely unconscious) guilt, conflict, and neurotic symptomatology which is being continually generated in large numbers of our populace because of their deeply repressed incestuous urges.

Precisely *because* incest is so roundly and universally condemned in our culture, and *because* our family system of child-raising necessarily leads to many (unconscious) incestuous desires, these desires are very poorly tolerated by the normal individual, must usually be deeply repressed or otherwise defensively handled, and therefore tend to result in widespread underlying self-conflict and neurosis. The irony is that even when society succeeds in reaching a unified, non-conflicting attitude against a given mode of sex behavior, this mode may still widely flourish in the form of unconscious urges and impulsions, which then may lay the groundwork for immense amounts of guilt, anxiety, doubt, self-punishment, inner discord, unhappiness, and psychopathological behavior. Even, then, when societies suppress overt sex conduct, they tend to super-press it into lower levels of consciousness—from whence it keeps pressing up to plague, bedevil, and neuroticize the same millions who are "successfully" coping with it. Sex behavior which is forcefully inhibited also tends to be forcefully inhabited—with trouble.

Attitudes Toward Incest in the 1960's

As noted in the first part of this chapter, there were very few references to incest in the mass media of the early 1950's and all of these were conservative. In the re-survey of this kind of material in the early 1960's, it has been found that there are now a good many more references to incest and that about a third of these are liberal or permissive.

On the negative side, more material was found in current best-selling novels than in any other medium. Grace Metalious's *Peyton Place* makes very much of the incestuous relationship between Selena and her stepfather, Lucas Cross. All the characters in the book, especially Allison MacKenzie and Matthew Swain, are horrified by Lucas's act; and Selena herself is so disturbed by it that when she is accused of murdering Lucas, and could save herself by confessing that he forced her to have incestuous relations with him, she refuses to do so:

"I'll never tell, thought Selena desperately. Not even when they take me out to hang me. They'll never find out why from me. Let them ask. They'll never find out."

In Robert Penn Warren's novel, *The Cave*, we are given no fewer than three separate instances of incestuous thoughts or acts—all of which are viewed with real alarm. Mr. Bingham, the banker, thinks of his daughter, Jo-Lea, with incestuous intent, and he becomes quite ashamed of himself. Mr. Hayworth, city editor of the Nashville *Press-Clarion*, thinks of his dead daughter "and wished she had not died when she was fourteen and promising to be pretty and well stacked. Then he felt ashamed, not saying to himself what exactly he was ashamed of." Sim Cutlick starts making passes at his daughter, Dorothy, while his wife is sick in bed; and we read: "Then a faint movement, for even if Sim Cutlick's woman was so sick she couldn't move, she was Dorothy Cutlick's mother, too; and then there was the voice, even weaker, saying: '. . . come in here—I'm up—you don't come in here right now, Sim, I'll blow yore brains out . . .' And there was the sound of an object being dragged on the plank floor. It sounded like a shotgun being weakly dragged."

In Morris L. West's religious novel, *The Devil's Advocate*, Paolo Sanduzzi "kept his eyes closed and breathed steadily because, although he wanted often to kiss [his mother], and have her hold him as she did in the old days, there was now a revulsion in him that he could not explain. It was the same thing that made him close his eyes and turn away his head when she undressed her thickening body or got up to relieve herself in the night. He was ashamed of her and he was ashamed of himself."

In William Inge's play, *A Loss of Roses*, published in *Esquire* magazine, there are also two separate negative references to incest. Helen says to her teenage son, Kenny: "All these years, you've felt I was neglecting you, that I was denying you, haven't you, son? Kenny:

176

Maybe. Helen: Oh, Kenny, I didn't mean to deny you. I didn't want to. But if I'd kept you any closer, I'd have *destroyed* you, Kenny. (She runs into the kitchen now, sobbing uncontrollably)." When Helen's friend, Lila, tells her that when she, Lila, married Ed, his father started coming to her room, trying to force himself on her, Helen says: "Your husband's *father*? ... Oh, that's shocking ... I've never heard of such people."

From *Esquire*, too, comes the cartoon depicting a movie producer growling at some of his underlings: "I don't care how much Faulkner knows about the South—in my pictures fathers *don't* marry their daughters!"

The general picture that we get from contemporary mass media, therefore, is that incest is still definitely taboo in this country and that anyone who engages in it is a low-down double-dyed bastard. But this picture is not entirely consistent. In at least two contemporary novels, incestuous relations are taken much more lightly. In Nabokov's *Lolita*, not only do we have the apotheosis of sex relations between a girl and her stepfather, but the girl herself initiates the act of coitus between herself and her stepparent. The male participant in this crime then pens this defense of his relationship with his stepdaughter: "Among Sicilians sexual relations between a father and his daughter are accepted as a matter of course, and the girl who participates in such relationship is not looked upon with disapproval by the society of which she is part. I'm a great admirer of Sicilians, fine athletes, fine musicians, fine upright people, Lo, and great lovers. But let's not digress. Only the other day we read in the newspapers some bunkum about a middle-aged morals offender transporting a nine-year-old girl across state lines for immoral purposes, whatever these are. Dolores darling! You are not nine but almost thirteen, and I would not advise you to consider yourself my cross-country slave, and I deplore the Mann act as lending itself to a dreadful pun, and revenge that the Gods of Semantics take against tight-zippered Philistines. I am your father, and I am speaking English, and I love you."

In *Hawaii*, James Michener has Dr. Whipple give another defense of incest to Abner Hale, who is horrified by the Hawaiian royalty engaging in brother-sister marriage. "Damn it, Abner," Whipple says, "two of the most completely civilized societies we've ever had were the Egyptians and the Incas. Now, no Egyptian king was ever allowed to marry anybody but his sister, and if I can believe what I've heard, the same was true of the Incas. They prospered. As a matter of fact, it's not a bad system, scientifically. That is, if you're willing to kill off ruthlessly any children with marked defects and apparently the Egyptians, the Incas, and the Hawaiians were willing to do so. Have you ever seen a handsomer group of people than the alii?"

In contemporary men's magazines there are also stories and features which show an unusually permissive attitude toward incest. In a story in *Ace*, a young boy's mother encourages his aunt to show him the facts of life. " 'Yes,' says the boy's aunt, Maria, glancing quickly at him with a smile. 'I have a lot to tell him about. All kinds of things.' Her smile widened. 'Maybe some things to show him, too,' she said, 'things from New York.'

"He looked away from her, glancing swiftly at his mother.

"She turned from the stove and said to him, 'That sounds nice. You always seem to be talking about New York. Now that your aunt is home, she can tell you all about it. She should know all the answers after three years.'

" 'Yes,' he replied quietly, looking away from Maria's knowing smile."

In a story in *The Gent*, a father wonders whether his young son is a homosexual; but his young second wife assures him that she knows, first hand, that the son is not. This gives the father a jolt, but apparently he is able to accept it.

Finally, we may quote the cartoon from *Texas Ranger* which shows a kindly old woman reading from *Lolita* to her grandson: "Once there was a nice man who loved his little daughter very much. . . ."

Incest, in the 1960's, has obviously become considerably less heinous than its depictions in the 1950's tended to make it out. This hardly means that every father's daughter had best now look with panic to saving her chastity nor that every mother's son should expect seduction at home. But it does probably mean that the strongly incestuous urges that most normal human beings experience at some time during their lives may now be experienced with considerably less conscious or unconscious feelings of guilt.

It should be remembered in this connection, as I have recently pointed out in *The Art and Science of Love* and several papers on rational psychotherapy, that the *complex* part of the so-called Oedipus complex is hardly innate or inherited (as the Freudians tend to believe), even though incestuous *desires* are so common among both young males and females, and among their parents in regard to them, as to be considered almost instinctive. What makes an individual with incestuous desires develop a full-blown Oedipus complex is his (or her) *belief* or *assumption* that it is wrong and heinous for him to lust after his parent of the other sex and to be consequently resented by his same-sex parent. If we did not bring up our children to *believe* this kind of nonsense—since, although incest certainly has many practical disadvantages, to *think* about committing it is hardly a dire crime— they would never develop Oedipus complexes, even though they very often would (as Freud and his followers correctly show) have

Oedipal feelings or attachments.

The more, then, we violently condemn and punish incestuous urges and ideas, the more we will tend to drive human beings into acquiring self-defeating Oedipus complexes. And the fact that today's literature seems to be emphasizing the horror of incest to a considerably lesser degree than did yesterday's is a sign that bodes well for the mental health of our youngest generation.

CHAPTER 21
Sex "Perversions"

Since this is to be a relatively grim chapter, we might as well, quite untypically, start it off with a few excerpts from the sexy joke magazines which overflow the shelves of present-day newsstands. *Laugh Book* tells us that "a dozen doctors tried Camels for a year and found out they still preferred women." *Joke Parade* prints the story of the spinster who complained to the steward that a sailor peeped into her cabin. "Sorry, madam," the steward replied, "but you're traveling tourist, you know. You could hardly expect the captain here." *College Fun* presents a quiz in sociology which includes the question: "According to Kinsey, which of the following are more popular among farm boys: (a) sheep, (b) pigs, (c) girls?"

Mark these tidbits well, for in perusing literally thousands of pages on sex material published (and widely read) in our day we could find only these attempts at dealing with sex "perversion" in an unequivocally humorous manner. The more material we read, the more evident it became that, in regard to the so-called "unnatural" sex practices, little comicality is allowed in contemporary American expression. Where other sex acts (as we have been seeing) are often publicly banned, denigrated, ridiculed, roundly condemned—and then backhandedly laughed off, overlooked, and even covertly admired and esteemed—sexual deviations are almost universally condemned, period.

One can, in fact, hunt through reams of public writings and utterances without finding any half-favorable reference to homosexuality, sadism, masochism, and other "unnatural" sex acts; and even neutral allusions to them are difficult to locate outside of purely scientific papers and books (where, indeed, they still are frequently described in prejudged, unscientific terms).

Thus we find Fulton J. Sheen (in *Peace of Soul*) and Thomas Merton (in *The Seven Storey Mountain*) terming all sexual deviations as "sins of lust," "perversions of natural appetite," "evil excesses of passion." An *Uncensored Detective* writer refers to the sex activities of

Martha Beck and Raymond Fernandez—who apparently indulged in certain spicy non-coital sex practices—as "unholy lusts and abnormal sex drives." And John O'Hara has the heroine of his *A Rage to Live*, who is a highly sexed adulteress, become greatly incensed when her girl friend insinuates that she might have allowed another girl to paint her while she was engaged in copulating with a man. To be thought capable of such deviational sex conduct is considered by her to be a rank insult.

On the surface, therefore, American writers are completely opposed to all kinds of sex "perversions." Nevertheless, if one digs deeply enough into contemporary lore, one finds a commonplace *use* of sexually aberrant behavior for the purposes of titillating and keeping the unflagging interest of prurient readers. One finds, in point of fact, so much (conscious or unconscious) employment of sexually "perverted" themes that one soon begins to suspect that the anti-deviational attitudes of the American populace serve as masks for deeply felt impulses toward exactly the kind of behavior that is so expressively excoriated. Or possibly things may be the other way round: perhaps the very fact that sexual "perversions" are so distinctly reviled and interdicted in modern America makes their description unusually exciting to many readers and listeners who might otherwise find them tangless and boring.

In any event, let us look at some of the facts of the case. Take first one of the leading "perversions"—sadism, or the inflicting of pain upon others for one's own sex pleasure. None of the hundreds of newspapers, magazines, motion pictures, plays, radio scripts, best-selling books, or popular songs examined during the researches on this volume was found to contain a single favorable reference to sexual sadism. Many, however, contained open or covert delineations of sadistic behavior which were obviously included to thrill or excite their perusers or auditors.

Torture scenes, for example, are common in contemporary fiction and drama and are frequently described at great length. Thus in a story in *Private Detective* magazine, gangsters, in order to force a girl to confess where she had hidden the key to her safe-deposit box, savagely cuff her, hit her on the mouth, and then "Jerry deliberately held the lighted end of his cigarette against soft flesh. Her scream was a piercing shock of agony. . . . Still Lorraine wasn't giving up. Jerry picked another soft warm spot for the end of his cigarette. Lorraine surrendered."

In the motion picture, *Pirates of Capri*, a beautiful, half-naked girl is agonizingly tortured with a huge spiked wheel for many minutes in a scene that has little to do with the main plot of the film and that could easily have been entirely omitted.

180

In Frank Slaughter's *Divine Mistress* the torture of the lovely model, Clarice, is described in vivid detail: "At a nod from Frey Ignacio, the torture master took up a pitcher of water and began to pour it slowly upon the *toca* [long strip of cloth], where it lay loosely across the *bostezo* [gag] in Clarice's mouth. And now Antonio could see the fiendish ingenuity of this method, for as the loose cloth filled with water, it was carried backward by its own weight, sinking ever deeper into her throat. Inevitably some of the water seeped through the cloth, and in the agony of near strangulation, she tried futilely to swallow and clear her throat for breathing. She could obtain air in no other way, for her nostrils were tightly plugged."

In the film, *Samson and Delilah*, there is a very gory and prolonged scene in which Samson kills a lion with his bare hands; at the end of which Delilah, who has been ecstatically watching, frenziedly screams: "You killed him with your hands—I love you!"

In a story in *Love Short Novels*, we read that "he gave her a long look that at once despised and desired her. His head swooped. A heart-beat later, he kissed her. He took her lips in a kiss that was brutal, bruising, and insulting. He crushed her to him with arms that offered no tenderness. Sheila could feel through her soft wool sweater every button on his jacket. They jabbed cruelly. She was sobbing beneath her breath with physical pain while her yearning arms crept up to his shoulders. They reached to encircle his neck, but never arrived. Ruthlessly, humiliatingly, he thrust her from him and laughed in her stricken face."

Lest it be thought that all modern sadism is merely fictional, let us refer for a moment to *Quick* magazine, which features a story about Ralph Edwards, famed producer of the radio show, *Truth or Consequences*, who has fabulously succeeded in life and property, driving his studio and air-wave audiences into literal gales of laughter by throwing pies in contestants' faces, sending them on world-circling wild-goose chases, shaming them in department-store windows, and forcing them to perform many other (to quote *Quick*) "contestant-torturing stunts."

Other examples of real-life sadism may be found (a) in the magazine, *Telecast*, which tells how boxing matches have become so popular over television that two chains of stations, CBS-TV and NBC-TV, paid three quarters of a million dollars for one year's right to indoor boxing matches; (b) in Botkin's *A Treasury of Southern Folklore*, where we are told that "people do not go to see the beautiful cave where Floyd Collins met his death, but do go see his horribly eaten-away body (which his relatives have preserved and now keep on display)"; (c) in the magazine, *Man to Man*, which features an article on human shrunken heads, with several gruesome pictures of these heads

181

—in one of which a blonde is shown holding a tiny head and stroking the hair; (d) in *Uncensored Detective* magazine, which on page 6 of one issue features a full-length photo of an old woman who has been bound, gagged, and murdered, and on page 26 of the same issue shows a large picture of the pajama-clad body of a man who has been stabbed to death.

One more illustration of real-life sadistic trends may suffice here. A classified advertisement in *Popular Photography*, after begging its readers to send in two dollars for twelve 5 x 7 photos of women's wrestling bouts, also wonders whether they would like "25 6 x 6 photos, German atrocities in France."

If the sexual element in the foregoing illustrations appears to be somewhat subdued, more specifically sexual varieties of sadism may also be commonly found in present-day literature. For instance:

In Mika Waltari's popular novel, *The Egyptian*, King Burnaburiash is made to speak of one of his concubines in this wise: "Truly I anticipate much delight with her, for I know that kind of girl; with them the stick is the best argument. I am still young, and my beard has not grown, and I am often weary in the arms of women; I find greater pleasure in looking on and listening to their cries when the eunuchs lash them with thin wands. Therefore, this stubborn girl pleases me well since she gives me occasion to have her whipped by the eunuchs, and I swear that this very night she shall be beaten until her skin swells up and prevents her lying on her back, whereby my pleasure shall be greater than before."

In the lavishly produced film, *Prince of Foxes*, Angela, madly enamored of the hero of the piece, Orsini, declares: "Andrea . . . Andrea . . . I can't help myself. I love you and I don't trust you. I never can read your mind and I'm not even certain you have a heart. If you do, it belongs to me from now on." (As she speaks, she runs her lips over the tips of his fingers, eventually reaching the fleshy base of the thumb. As she finishes, she savagely bites the fleshy base of the thumb."

From Alberto Moravia's passionate novel, *The Woman of Rome*, we have this sadistic bed scene: "When I drew close to him and bent over the bed to stretch myself beside him, I suddenly felt him grip my knees with his arms and then bite me savagely on the left hip. I felt an acute spasm of pain while at the same time I realized absolutely that the bite expressed some indefinable despair he was experiencing. It was as though we were two cursed souls driven by hatred, rage and sadness to bury our teeth in one another's flesh in the depths of some new hell, rather than two lovers about to make love."

In Nelson Algren's *The Man with the Golden Arm* John's specifically sexual sadism against his wife, Molly, is made crystal-clear: "All she had ever yet extracted from John was a promise to stop kicking her.

182

A promise seldom kept. Sophie had heard John telling Molly, coming past the door late at night, 'I'm not layin' you, sister—I'll never lay you. Just let me get in those kicks.' They had passed to the sound of her crying, 'All I want from you is to be left alone.' "

Finally, in Nick Joaquin's short story, "Three Generations," in *Wake* magazine, we have a frenzied middle-aged son desperately trying to keep a young girl away from her dying lover, his father, and maddened at his own son's bringing the two together again: "He had a sudden, delirious craving to unloose his belt and whip her again, to make her suffer, to tear her flesh into shreds, to mutilate that supple, defiant, sweet, animal body of hers. His hands shook and his desire became an anger towards his son who had brought this voluptuous being so near."

Note, in these illustrations from contemporary literature, how very explicit the voluptuous element in the sadism is made; how the details of the actual acts are painstakingly, lovingly drawn; how the reader's emotions are deliberately roused and his senses distinctly excited. The one thing, indeed, that some of this sex brutality type of writing seems to represent is a thinly disguised pornography that is ingeniously designed so that it will have little trouble getting by the censors, whereas the same descriptive intensity and realism, if used for depicting, say, straight, "normal" sexual intercouse, would doubtless be banned in Boston and many points north, south, and west.

So much for sadism. Its psychological counterpart and correlate, masochism, also comes in for some lurid handling on the part of contemporary writers, who, without ever seeming to approve of or encourage it in any way, nevertheless manage to exploit its sex content for all the traffic will bear.

A fairly light—and transparent—degree of masochism is exhibited in the popular song entitled "Why Don't You Haul Off and Love Me?" in which the heroine asks her boy friend why he doesn't squeeze her until she turns blind.

Going a little further, we find *New Love* magazine with no less than four stories out of six in one issue depicting a scene in which the hero, a swaggering, brash character, forcibly, brutally kisses the heroine after knowing her for about five minutes. But does our Nell take too unkindly to this type of battering at her portals? Oh no: "It was a hard, angry kiss, a kiss a man gave a girl he hated and wanted to hurt. Yet, even knowing that, it made the blood skyrocket through her and her foolish heart sing. There was magic in the touch of his lips, in the beat of his heart against her own."

Let it not be erroneously thought, however, that masochistic feelings, in modern literature, are confined only to women. We may turn to a scene in Kingsley's play, *Detective Story*, to find Charley, a hoodlum, and Callahan, a detective, conversing thus:

CHARLEY: Go ahead! Beat me! Beat me unconscious. Go ahead!
CALLAHAN (*laughs, puts the "persuader" away*): You're too eager,
Charley. Some-a them creeps like it, you know. Gives 'em a
thrill. Look at that kisser! I'm a son of a bitch, I'm right.

Masochism is delineated, significantly enough, by two of the same
writers who, a few pages back, we noted giving torrid illustrations of
sadism, Nick Joaquin and Alberto Moravia. Here is Joaquin's contribution: "As for the women, he had suspected that they even took a
certain delight in the barbaric cruelties of their lords. His father was
never without two or three concubines whom he had whipped as
regularly as he did his sons; but none of them, once fallen in his power,
had bothered to strive for a more honorable status."

Here, finally, is the manner in which Moravia describes the female
of the affair between his heroine, the Woman of Rome, and the
murderer, Sonzogno: "At last he took me and I felt a pleasure made
sinister and atrocious by fear. I could not restrain a long, wailing cry
in the dark, as if the final clasp had been the clasp of death, not of
love, and my cry was life departing from me, leaving behind a
tortured, motionless body."

Obviously, then, the abhorrence of sadism and masochism which is
so unanimous in American sexpression does little to discourage their
detailed, lascivious depiction. Quite, it would appear, the contrary.

This same theoretical unity and practical ambivalence of attitudes is
also seen in the case of public references to homosexuality, and nowhere more clearly is it shown than in the featured writings and
advertising matter of magazines devoted to the seemingly popular
sport of weight lifting or bodybuilding. Bodybuilding, it may surprise
some readers to know, has thousands upon thousands of adherents in
the United States and boasts a national organization as well as several
flourishing periodicals which are packed, from cover to cover, with
the almost-nude pictures of well-muscled males. As far as is known,
these magazines have an almost exclusively male clientele.

One of the bodybuilder publications features an article which
frankly discusses the question of whether homosexuals "are invading
our physique shows and lifting contests . . . . getting into our gyms and
into the profession of physique photography and . . . are polluting our
bodybuilders and bringing a bad name to the profession of bodybuilding." The writer of the article, who makes it clear that he considers
homosexuality a nasty, immoral, abnormal practice, vigorously con-
tends that only a small minority of American weight lifters, their
photographers, and their devoted followers are homosexually inclined.

Perhaps so. But, aside from displaying advertisement after advertisement hawking the most gorgeous, graceful, and aesthetic poses of bare-chested males imaginable, bodybuilding magazines also contain two ads for "a magnificent dual series" of photos of lithe and muscular bodybuilders posing together. In one series, "these superb photographs" include (for only $3.00, air mail 25¢ extra) eleven different sets of magnificently torsoed men wrestling each other; and, in the other offer, "two of America's greatest young models" go through five artistic poses for only $5.00 in the jumbo 8 x 10 size or $2.50 in the regular 4 x 5 photos. This last ad also proclaims: "Don't miss this great set of Photos! Send now—Limited Quantities—Get yours!"

For the rest, public attitudes toward homosexuality seem to be universally negative in twentieth-century literature. Thus in Margaret Landon's *Never Dies the Dream* the heroine's reputation is almost ruined because she nurses a young girl back to life and is therefore suspected of lesbianism. In Paul Bowle's story in *Wake* magazine a thoroughly sophisticated college instructor, as well as a villageful of British West Indian natives, is scandalized by the homosexual leanings of the instructor's son. In Nelson Algren's *The Man with the Golden Arm* even a hard-boiled police captain is shocked by a prisoner's saying that he has not been picked up for molesting a ten-year-old girl—but a ten-year-old boy. And *Pace* magazine takes it very much for granted, in one of its feature articles, that Los Angeles vice-squad officers should be caught shaking down homosexuals for from $20 to $50, in lieu of carting them off to jail.

Even the jokes about homosexuals in modern America take on a somewhat sadistic, ridiculing tinge—which is not at all evident in regard to anecdotes about adulterers, fornicators, and other heterosexual offenders against public morals. Thus *Laugh Book* notes that "ever since Percy received a pair of pink pajamas and a military brush for a present, he doesn't know whether to enroll in Agnes Scott or make a try for West Point." And Nelson Algren, doing a beautifully realistic take-off on a floor-show performance in a Chicago night club, describes how "Mr. Floor Show . . . resumed his fluttering about in the orange shorts for want of anything better to do, like a crazed burlesque queen, pausing only to stamp his foot with a girlish petulance and assert, 'I'll have you know I'm every inch a man!' "

Even when the contemporary American laughs at sexual "perversion," then, he tends to do so in a rather nasty, sickly way. When deviant sex behavior is not faced antagonistically or with morbid humor, it is rarely faced at all. It does, as we have seen, come prominently out on many occasions: but then its expression tends to be either unconscious or overly self-conscious; on the one hand, it shows itself in the form of sadomasochistic or homosexual characterizations

185

or manifestations of whose basically sexual content neither the writer nor reader may be aware; or, on the other hand, it finds expression in frankly shocking and titillating fictional or dramatic scenes which the writer may consciously employ but whose sexuality the reader is probably much less conscious of enjoying.

American attitudes toward other sex perversions than sadism, masochism, and homosexuality are most difficult to derive from popular writings and utterances, since virtually no mention whatever is therein allowed them. Fetishism, transvestitism, pedophilia, voyeurism, exhibitionism, and various other aberrant sex practices (at least some of which seem to be fairly widely practiced, if Kinsey and other students of sex behavior are to be believed) are rarely mentioned in the popular prints. The one significant exception to this rule is that some popular magazines are full of advertisements of sex books which, according to the lurid invitations of the copy writers, go into every possible gory detail of every possible sexual aberrancy. Here too, then, the general rule about sexual perversion in twentieth-century America seems to hold true; namely, that although no conscious, or even left-handed, sanction of such "perversion" is publicly tolerated, the very horror in which it is held makes mention of sexual aberration unusually exciting and interesting to the average American reader.

In summation: sexual "perversion" is so universally condemned and deliberately suppressed in American society that very little frank, sly-dog, or ribald undercover enjoyment of it is permitted. When it does express itself, it generally does so in an anxiety-ridden, morbid, or ridiculously exaggerated way (e.g., the mincing manners and garish displays of Greenwich Village homosexuals). This may be one reason why, while adultery, fornication, whoremongering, and other "immoral" sex outlets are utilized by millions of fairly normal Americans, homosexuality, sadomasochism, and other "abnormal" sex practices, when they are habitually and exclusively used as modes of sex participation, are so frequently concomitants of seriously neurotic behavior. It may not be sexually perverted acts which make a society sick or decadent, but society's own mores which, by their expressing unduly harsh attitudes toward certain sex acts, render these acts "perverted" and "abnormal" and thereby encourage their habitual or exclusive employment by many of society's neurotic members.

Attitudes Toward Sex "Perversions" in the 1960's

It was found, in our survey of the 1950 material, that there were few expressed or implied attitudes toward sexual deviation in the mass media of that day and that these attitudes were preponderantly conservative. In the follow-up study of attitudes in the 1960's, a great

186

number of references to homosexuality and other sex deviations were found and most of these references were liberal or permissive.

Anti-perversion attitudes in the 1960's are largely to be picked up in the best-selling fiction works and in the men's magazines. In the novel, *Poor No More*, Philip duFresne's mother says that he "has more or less degenerated into a nasty child," since he started picking up sailors in *pissoirs*. Carol Craig and Jimmy Wilbur both show disdain for fags and lesbians. In *Hawaii, Return to Peyton Place, On the Road*, and *Lady Chatterley's Lover* there are also snide and open digs at homosexuals by various characters.

In Allan Drury's *Advise and Consent*, one of the main themes of the book revolves about the discovery that a United States Senator has had a homosexual attachment early in his life; and he feels so disgraced and politically lost by this revelation that he finally commits suicide. In Morris L. West's *The Devil's Advocate*, a considerable portion of the book involves the attempt of Monsignor Meredith and others to break up the homoerotic relationship between Nicholas Black and Paolo Sanduzzi. At one point, the Monsignor says to Black: "You are doing a detestable thing. Your private vices are a matter between you and the Almighty. But when you set out to corrupt this boy, you are committing a crime against nature. . . ."

Contemporary men's magazines—which we shall see later often take a most permissive view of sex deviation—contain some of the nastiest gibes against homosexuals and other kinds of perverts. *The National Enquirer* goes out of its way to dig up the story of Oscar Wilde whom, it headlines, "WOMEN ADORED, BUT HE WAS JAILED OVER HIS AFFAIRS WITH MEN." *Confidential* has a letter noting that there is a "proportionately high rate of turnover among fellows of [Harvard] University who are retained in the various houses as advisers to the students. Evidently, in quite a number of cases, parents have complained to the administration about these advisers. There have even been rumors of molestations of the younger boys."

The *Saturday Review* contains a review of George Axelrod's play, *Goodbye Charlie*, in which the protagonist, George Tracy, falls in love with Charlie Sorrell who, after his death, has returned to earth in a woman's body. Says the *Saturday Review*: "But the main flaw is the failure to exploit audience reaction to a special situation. For every time George finds himself drifting toward romantic involvement with the retooled Charlie, he and the audience recoil in horror at the thought of physical relationship between a man and a male personality in a female container."

Errol Flynn, after boasting in his serialized autobiography in *True* magazine about his innumerable heterosexual affairs, has this to say about his escape from a fate worse than death: "There was another,

Coombs, a young faculty member. I hadn't been there a week when this splay-footed individual wanted to bugger me. I never felt such panic as when I found myself in a corner. Coombs approached stealthily, with an evil and lecherous smile, and an intent of which I had no idea at the time. Yet I sensed something highly ominous."

In the film, *Suddenly Last Summer*, Mrs. Venable, who has often helped her dead son, Sebastian, procure men by acting as a beautiful female decoy, is outraged when Catherine, who was also used as a decoy by Sebastian, exposes his homosexuality. " 'Stop her,' wails Mrs. Venable. 'See? *See* how she destroys us with her tongue like a hatchet?' " And she tries to induce a brain specialist to cut out a large slice of Catherine's brain.

One magazine contains a letter which remarks: "Due to present shortsighted policies, Uncle Sam does not want homophiles in his service. Homophile organizations consider these policies discriminatory—but they do exist, and can seriously hurt the unwary individual. . . . I know of one sad case of a handsome corpsman in the Navy who was trying desperately hard to avoid difficulties when some young queen he had spurned reported him for 'lingering too long' over the dressing of a patient's leg, and although no overt act had been committed, the corpsman received a blue discharge. Subsequently, he found difficulty in obtaining satisfactory employment and had to accept menial jobs. Finally, he changed his name and secured ministerial training where he is converting his rough experiences into understanding guidance of many who have been 'down and out.' "

Other negative attitudes toward homosexuality may be found in articles and stories in such diverse publications as *The New York Times, Mystery Digest, The Commonweal, Scamp, Saga, Vue, Esquire,* and *Cavalier.* Anti-deviational attitudes in regard to other forms of sexual "perversion" are also found in modern mass media. Thus, in a story in *Tan* magazine a woman's physician tells the heroine that she is a hermaphrodite (that is, an individual with genital organs of both sexes) and she reports that "If he had killed me, I don't think the moment would have been worse." And in William Inge's play, *A Loss of Roses,* published in *Esquire,* Helen is quite shocked because her son Kenny is a fetishist who steals little items, such as gloves, from girls to whom he is sexually attracted.

Liberal attitudes toward sex deviation are even more prevalent in today's literature than are disapproving attitudes, especially in the best-selling novels and men's magazines. In *Advise and Consent,* Senator Brigham Anderson, just before he kills himself because of a homosexual scandal in which he is involved, thinks back to the joys of his homosexual experience. In *Return to Peyton Place,* Anne Harvey

188

is entranced with Jennifer Carter and worships her despite Jennifer's coldness. In *Lolita*, the young heroine has a fine time having an affair with Elizabeth Talbot and is not in the least guilty or disturbed about it.

The same novel, *Lolita*, has probably the most detailed and most persuasive defense of extreme heterosexual fetishism—the compulsive-obsessive attachment of a male for a young adolescent female—that has ever been penned in any language. Not only does the narrator of this story wildly love his nymphet, Lolita, but also remains obsessed with watching and thinking about other nymphets of her age. As he says: "I would park at a strategic point, with my vagrant schoolgirl beside me in the car, to watch the children leave school—always a pretty sight. This sort of thing soon began to bore my so easily bored Lolita, and, having a childish lack of sympathy for other people's whims, she would insult me and my desire to have her caress me while blue-eyed little brunettes in blue shorts, copperheads in green boleros, and blurred boyish blondes in faded slacks passed by in the sun."

Return to Peyton Place, in addition to its condonation of homosexuality, has some particularly sadomasochistic scenes which are used for salacious titillation and which apotheosize the great pleasures to be derived from such sex encounters. The same Jennifer whom we saw, two paragraphs back, having a homosexual affair with Anne Harvey, also has this kind of a sexual relationship with her husband, Ted:

"She laughed up into his face and taunted him. 'Listen to my big brave man begging for favors. Sit up, Fido, Mama give you liver.' Ted jumped out of bed and yanked the blankets off her. 'You little bitch,' he said harshly, his hands trembling. 'You little bitch.' He grabbed her nightgown at the neckline and tore it from her body and his hands left angry, red marks against her white skin. 'You love it,' he said into her mouth, bruising her lips as he bit into them. 'You love it and you know it.' And then it was Jennifer who was insatiable. Her body heaved and her eyes glittered. 'Hit me,' she cried. 'Hit me.' 'You're goddamned right I'll hit you,' said Ted. 'I'd like to kill you.'

"He used his belt on her until her back and buttocks and thighs were covered with welts and when he finally took her, her lips were red with blood from his shoulder and she fainted. 'Dear God, what have I done,' cried Ted. He began to weep. 'I'll never do it again, darling. Never. My God, I'm no better than an animal. I'll never do it again. Please. Please forgive me.' Ted slept at last, the sleep of exhaustion, and for a long time Jennifer lay awake in the dark smiling. She touched the welts on her thighs, running her fingers over them hard so that the pain burned all through her and her teeth gleamed white in the dark room. She moved so that her back scraped against the sheet, hurting her, and her nipples grew rigid and she felt the tightening of excitement between her legs. 'Again,' she whispered into Ted's ear, 'Again.' "

The men's magazines contain more than their share of items that show unalloyed or at least mild approval of various aspects of sexual deviation. In fact, many special men's magazines exist which are almost entirely filled with photographs of nude or almost-nude males, many of them posing amiably with another nude male; and there would seem to be no doubt whatever that these magazines are purchased almost exclusively by homosexuals, just as the girlie magazines are purchased almost exclusively by highly heterosexually oriented males. One of these magazines, *Tomorrow's Man*, has 56 photographs of nearly-nude "bodybuilders" in its 48 pages. Another, *Popular Man*, has 50 similar photos; *Man Alive* has 35; and *Zing* has 29.

These same kinds of magazines have numerous advertisements for large collections of photos of males, for "the best—and briefest!—in male attire"; for movies of two or more males having intimate physical contact with each other; etc. Again, there is no doubt whatever that these items would only appeal to homosexuals and that they indicate a favorable acceptance of the sex behavior of these homosexuals.

Articles favoring or condoning homosexuality are also to be found in such periodicals as *The Dude*, *Twenty-One*, *Sexology*, and *Realife Guide*. In a case study of two homosexuals in the last-named magazine, the author writes: "They have strong, beautiful bodies, and they have active, intelligent minds. Their Greek love is truly an idyll. Nature's mistake was putting them into the wrong society in the wrong age of history, but with the understanding of myself and my associates, and with the necessary discretion, these young men will overcome the demon Guilt and will 'live happily ever after.' "

During the last decade three publications have come into existence in the United States which are published by homosexuals and which are devoted to defending and protecting homophiles against persecution. These are *One*, the *Mattachine Review*, and a Lesbian publication, *The Ladder*. Every issue of these publications contains stories, articles, or poems indicating that homosexuality is a fine, enjoyable state of existence; that homosexuals are nice people; and that laws and mores which are directed against homosexuality should be changed. In *One*, for example, the advisability of using the magazine to encourage pen pals among its readers is discussed; and most of the correspondents definitely favor this idea, although some of the editors do not.

Other aspects of sexual deviation are also endorsed or approved in contemporary mass media. Sadism is approvingly mentioned in advertisements in the *New York Times*, and in articles in *Comedy* and *Rapture*. In the last-named periodical there is an article on how a man can pick up girls with a cane, which has all kinds of sadistic allusions and which concludes: "Seriously, the cane is a disappearing element of American life—and one that needs revival badly. Won't you be the one to raise cane in hand and raise Cain in bed?"

Other ads for sadistic photographs, stories, and paraphernalia appear fairly frequently in the men's magazines. To illustrate:

From *Frolic*: "BONDAGE STORY DRAWINGS OF DAMSELS IN DISTRESS THAT ARE BOUND TO PLEASE. List of illustrated serials in stock! 'Sold in Slavery,' 20 chapters, all for $11.00, 'Fighting Girls Fracas,' 25 chapters, all for $13.75, 'Yolanda's Bizarre Experience,' 15 chapters, all 15 for $8.00. . . ."

From *Follies*: "SPANKING. BOOKS/PHOTOS—STORIES. Illustrated lists on C.P., T.V., etc."

From *Vue*: "SWEET GWENDOLINE & SIR MYSTIC D'ARCY. A COMPLETE FULL SIZE 52 PAGE MAGAZINE MELODRAMA DRAWN BY JOHN WILLIE. INCLUDING FOUR PHOTOS OF THE MODEL IN TYPICALLY—WELL, should we say RESTFUL? poses . . ." [with illustration of a buxom beauty bound to a post, obviously as a prelude to being beaten].

From *Frolic*: "SPANKING NEW. We have what we know you'll enjoy—The Battle of the Sexes" or "She Got it on the End. . . . 3 different sets of 10 4 x 5 glossy photos each of how man keeps the upper hand."

From *Tab*: "EXPOSED! Conditions in Women's Prisons. Correspondence from overseas tells an extremely interesting story, well documented with many illustrations. Ancient corrective methods still in use, scenes of Beauty in Penitence. For all seasoned collectors of curiosa. . . ."

Masochism is another sexual deviation that is favorably referred to in modern magazines. *Twenty-One* features an article which shows that masochism is widespread among American males and that many "magazine covers cater to masochists who love to suffer at the hands of women, as also may the magazine's readers." *The National Enquirer* has an article about Georgia Moll, the sexy Italian movie queen, which is entitled "I'll *Fight* The Man I Love!" and which quotes Miss Moll as saying: "Oh, I can hardly wait for the wonderful war to begin . . . I mean when I get married. It will be an all-out, knock-down series of pitched battles, thank goodness."

Several magazines, including *Frolic* and *Follies*, feature masochistic ads such as this one: "MUSCLE GIRLS. Strong women, boxers, wrestlers, etc. Action photos, cartoons and movies from all over the world. Write for free list." *True Adventure* also has an ad for "RARE THIGH STILETTO," with a photo showing how it is worn by a girl. The copy reads: "You may have read about this before, but until now it has not been available. With a sword handle and razor keen Solingen steel blade, it was designed by an adventurer who knows the art of self-defense. Black or pink velvet sheath and garter make it a glittering gift for milady." *Hit Show*, in an ad featuring sadistic booklets, also features many masochistic ones, including "RITA'S SCHOOL FOR DISCIPLINE" and "DUCHESS OF THE BASTILLE."

Fetishism, such as foot fetishism, hair fetishism, breast fetishism, etc., is also favorably featured in a number of current men's magazines. Both *Candid* and *Twenty-One* Magazines have articles showing how popular fetishist publications have been in recent years. A special magazine devoted to fetishism, *Fantasia*, is advertised in *Follies*. And *Hit Show* has these two fetishistic advertisements: (a) "TERROR AT THE BIZARRE ART MUSEUM. A brand new publication devoted to Damsels in Distress. Appealing and unusual drawings that tell a story about girls in boots, high heels that you will find captivating and are bound to please." (b) TATTOOED PHOTOS. Twelve 5 x 7 photos highly tattooed men or women (choice) two dollars. Fifty for five dollars."

Extravaginal sex relations—which are *not* sex deviations but are often wrongly considered to be by puritanically minded persons— are also approvingly mentioned in several different kinds of con- temporary publications. Thus, in the religious novel, *The Devil's Advocate*, Monsignor Meredith asks Nina Sunduzzi: " 'Your relations with this man (Giacomo Nerone)—were they normal? Did he ever ask you for what should not be done between men and women?' " And, we are told: "She stared at him in momentary puzzlement. Then her head went up proudly. 'We loved each other, Monsignor. We did what lovers do and were glad of each other. What else could there be?' "

In the magazine, *Realife Guide*, an article by Harold Kenneth Fink has this to say about extravaginal sex relations: "So many positions and sexual technics are considered 'wrong' or 'wicked' by many other- wise intelligent people. The result is that they refuse to experiment in order to find the ways in which they can best give and receive satisfaction, and they remain frustrated, hating and blaming the part- ner and sometimes even ending in a divorce. It should be remembered that nothing is a perversion unless it is the *only* method of sexual satis- faction that the person can enjoy. As Dr. Albert Ellis has pointedly remarked, traditional intercourse (with the husband on top and facing his wife) can become, technically, 'perverted' when it is the *only* position and technic the couple ever use because they are afraid to be free enough to try other methods for variety and improved orgasms and greater satisfaction." Another article in the same magazine also approvingly notes: "Dr. Albert Ellis, one of our best-known sexologists, states that there is nothing abnormal in any type of sex-play between the man and woman as long as it is *mutually agreeable* and does no harm to either."

Men's Digest reprints the joke about the beautiful girl and the fellow who were applying for a job as a lion tamer. Asked to show what she could do, the girl walked into the cage without any weapons, snapped her fingers and had the lions go into a little dance. Then, to crown her act, she stripped to the bone, and got the biggest male lion to lick her feet, her legs, her entire body just like a sweet little kitty. The owner of the carnival was delirious with joy and didn't want to give the male lion tamer a chance; but the fellow calmly said: "Oh, I can top that." "You can?" asked the owner. "Show me!" "O.K.," said the fellow, "but first, mister, get those goddam lions out of there!"

Many other references were found in the literature of the 1960's where sexual deviation was neither endorsed nor condemned but where it was patently employed for lascivious purposes, in order to stimulate readers. Publications including this kind of reference to sexual "perversion" included *Scamp, Coronet, The Texas Ranger,* the novel, *Return to Peyton Place, Off Beat Detective Stories, The Gent, Swank, Mystery Digest, Hi-Life, Twenty-One,* the novel, *Darkness and the Dawn, Cavalcade, The Police Gazette,* and the *New Yorker.*

All this recent material would clearly tend to indicate that there has been a considerable liberalization of the attitudes toward publishing material on sexual deviation in American mass media during the last decade. Although there is no evidence that deviation itself has significantly increased, there is more reason to believe that those who practice "perversion" are often much less guilty and ashamed than they previously were.

This is particularly true (as shown in my recent book, *The Art and Science of Love*) in connection with extravaginal heterosexual relations, which are not true sex deviations but are often erroneously considered so. Whereas, in the early part of this century, anyone who practiced fellatio or cunnilinctus with his or her spouse would almost certainly consider himself or herself to be some kind of "pervert," today's educated mate who does *not* to some extent engage in these kinds of practices is likely to consider himself or herself to be "abnormal."

Even in regard to true sexual deviations, such as exclusive homosexuality and extreme sadomasochistic tendencies, much more acceptance and permissiveness now seems to be the rule than existed a decade or two ago. Negative and mixed attitudes are still extant and color our thinking in this respect; but many of them slowly but surely seem to be dying and are being replaced by a more scientific and objective view of deviation—which augurs, from a psychological standpoint, well. One cannot guarantee that the more liberal attitudes toward sex deviation tend to be, the less fixed, obsessive-compulsive

193

deviates tend to exist; but, on the basis of many years of experience as a psychotherapist, I would certainly be willing to uphold this hypothesis.

CHAPTER 22

Censorship

On the surface, American attitudes toward the censorship of sex material are amazingly one-sided, since, if we are to take seriously contemporary public expressions in this connection, almost everyone favors censorship, while only a few courageous souls have the temerity to oppose it.

By way of illustration, consider the motion-picture situation. Sexy films, as everyone knows, are very popular. But the Motion Picture Production Code insists that overt sexuality be minimally displayed in Hollywood productions. This, says an occasional Hollywoodite like the outspoken Samuel Goldwyn, is an artistic blunder and a damned shame. To which, one might expect, all the motion-picture producers and exhibitors would chorus: Amen!

But no. *Variety*, asking some of the leading film moguls to comment on the censorious Production Code, got responses like these: "I am firmly in favor of the Production Code" (Barney Balaban, Paramount Pictures). "Tampering with the Code is a dangerous practice" (Dore Schary, Metro-Goldwyn-Mayer). "I have yet to be convinced that the Code isn't a good idea from every point of view, artistic or commercial" (Nicholas M. Schenck, Loew's). "There is nothing wrong with the Production Code" (Gradwell Sears, United Artists). Without the Production Code, I doubt whether our industry could have attained its present position of world-wide importance and influence" (Spyros Skouras, 20th Century-Fox). "I definitely believe in the Production Code" (H. V. Harvey, Pacific Coast Conference of Independent Theatre Owners). "Hollywood is producing pictures quite successfully of all types within the framework of the Production Code" (Robert J. O'Donnell, Interstate Theatres). "Our industry must police itself if it is to retain its identity; rather, we should strengthen the Code even to a point where it can act as a policing agent for stars and others in the industry who bring discredit to this great business of ours" (Truman T. Rembusch, Associated Theatre Owners of Indiana).

In view of this near unanimity of opinion, Hollywood's toleration of censorship is hardly surprising. Still, it may come as something of a shock for one to realize that even in stills made for publicity purposes film beauties must be bosomless. As reported by *Variety*: "Hollywood is the only place in the world where women don't have 'em and mustn't be caught with 'em—when a studio lenser presses the bulb. When an outside photog takes art for the mags, that's a different story."

Speaking of movie publicity, it is interesting to note that in an interview with Hedy Lamarr, published in one of the romantic comic magazines, Hedy's film career is reviewed in detail, and several of her hit movies are prominently mentioned. Conspicuously unmentioned, however, is her most famous picture, *Ecstasy*, whose notorious sex scenes Hedy and her public relations men are apparently doing their best to annihilate from the public's consciousness.

Not content with censoring movies and publicity photos, film producers have made many attempts in recent years to regulate the private lives of their stars. This kind of censorship has been recently highlighted by the scandal aroused by the Ingrid Bergman-Roberto Rossellini affair, with Miss Bergman's being forced, obviously under pressure, to retire from all screen activities because of her extramarital union with Signor Rossellini. Long before this, however, as *True* magazine tells us, it has been "a general Hollywood policy to encourage actors to spend their off-screen time trimming the hedges and working in the kitchen with the Little Woman," when, in fact, they had ideas of a somewhat contrary nature.

As a final illustration of movieland's propensity for censorship, we may mention a scene from the film, *Battleground*, when an army sergeant, waking up the soldiers of his outfit in the morning, sings out: "Leave your cots and grab your socks." This, as any veteran of World War II will gladly tell you, is a sorry take-off on a somewhat more pungent contribution to American folklore.

Contemporary sex censorship is not, of course, confined to the movies. The New York *Herald Tribune*, in reviewing theatrical events at the turn of the half century, notes that "Chicago police censored *The Respectful Prostitute* off the boards," and that the League of New York Theatres barely managed to stop a proposed "morals" bill that would have almost completely emasculated Broadway dramas. At the same time, the National Capital Sesquicentennial Commission promised in *Variety* that its theatrical productions would be "on a wholesome basis" and would include "a clean show which will not detract from the dignity of the occasion we are celebrating."

The most drastic form of stage censorship is done by the National Legion of Decency, which every week lists Broadway shows which are partly or wholly objectionable and which are supposed to be boycotted by all good Catholics and others who uphold the Legion's views. Thus *The Tablet*, in one issue, prints a list of sixty objectionable and twenty-five condemned motion pictures; and, in the same issue, publishes a list of sixteen objectionable and two condemned shows. Included in this list are virtually all the plays and musicals reviewed for this study, with the exception of *Howdy, Mr. Ice*, which was passed for general patronage, and *Where's Charley?*, which was put in Class A2—for adults only. In other words, out of twenty Broadway shows rated by the Legion of Decency, eighteen (or 90 per cent) were found to be sexually objectionable and were banned to all believers in the Legion's censorship proclivities.

Printed matter is no exception to the censorship rule. When the author is not discreetly censoring his own material to escape public embarrassment, or the publisher is not forcing him into line, more official agencies are apt to step in to make up his mind for him. Thomas Merton, for example, frankly tells us that, out of religious motives, he cut a good deal of the autobiographical ground from under himself in writing *The Seven Storey Mountain*. The *Atlantic Monthly* reviewer congratulates Francis Steegmuller on his "tact", in dealing with De Maupassant's "scandalous career, with its sexual excesses and its terrible battle against syphilis." The *Saturday Review of Literature*, after more than one tussle with the authorities, now insists that only "communications of a decorous nature" be submitted to its classified columns. An *Uncensored Detective* writer, after titillating his readers with hints about the "various strange and exotic love practices" indulged in by Martha Beck and Ray Fernandez, explains that these practices had to be told at their court trial "in terminology that was comprehensible to physicians and psychiatrists"—and he never does give any description whatever of their sex behavior. And in his *Baghdad-by-the-Bay*, Herb Caen tells us about "the time the Los Angeles Police Department was ordered by a blue-nosed district attorney to confiscate all copies of *Lysistrata*. A conscientious, clean-minded police captain went one step further. He sent out a detail to arrest the author."

American attitudes favoring censorship have now gone so far, in sum, that a men's magazine satirizes them with a cartoon showing a man on the operating table being told by his surgeon: "Watch what you say under ether. This operation is being televised."

Has, then, nobody an *un*kind word to say for the sex censor? Not too often, or very publicly, it would seem. For in our survey of literally hundreds of newspapers, magazines, books, movies, plays, radio scripts, and popular songs extant at the turning point of the mid-century, we could only find two serious references to the evils of sex censorship: (1) The *World Almanac* reports that, in denying the contention of the Philadelphia police that a certain book was obscene, Judge Curtis Bok said: "I should prefer that my own daughters met the facts of life and the literature of the world in my library than beind a neighbor's barn, for I can face the adversary there directly."

(2) John Mason Brown, in the introduction to the printed version of *Mister Roberts*, vehemently defends the "un-Gideonized, pro-Kinsey anguage its sailors talk" by pointing out that these sailors are Blue ackets and not blue stockings. The implication here is that their anguage was permissible only *because* they were sailors.

In all the material surveyed for this study it was found that only the artoonists seem to be chancing unequivocal criticism of sex censorhip. Thus Peter Arno depicts in his *Sizzling Platter* one member of he Society for the Suppression of Vice saying to another: "Did you ver have one of those awful days when everything just seems to go ight?" Pearson, in *Liberty* magazine, shows a policeman who is being idden in the center of a huge cake asking his captain what to do in ase the party is not having an indecent show. And Sharp, in *Sir!* nagazine, portrays a salesman showing a customer a tie on which is he picture of a well-curved naked girl. "This one," he says encouragingly, "was banned in Boston."

A non-cartooning gibe at censorship was also found in one of the college periodicals surveyed, *The Old Line*, which printed this appropriate note:

> *In Boccaccio, it's frankness.*
> *In Rabelais, it's life.*
> *In a professor, it's clever.*
> *But in a college magazine, it's smutty*

Aside from these backhanded humorous slaps at contemporary ex censorship, the censors themselves, both official and unofficial, eem to be having quite a field day. Supported by several national rganizations, especially the Legion of Decency, which publicly condemn large numbers of current books, films, and plays as "morally bjectionable," these sex censors appear to be becoming more powerful and less opposed.

With, it would seem, one significant exception. While the organized opposition to sex censorship appears to be currently weak, the unorganized opposition to it is stubborn and robust. The same ilms and plays which are condemned by the Legion of Decency and other censorship groups are, by virtue of that very condemnation, ometimes converted into box-office smashes.

To illustrate this unorganized resistance to sex censorship, we may quote the columnist, Sheilah Graham, who, in making her weekly broadcast over the Mutual Broadcasting System, reported that the film, *The Outlaw*, when finally released at the end of 1949 "with the hot stuff left in ... is breaking records and expected to gross from eight to ten million dollars." *The Outlaw's* release had previously been held up for three years because of Motion Picture Production Code censorship.

Laugh Book, in commenting on the fact that nothing raises sales like the censors' raising hell about a work, noted that "people easily shocked seem to have an instinct for finding books, plays, movies, and other things that easily shock them."

Once again, then, we have the story we have been seeing repeated so often throughout the chapters of this book: Ban a mode of sex expression, if you will; get all possible unanimity of public opinion against it, if you wish—and then be prepared for at least a tenfold increase in its popularity.

Attitudes Toward Censorship in the 1960's

As has been noted in the first part of this chapter, in the early 1950's American mass media included relatively few attitudes on sex censorship and these were preponderantly conservative. In the re-survey of attitudes in the same kinds of mass media in the 1960's, it has been found that there are a greater number of references than in the previous decade and that the majority of these are clearly on the liberal or permissive side.

Censorship influences of past years are still distinctly present in contemporary life and literature. *Candid* magazine reports that "According to Bernard P. Gallagher, New York City magazine consultant, local committees in 'more than 235 communities are yelling for action against the sex heavy magazines.'" The Catholic periodical, the *Sign*, still prints, week after week, its list of partly objectionable and completely objectionable plays and films. In January, 1960, for example, it found the following plays completely objectionable: *Goodbye, Charlie*; *Gypsy*; *A Loss of Roses*; *The Marriage-Go-Round*; *Silent Night, Lonely Night*; *Sweet Bird of Youth*; *Threepenny Opera*; *Two for the Seesaw*; and *The World of Suzie Wong*.

According to the *New York Times*, Jack Paar's television show, even though it goes on the air late at night when children are presumably not listening, was censored by the National Broadcasting Company because its Department of Standards and Practices thought it was "not in good taste." Almost five minutes was cut from the television tape of the show before it was broadcast; and a great to-do was later made by Paar about this cut.

America has an editorial praising the stand of three Baltimore newspapers which have said that they will censor movie-ad copy when it "borders on indecency." The same publication also lauds NBC's snipping of Jack Paar's programs.

The *New York Daily News* reports an attempt by Albany, New

York, legislators to bar the showing of "improper" movies to viewers under eighteen. The *New York Times* tells of a ban against *Playboy* magazine by Connecticut newsstands. This same paper also reports that in the standard English translation of the famous Chinese novel, *The Golden Lotus*, "whole pages are reproduced in the curious chastity of Latin, for Chinese obscenity is something to wonder at."

We may finally note that in the best-selling autobiography by Moss Hart, *Act One*, there are numerous details about the author's family and professional life but hardly a word about his sex relations during his entire youth, when there is every reason to believe that he was having, during this period, reasonably active sex adventures. *Act One* is highly typical, in this respect, of many other autobiographical best-selling works by a variety of well-known individuals.

It may be clearly seen, from evidences such as these, that sex censorship is hardly dead in the 1960's and that more than slight vestiges of it still remain. Much has happened, however, since 1950 in this respect, and easing of bans on movies, TV shows, novels, magazines, etc., is evident in many quarters.

Thus, *Tab* has an article entitled "Are Movies Getting Too Naughty Again?" The article begins: "Thanks to a recent decision by the U. S. Supreme Court, adults (male and female alike) in this country soon may view in public theatres some of the scorching sagas and scenes hitherto limited to furtive showings at smoke-filled stag sessions. . . . Last June nine black-robed justices, after a private screening of the controversial epic [the film version of *Lady Chatterley's Lover*], slapped down the censors and ruled the ban on Lady Chatterley and her lover unconstitutional. In effect, the highest court in the land solemnly decreed that pure and unadulterated adultery can be proper and moral under certain circumstances, and that a frank portrayal of the same can be shown on screens in New York and points north, south, and west."

Twenty-One magazine reports that Federal Judge Julius H. Miner of Chicago "recently ruled that Otto Preminger's film, *Anatomy of a Murder*, is not immoral and obscene, as charged by local authorities. The film opened two hours later." The *Saturday Review* editorializes: "Today, thanks to a number of Supreme Court decisions, the censorship boards have all but disappeared. Thanks to another Supreme Court decision that divorced theatres from the production companies, the teeth have been pulled from the Production Code (which formerly enforced its rulings by seeing to it that no film denied a Production Seal played in any of the major chains controlled by its member companies). Now, because of the need to attract a newer, wider audience, some producers are even daring to defy the Legion of Decency. The postwar years, the years since World War II, have produced a new frankness in literature. Inevitably, with the loosening of these restrainings, some of that has begun to rub off on films."

Life magazine, early in 1960, ran an article entitled "The Bold and Risky World of 'Adult' Movies." The article is mainly concerned with the breakdown of film censorship in recent films and states, in part: "This year, in *Suddenly Last Summer*, Miss Hepburn plays a mother whose attachment to her late son seems to border on the incestuous. Actually her function, as the plot reads its way through various types of insanity, was to procure young men for him by first luring them to herself. The film concludes with a scene in which the son is literally devoured by a pack of boys whom he tempted too far. . . . *The Best of Everything* and *A Summer Place* deal not only with unmarried young people faced with pregnancy, but also with their adulterous elders, proving, if nothing else, that the different generations have some interests in common after all. *Blue Denim* also involves a girl well this side of voting age who gets with child. As in *The Best of Everything*, there is talk of visiting the kindly old abortionist. *It Started With a Kiss* seeks its laughs in the notion that a bride would hold her bridegroom at bay for a month to prove that he did not marry her for the wrong reason—an embargo that drives him to cold showers and other desperate measures."

On the book front, more progress has recently been made in reversing previous sex censorship edicts than has been made in the past century. *Lady Chatterley's Lover* and *Memoirs of Hecate County*, both completely banned only a decade before, have now been released for public sale; and many books, such as *Lolita*, which previously would not have been published, are going through the presses without official or quasi-official opposition. In a historic decision, Supreme Court Justice William J. Brennan reversed the conviction of a Los Angeles bookseller for "illegal possession" of obscene literature under a local ordinance, holding that the Los Angeles statute would so frighten booksellers as to eliminate all kinds of books from their shops and thus seriously restrain freedom of expression.

Articles and editorials against literary sex censorship have recently appeared in such publications as *The New York Times*, *The Realist*, *The Ladder*, *One*, *The Mattachine Review*, and *Commentary*. And *Cue* magazine defends such recordings as Pearl Bailey's *For Adults Only*, which are "restricted from TV and radio air play" and therefore become sensationally popular, in many instances, with record buyers. The ultra-new public attitude toward sex censorship is nicely summed up by Harriet F. Pilpel, well-known New York attorney and the individual most responsible for the United States Supreme Court decision to allow scholars, such as the Kinsey research group, to import "obscene" materials for investigatory purposes. Writing in *Variety*, Mrs. Pilpel notes:

"... In the 'Chatterley' book case, Judge Bryan, speaking for the Federal District Court in New York, reiterated the rules that a book must be judged as a whole, that the group to judge it by is the average man of ordinary susceptibilities, and that erotic scenes integrated into a worthwhile work of literature (as opposed to 'hard core pornography,' whatever that is) do not 'appeal to the prurient'—hence they cannot be adjudged obscene and suppressed. As of the end of 1960, some court or courts may go further, and ask—who says it's bad for readers or viewers to be sexually titillated? Why isn't it an equally sound hypothesis that it's good for people to be sexually aroused? At best maybe it makes them more alive as the sex-oriented culture we live in certainly assumes. At worst maybe erotic art, literature, movies and plays afford a necessary stopgap and safety valve for people who would otherwise erupt into open violence. Increasing recourse will be had to the social sciences whose researches have begun to 'dig' the question whether even pornographic material gives rise to antisocial conduct and if it doesn't why should it be suppressed? In a free society, some court will say, it's about time we stopped trying to prevent or punish anti-social (in this context meaning erotic) thoughts and words and concentrated on what people *do* and what makes them *do* it. Otherwise, Mr. Orwell's '1984' may not be so far away."

Although, then, sex censorship is hardly on the way out in America, and in many quarters there are still campaigns to make our censorship laws stricter and more punitive, the general tendency is clearly on the side of liberalization. Censorship laws have not, and apparently never will, stop the dissemination of "hard core pornography"; and even if they could, it is highly questionable whether this would be desirable. Instead of preventing antisocial sexual behavior, laws against the dissemination of "obscene" material are more likely (as I have testified in court on several occasions and indicated in *Sex Without Guilt* and other writings) to help make human beings so obsessed with sexual thoughts (since banning a sex mode almost invariably adds obsessive-compulsive excitement and interest to it) that they are much more likely to commit sex misdeeds than if sex acts and representations were more freely available.

People who commit sex crimes, in other words, are virtually never made criminals by reading or witnessing highly sexualized material per se. They first become emotionally and sexually disturbed because their society unduly restricts their sex interest and behavior; then, because of their disturbance, they sometimes become obsessed with collecting pornographic or erotic material; and, concomitantly, instead of participating in regular heterosexual activity, they sometimes commit exhibitory, homosexual, rapist, and other legally proscribed acts. Sexual permissiveness, almost by definition, leads to sexual participation—but very rarely to sex crimes. Sexual inhibition and the banning of sex materials and satisfactions frequently (as Dr. Ralph Brancale and I showed in our book, *The Psychology of Sex Offenders*) motivate sex offenses. Putting up barriers against sex arousal and activity rarely destroys human sexuality; what it does sabotage is *healthy* and fully *satisfying* sex participation.

CHAPTER 23

Puritanism

PURITAN—one who . . . practices or preaches a more rigorous or professedly purer moral code than that which prevails.
—*Webster's International Dictionary*

While anti-sexual acts are, as we have been seeing throughout this study, common enough in America, they are normally ameliorated to some degree in theory or practice. Thus the very same people who believe that, say, kissing and petting are generally undesirable habits will frequently acknowledge that, under *certain* circumstances—e.g., when not indulged too intensely or promiscuously—these practices are permissible.

Moreover, most people who are under all circumstances unalterably opposed to various sex acts—such as fornication or adultery—will still deal fairly tolerantly with those who break the rules and who do engage in such acts. They will definitely say that, in their opinion, John Jones or Jane Smith is wrong for fornicating or committing adultery—but they will not insist that John or Jane, merely because of his or her sex misdeeds, must positively be fired, socially ostracized, jailed, or otherwise severely punished.

Some people, however, will condemn virtually all infractions of sex codes, no matter how minor. Or, when sex misconduct does occur, they will attempt most rigorously to punish its perpetrators. Such individuals, even in a generally anti-sexual culture like our own, may justly be called puritans or prudes.

To what extent do puritanical attitudes flourish in modern America? To quite an extent. Even a cursory persual of nonfictional contemporary writings soon elicits ideas like these:

1. "Dancing, swimming, smoking, and drinking are 'wrong—it says so in the Bible'; swimming is a good sport only if boys and girls

go separately. People in bathing suits are guilty of indecent exposure."
—Typical American small-town parents, quoted in the *Ladies' Home Journal*.

2. The soul of man must suffer and be guilty for virtually every sex act he commits, "since the incurrence of original sin and because of it, man lost the privileged balance whereby carnal inclinations were under the thorough control of reason and grace."—Columnist in *The Sign*.

3. In small religious communities in America people have often had it drilled into them "that nothing but procreation justified relations between husband and wife and that the use of contraceptives was a crime against Providence."—H. K. Repete, in *Your Psychology*.

4. Anyone who shows interest in the personal life and sex escapades of Hollowood stars is not a decent American.—Charles Laughton, interviewed by the Associated Press and quoted in the New York *Herald Tribune*.

5. Writing a book like Alberto Moravia's *The Woman of Rome* is akin to "peddling dirty post cards."—Book reviewer in the *Catholic World*.

6. Details of a man's sex life are exceptionally sordid and are not fit to print.—Staff writer in *Uncensored Detective*.

7. Any girl who goes to a bar with a girl friend, but with no male escort, is damnably immoral and does not deserve to be steadily dated by a boy.—Love-problem columnist in *Revealing Love Stories*.

8. A motion picture like *All the King's Men* may be a vivid, stirring dramatization, but "unfortunately for the film's effectiveness, the bland acceptance of divorce and a generally low moral tone detract from its value both as entertainment and a social document."—Movie reviewer in *The Sign*.

9. Any movie star who flaunts public morals "should be eliminated as a cancerous growth on the heart of Hollywood."—Jimmie Fidler, broadcasting over the American Broadcasting System.

10. In the musical play, *Kiss Me, Kate*, some of Cole Porter's lyrics are utterly wicked; and in *Mister Roberts*, "the seagoing language smears a very sound story."—Play reviewer in the *Catholic World*.

11. The "easy morality" and sexual "broad-mindedness" of modern life are entirely unchristian and corrupt.—Peter Marshall, in *Mr. Jones, Meet the Master*.

12. Because of attitudes which are very prevalent in the United States, "there are cases on record where a 'virgin' wife has completely refused to submit herself to her husband at any time after the first experience of the wedding night. There are many cases wherein a wife has refused to submit herself to her husband for some time after marriage, and thereafter infrequently. Thousands of hapless husbands

have experienced the disappointment and chagrin of 'kissless honeymoons.'"—H. K. Repete, in *Your Psychology*.

13. Sex expression of any kind outside of conventional intercourse in marriage is pagan, sinful, degenerated, nasty, debauched, and corrupt, implies Fulton J. Sheen, in *Peace of Soul*.

14. It is iniquitious for any girl to have dates with boys on Sunday.—Editorial in *Integrity*.

15. Premarial sex relations, even between two persons deeply in love, constitute a horrible sex sin and can be forgiven only by prolonged spiritual treatment.—Norman Vincent Peale, in *A Guide to Confident Living*.

16. The lusts of the world are so common and frightful that the only effective way to conquer them is to get thee to a Trappist monkery.—Thomas Merton in *The Waters of Siloe*.

Writers of modern fiction, following closely on the heels of the nonfictionalists, also have more than a few puritanical notions to express. Contemporary short story writers, for example, inform us—

That a woman who sings risque songs is "a tramp."—*Today's Woman*.

That it is all right for a woman to talk to a stranger in a restaurant, but no matter how nice he is to her, she must never let him take her home in a taxi.—*I Loved*.

That any husband who kisses a woman other than his wife is an unspeakable cad and deserves to have his wife leave him immediately.—*Intimate Romances*.

That any girl engaging in premarital sex relations should be fired from her job.—*Revealing Love Stories*.

That no electorate would ever think of putting a politician in office if it were known that he had written some passionate love letters to a girl.—*Private Detective*.

That any father who finds his daughter being kissed by a fellow will of course force this fellow to marry her.—*True Story*. That any mother who catches a young man petting mildly with her daughter should scream at him: "Get out before I beat you within an inch of your life!"—*Intimate Romances*.

That no respectable woman ever goes up to a man's hotel room.—*Redbook*. That nice women will not even visit a physician who works by himself and has no reputable woman around his premises.—*American* magazine.

That any fellow who suspects a girl of having an affair with another fellow should naturally despite her and refuse to speak to her.—*Intimate Romances*.

That parents have a perfect right to forbid seventeen- and eighteen-year-old girls from dating any boys.—*Revealing Love Stories*.

That a truly refined man will never fully accept sex, even with his own wife, and will despise any woman who does accept it.—*Wake*.

Finally, if we would look for some illustrations of puritanism in twentieth-century films and novels, we quickly find ones like these:

In *East Side, West Side* an adulterer who is mistakenly accused of murdering his mistress is unsympathetically told that, even if he is innocent, he may well expect, because of his heinous sex habits, to be punished for the murder.

In *One on the House* three old hags take unusual precautions, while riding in a New York subway car, to make sure that no man gets close to them.

In *The Peaceable Kingdom* a bigamous Mormon wife thinks it horrible for a widow to have sex relations with two men.

Puritanism, then, not only exists on a large scale in American mass media; it almost runs riot. And dissenting voices—are there none? Well, not entirely. Hartnett Kane, for instance, after pointing out that puritans term New Orleans "a hell-spot, dripping with scarlet wickedness," goes on to say that "to this the Orleanian would retort that life is meant to be lived and that he cannot find it in himself to blame human beings for being—well, human."

Edison Marshall, in *Gypsy Sixpence*, has one brother say to another: "He's a real aristocrat, Rom. Born one—bred one. What in the hell need he care for Mrs. Grundy or any of her works? There are only two classes who are free to be happy. The 'way up and the 'way down. It's we middle fellows who get it in the neck."

Alberto Moravia, in *The Woman of Rome*, includes a scene in which the heroine's mother, defending her against a charge of immorally posing in the nude, exclaims: "It isn't moral, isn't it? . . . Not moral—what *is* moral, I'd like to know. Perhaps it's moral to work your fingers to the bone all day, wash up, sew, cook, iron, sweep, scrub floors and then have your husband turn up in the evening so deadbeat that as soon as his meal is done he goes to bed, turns his back on you and sleeps? That's what you call moral, is it? It's moral to sacrifice yourself, never have time to breathe, to grow old and ugly, then croak? Do you want to know what I think? It's that you only live once, and when you're dead, you're dead, and you and all your morality can go to the devil."

Renato J. Almansi, reviewing Rene Guyon's "The Ethics of Sexual Acts" in the *American Journal of Psychotherapy*, does not quite agree with Guyon's ultra-liberal views on sex, but he does state that "we all agree with Guyon, of course, that many of the commonly accepted standards regarding the relationship of the sexes are in need of revision, clarification and, often, of liberalization."

Puritanism, then, has some opposition in our culture. But this opposition does not frequently make itself felt in our most popular mass media, since few passages other than those just quoted could be found

205

presenting clearly anti-puritanical ideas, while about seventy-five exceptionally prudish viewpoints were disclosed in the course of this study. At least in print, therefore, puritanical attitudes have a clear-cut majority and, vocally, the anti-puritans have as yet made relatively little headway. Indeed, if there is any move presently on foot to campaign for considerably more liberal sex attitudes and practices, it seems to be pretty well stymied in its public expression. The rabid antipuritan gets about as much access to American mass media as does, say, a democrat to the press of any totalitarian state.

Since, as much of the material examined elsewhere in this survey makes quite obvious, few Americans seem actually to abide by the rules which the puritans prescribe for all of us, a conflict exists between what people think they should do and what they really do in regard to puritanical sex notions. Thus, in contradistinction to some of the viewpoints quoted at the beginning of this chapter, few would deny that literally millions of American girls, every single day of each year, keep petting with boys, going unescorted into public bars, visiting males in their hotel rooms, telling risque stories, dancing, dating on Sunday, picking up strangers, and doing hundreds of other things which, according to widely prevailing puritanical viewpoints, they definitely should not be doing. And that, of course, goes double or triple for myriads of American males.

The most common result of unmitigated prudery, in fact, seems to be an unrivaled degree of prurience. It would be repetitious to catalogue the facts of contemporary American prurience here, since we deal with them at length in several other chapters, especially those on lasciviousness, nudity, sex organs, and "obscenity." Suffice it to say that the contents of American mass media, as we have been consistently seeing, are as sexy as our censorship will allow. The real opposition to American prudery comes not in frank anti-puritanical statements for public consumption—but, much more effectively, in a veritable cascade of luscious fiction, ribald anecdotes and cartoons, sensational news stories, half-dressed women strolling the streets, bawdy songs, revealing brassiere ads, lascivious conversations, and a thousand other everyday manifestations of American sexuality besides which an unadulterated essay favoring free love would seem as exciting as a Sunday-school picnic.

Apparently, then, while—in theory—American puritanism rules the roost, in practice the cry of the populace seems to be: Long may it waver!

Attitudes Toward Puritanism in the 1960's

Relatively many references to puritanism were found in the study of sex attitudes in the early 1950's and these were preponderantly conservative. Exactly the same tendencies are to be found in the references to puritanism in the 1960's, but the puritanical views that still are fairly widely published tend to be somewhat less frequent and considerably less definite. Whereas previous upholding of antisexual philosophies was frequently unequivocal, it today tends to be much more equivocating.

Nonetheless, there are still many distinctly puritanical attitudes prevalent in contemporary mass media. Thus, we learn that

—it is natural for a man to shoot another man for flirting with his wife (film, *Hound-Dog Man*).

—a boy who is found in bed with a girl when police raid a party should be sent to reform school on a morals charge (*Secrets* magazine).

—a boy and a girl who have premarital sex relations should be "ashamed to meet each other's eyes" (*Teen Secrets* magazine).

—a husband who is unfaithful to his alcoholic, unappealing wife is a "bastard" (novel, *Poor No More*).

—getting a girl illegitimately pregnant is a "sinful shenanigan" (*Man's Magazine*).

—a man must not allow himself to be rescued from a fiery volcano by a group of nuns until he persuades them to get him a pair of pants (film, *A Journey to the Center of the Earth*).

—a girl who is in a boat with her boy friend and has to spend the night on the beach because their boat capsizes should be forced, by her mother, to be medically examined to prove that she is still a virgin (film, *A Summer Place*).

—the police should arrest a girl who is undressing next to her open window (*Snappy* magazine).

—it is entirely alarming that young people should have any sex relations divorced from spiritual or love feelings (*Real Confessions*).

—a girl who is promiscuous should be despised by all fellows and no one should attempt to defend her (novel, *The Cave*).

—casual sex encounters can never possibly lead to any worthwhile life experiences (novel, *Advise and Consent*).

—kissing is a wicked pastime that leads to the most soul-searing consequences (*Personal Romances*).

—a girl had better die than accept money for her sexual favors (*Secrets*).

—learning that one has acquired syphilis is like being hit by the whole back line of one's high school team (*My Love Secret*).

—anyone who employs mechanical methods of birth control commits "a sin against nature and commits a deed which is shameful and intrinsically sinful" (*The Sign*).

—homosexual actors are disgusting individuals (novel, *Return to Peyton Place*).

—no matter how much a boy and girl love each other and are able to live happily together, having nonmarital sex relations is entirely wrong and they should be severely punished for doing so (*Revealing Romances*).

Many antisexual attitudes such as these still exist in today's mass media. As persistently noted, however, throughout the various addenda to this book which show sex attitudes in the 1960's, prosexual opinions and philosophies are rapidly overtaking the puritanical notions which were ubiquitous in the early part of the twentieth century and which were still widely extant in the early 1950's. According to *Cavalier* magazine, the famous movie producer, Sam Goldwyn, was reputed to have said that "there was never a bad woman who wasn't good box office." Similarly, there now never seems to be a "bad" or a "lewd" or a "sexy" situation in our novels, films, plays, newspapers, magazines, or other popular media that doesn't capture the attention of numerous readers and viewers and make them clamor for more of the same.

This continual use of highly unconventional and highly sexed circumstances and characters to spice up today's mass media has had a curious boomeranging effect. Where, originally, this kind of material was deliberately employed because it *was* novel and risque, its frequent employment has made it lose much of its novelty and spiciness; so that today it is almost commonplace. But what is commonplace cannot, for very long, be felt to be too "wrong" or "unconventional." Ultimately, therefore, the same material that is employed because it is *not* "acceptable" or "right" becomes, by its very employment, at least tacitly acceptable.

Put differently: sex puritanism puts a high premium, in terms of interest and excitement, on certain condemned acts. These acts consequently are used for purposes of literary arousal; and the more they are used, the less wicked they seem. The reading public, therefore, quite unconsciously and unwittingly, ends up by becoming less puritanical. Which is exactly what seems to be increasingly happening today. "Virtue" is not only its own reward, but it appears to be creating a redefinition of "virtue."

CHAPTER 24

Romanticism and Sex

The basic American attitude toward sex and romantic love which is ostensibly held by just about all publicists who in any manner, shape, or form mention sexuality in our culture is that sex without love, sex

208

for its own sweet sake, sex devoid of feelings of mutual admiration, respect, love, or marriage, is just about the cheapest and most disgusting thing in the world. Whoever enjoys sex pleasure with a mate he or she does not love is, according to this view, a crass, low-living, soulless apology for a human being.

One of the best illustrations of this attitude toward sex is found in John Sedges's novel of love and marriage, *The Long Love*. The hero of this novel hints that his wife may possibly be physically attracted to one of their friends; and she, hurt to the quick that he should even consider such a possibility, immediately retorts: "What you say is an insult to me. I will not endure it, do you hear me, Ned? If ever again you accuse me of being—physical—with a man I don't love, that day I will leave you."

Sex without love, in fact, is such an anathema to the modern romanticist that an advertisement for Taylor Caldwell's *Let Love Come Last* headlines the query: "IS IT A SIN TO MARRY BEFORE FALLING IN LOVE?" and goes on to imply that any woman who would dare sleep even with her husband before falling violently in love with him, or any husband who would cohabit with a wife he did not romantically adore, would be committing a major crime against herself or himself as well as against society.

Even in the more sophisticated and sexually liberal stories of our day, this sex-without-love-equals-iniquity theme is for the most part stoutly supported. Thus in her *Esquire* story of a promiscuous camp follower, one of the "whores de combat" of the Spanish civil war, Martha Gellhorn lets us know that she really "loved all these passing men"—and hence was not such a bad egg after all. And in his sexcapade, *A Rage to Live*, John O'Hara has his adulterous heroine refuse a would-be-lover with these words: "I'm sorry, too. It has to be love with me, Paul. Or the other so much that I don't know where it comes from, and can't help it."

No wonder is it, then, that in considering the philosophy that sex is largely a biological urge, and that it is therefore proper for men and women to cohabit with no thought of love and marriage, Fulton J. Sheen, in his *Peace of Soul*, violently rejects this view and implies that, while pigs and snakes may freely copulate on a biological basis, any human being who does so must have a pig's or a snake's sensibilities and soul.

The theme that sex without love is unlovely has numerous variations in modern literature. One of these is the romantic attitude that sex pleasure, though real and enjoyable enough, simply cannot compare with the ecstatic joy of love. Thus in *The Egyptian* the hero follows his beloved, Minea, over half the ancient world; and when she offers herself to him, although she admits that she will be sad and guilty at

209

the loss of her virginity, he refuses her with this romantic declaration: "For me it is enough that you came here tonight as you were when we stalked the roads of Babylon together. Give me the golden ribbon from your hair; I ask no more of you than that." And, he informs us: "I did not possess her, for what was no joy to her was none to me. I fancy that my joy was sweeter and more profound than if she had been mine...."

In a story in the *American* magazine, a supposedly sophisticated and hardheaded young man refuses to enfold the charms of a beauty who offers herself to him and tells her: "You don't understand, I don't know if I can explain, but there's something beyond physical attraction, Dorcas, something you and I haven't reached together."

Even in *The Woman of Rome*—a sex-filled tale if there ever was one—one of the heroine's lovers tells her that he left her "because I realize I felt nothing for you. Or rather, all I felt was the kind of desire my friend felt for your girl friend that evening."

Curiously enough, however, the same romantic love without which sex becomes suddenly wicked also serves to make sex wickedness good. That is to say, in a good many modern novels and stories the heroine is allowed to have fornicative, adulterous, or other usually forbidden relations with some man *because* she loves him and because, presumably, love sanctifies anything. Thus in a tale in *Revealing Love Stories* the heroine, when asked to run away with a married man, exclaims: "Oh ... John ... John darling ... what are we going to do? I know it's wrong ... that it isn't fair ... and yet I'm so much in love with you ... I can't live without you!" And in a *Real Romances* story, Jane, a married woman, wakes up in bed with Jack, who is not her husband, and informs us: "I told myself I was silly to feel ashamed. Jack and I loved each other. We'd be married as soon as I got my divorce. I shut my eyes, tried to recapture the blissful surety in which I'd drifted off to sleep, my head pillowed on Jack's arm. Nothing so wonderful as what we'd had together could possibly be wrong."

The rationale that makes unconventional sex behavior sinful in one instance and not in another seems to be the romantic notion that love somehow so transforms a sex act as to make it entirely different from the same act performed on a non-loving basis. In one *True Confessions* story, for example, the heroine tells us that her truelove's kisses were entirely different from those of the man she thought she loved, because "his kisses just blotted out everything. When he took me in his arms, I'd sort of sprout wings and fly out of this world." In still another *True Confessions* tale the minute the heroine finds the man whose "lips crushed down on mine with longing and love," she responds "in a strange way ... as I had never done with Ray Shand or any other man." In an *Intimate Romances* narration the beautiful protagonist, of course impelled only by a beautiful love, almost breaks her lover's neck with a passionate clutch, appears to go into an orgasmic trance, and then apologizes: "I didn't know I could feel like that, honest I didn't."

The apotheosis of the view that sex becomes entirely transformed by love is the concept that, once love does come to the hearts of men, their imperious and promiscuous sex desires suddenly become rigidly channeled, and they want to have relations only with the one truelove of their life. Thus in the novel, *Prince of Egypt*, the previously gay-blading Amon-nebet tells Moses that since he has loved Nefertiti, "I haven't wanted to possess another woman. Is that strange?" And Moses replies: "No, it's not strange at all. I—I think I would feel the same way."

In Paul Gallico's *The Lonely* we learn that when the heroine, Patches, gives herself to the hero, he immediately feels that "the young breasts were tender, swelling, lovable breasts of Patches, and not the mere stimulating and exciting paps of women.... No one but Patches could have done it so or made him such a sweet and gentle gift."

In Edison Marshall's *Gypsy Sixpence* the hero, Rom, lets us know full well that, as soon as he can have his one real beloved, Sukey, he will immediately give up his widespread woman chasing, will kick out of his bed the incredibly lovely and loving Sithy, and will settle down for the rest of his days to one woman's arms.

Lest it be thought that this ideal of love automatically making for sexual monogamy is confined only to romantic fiction, let it be noted that Dr. H. A. Overstreet, in his book, *The Mature Mind*, makes it a cornerstone of his philosophy and strongly implies that any man in our society who cannot strictly follow this romantic monogamous pattern in his sex life is distinctly immature.

It would seem, then, that the romantic philosophy as regards human sex behavior runs something like this: (1) Sex is only good, beautiful, and proper when it is accompanied by deep feelings of love. (2) Sex without love is a relatively mild, purely animal pleasure; with love, it is soul-stirring, ecstatic bliss. (3) The same kind of sex relations that, without love, would be indubitably and indelibly shameful may be indulged with relative impunity when experienced as part of a heavily romantic attachment. (4) This follows because sex, with love, becomes entirely transformed and is simply not the same kind of feeling at all as one derives from (perfectly enjoyable) sex relations with someone you do not really and truly love. (5) Sex, in fact, becomes so changed by love that, once a man finds his one and only beloved and mates with her, never again does he give a serious thought to copulating with another woman.

What this romantic philosophy adds up to, altogether, is the attitude that sex desires should be thoroughly controlled by and under the influence of love feelings, and that whenever they are not so controlled and influenced they are more or less reprehensible. Ostensibly, it is a quite consistent philosophy and has no serious contemporary opposition, since stories, plays, movies, or nonfictional works in which men and women consciously enjoy sex without love and do not suffer any dire consequences are quite rare in our culture. The key word here is *consciously*. Unconsciously, the situations seem to be different.

That is to say, while virtually every girl in every American novel and magazine story who is having sex relations with some fellow is either distinctly in love with him or temporarily imagining that she is, and while virtually every nonfictional discussion of sex that is nowadays published points out the necessity of not "cheapening" sex relations by confining them to affectional ones, there can be little doubt that *unconsciously* this basic sex-must-go-with-love rule is continually being publicly as well as privately flaunted.

Take, for example, the lasciviously arrayed and disarrayed women who ubiquitously adorn our advertisements, occupy our stages, embellish our cartoons, smile out from our picture magazines, and thicken the plots of our stories and novels. Does anyone pretend that the millions of American males whose ardor they are obviously designed to—and do—arouse are *in love* with these beauties? Take the hundreds of thousands of American girls who, every night of each year, are ardently kissed, hugged, petted, and so forth, in public parks, movies, cars, and parlors of this great nation. Is there any likelihood that they are all romantically attached to their swains? Take the myriad American wives who legally cohabit with their husbands week after week, year after year. Does anyone suppose that every time (or, in many cases, *any* time) their spouses touch them their hearts continue to go romantically clippity-clop as once (perhaps) they did in the earliest days of their mating?

Which means?

That, patently, the consciously indited views on love and sex which may be had for the reading in almost every imaginable type of publication are, in actual American life, unconsciously ignored by literally millions of very active sex participants. Indeed, it may be confidently predicted that, if the facts could ever be truthfully known, only a small part of the heterosexual kisses, embraces, and copulations which take place in this country from day to day are accompanied by the deeply experienced feelings of love, comradeship, friendliness, and romance without which—so the story writers tell us—these sex affairs are not truly ethical and good.

If, however, the average American is supposed to enjoy sex only when it is a concomitant of specific love feelings; and if, as would seem clear, he or she frequently enjoys it on a fairly non-loving or neutral basis, the result is inevitable; namely, a piling up of an enormous burden of guilt and regret that will tend to inhibit or destroy sex pleasure and to sabotage the mental—and perhaps physical—health of the common-garden-variety human being who should not, but obviously still does, like his sex affairs with little or no love.

Attitudes Toward Romanticism and Sex in the 1960's

In the study of sex attitudes in the early 1950's, it was found that there were relatively few clear-cut references to romanticism and sex and that almost all these were conservative—that is, they took the position that sex and love should or must go together and that sex without love is a more or less odious offense on the part of those who engage in it. In re-studying sex views as expressed in mass media in the 1960's, it has been found that much the same conditions prevail, in that there are still relatively few published views on sex and romanticism and that most of these are still on the conservative, or sex-is-no-goddam-good-without-love, side.

At the same time, however, there are literally scores of attitudes in today's mass media, particularly in the men's magazines, where romantic love is not mentioned at all, but where it is conspicuous by its absence when pleasant sex escapades are described. In these sex-is-great-for-its-own-sake references, there is no implication, most of the time, that sex with love is a bad thing; but there is an almost crystal-clear implication that when sexual participation is had by, for, in, and of itself it *still* may be entirely harmless and satisfying.

The conservative side of the romanticism and sex issue may perhaps be best seen in various references in modern best-selling novels. In *Exodus*, by way of illustration, we have this passage concerning the love and sex relations of Kitty and Ari: "'Why do you and I always have to confront each other with our guards up, ready to swing ... ready to run?' Kitty regarded him steadily for a moment. 'Maybe because I don't live by your simple, uncluttered standards of I-like-you-and-you-like-me-so-let's-go-to-bed. Page four forty-four of the Palmach manual: boys and girls should not indulge in coyness. Women of Palestine, be forthright. If you love him, sleep with him.' 'We aren't hypocrites.' 'I'm not so advanced in my thinking as Jordana or your immortal Dafna.' 'Stop it,' Ari snapped. 'How do you dare to imply that my sister and Dafna were—tramps? Jordana has loved only one man in her life. Is it wrong to give her love when she does not know if either of them will be alive at the end of the week? Don't you think I would have preferred to live in peace at Yad

El with my Dafna than have her killed by Arab gangs?' 'I don't live my life as a noble mission. It is very simple with me, Ari. I have to be needed by the man I love.' "

In this passage, it can easily be seen, neither Ari nor Kitty is asking for sex without love, although he is asking for sex without marriage. But both the American girl and the Israel man obviously feel that it is not quite kosher to fornicate for its own sake. Similarly, in *Poor No More*, Libby has no hesitation in going to bed with her boss, Craig Price; but she is horrified at the notion that he might also be having intercourse with his wife, whom he no longer loves. In *The War Lover*, a strong distinction is made between Daphne's having sex relations with a male—which she has often done, at practically the drop of a hat—and her copulating *with love*. Only under the latter cirumstance does she really let herself go and fully enjoy herself sexually.

In *The Cave*, Nick Pappy, a whoremonger and a semi-rapist if there ever was one, who has literally blackmailed and bullied Dorothy Cutlick into having coitus with him regularly, is utterly shocked when he discovers that their sex relations have not *meant* anything to her; and, as Robert Penn Warren tells us, "he was not prepared to face the awfuller fact that it had never meant a thing to him, either." In *Lady Chatterley's Lover*, we have this passage which indicates how important a part love is supposed to play in human sexual affairs:

" 'I believe in being warm-hearted. I believe especially in being warm-hearted in love, in fucking with a warm heart. I believe if men could fuck with warm hearts, and the women take it warmheartedly everything would come all right. It's all this coldhearted fucking that is death and idiocy.' 'But you don't fuck me coldheartedly,' she protested. 'I don't want to fuck you at all. My heart's as cold as cold potatoes just now.' 'Oh!' she said, kissing him mockingly. 'Let's have them sauteed.' He laughed, and sat erect. 'It's a fact!' he said, 'anything for a bit of warmheartedness.' "

Quotations such as these show most convincingly that the idea that sex is sinful sans love is still widely prevalent in our literature. On the other hand, as noted in the beginning of this chapter, the proposition that loveless sex cannot be sacrosanct is heartily contradicted in most of our highly popular men's magazines. Stories, articles, jokes, cartoons, and other items strongly favoring sex for its own sake, including arrant promiscuity, are to be found in recent issues of *Revels*, *Scamp*, *Modern Man*, *Man's Conquest*, *Harem*, *Man's Magazine*, *Candid*, *Joy*, etc.

An article in *Man's Conquest*, for example, tells with great relish of teenage sex clubs in Philadelphia; Morris Country, New Jersey; Pine Island, N.Y.; Panama City, Florida; Borger, Texas; and Matoon,

Illinois. One of the girls who fervently engaged in the membership proceedings of one of these clubs, including wild sex orgies, is quoted as saying, when asked her reasons: "Strictly for kicks. I *love* my loving."

Revels carries a typical cartoon—one of a great number to be found in almost every issue of this type of magazine—showing a beautiful young girl in bed with a passenger on a ship being bawled out by the ship's captain, who has several other males waiting behind him. Says the captain: "As social director, Miss Nulty, there's a responsibility that you have to our other 247 passengers!"

Many other examples of today's permissive attitudes toward promiscuity and sex sans love may be found in the addenda to previous chapters in this book on fornication, adultery, prostitution, promiscuity, and various other aspects of human sexuality. These numerous and typical illustrations indicate that many American editors, publishers, and writers on the one hand, and presumably readers on the other, distinctly endorse the view which I examined and defended a few years ago in my book, *Sex Without Guilt*: namely, that although sex with love is indubitably a fine experience, and for most people perhaps superior to the experience of loveless sex, sex without love is nonetheless *also* a great and glorious thing and may most profitably be experienced in its own right.

Summing up: the wedding of romanticism and sex still goes on in American mass media; and sometimes a happy marriage of the two ensues. But the wedding of sex with sex (and, often, with still more sex) is a relatively newly enthused-over phenomenon in our most widely distributed communications. And the enthusiasm for sinless sex for its own sweet sake seems to be waxing and waxing. . . .

CHAPTER 25

Sexuality of Women

American attitudes toward the sexuality of women, as they are expressed in modern fiction and non-fiction, are so clearly dichotomous as to result in a classic case of split personality on the part of any man (or woman) who encompasses both sides of them. And that, it would seem, means you and you—and me.

On the one hand, the time-honored double standard of morality would still appear to be very much with us; which means that most Americans still seem to believe that man may be allowed considerably more sex freedom than woman. As Judson T. and Mary G. Landis, quoted in *Your Marriage*, put it: "If boys are punished for their early experimentations, it is seldom with the zeal that is applied when girls are the offenders. Some parents tend to view boys' infractions of rules on sex behavior as evidence of potential virility, and to be lenient."

This assumption that what *is* sexually right for American boys and men may be entirely wrong for American girls and women is mirrored in numerous publications and presentations. Thus in the popular film, *Adam's Rib*, it is ironically shown how a district attorney and a jury will ordinarily consider it not nice if a man commits adultery—and perfectly horrible if a woman does. In *New Physical Culture* women are told by Mrs. Bernarr Macfadden that they must never try to "prove your equality to man by having as many romances as the male may have." In the film, *Quartet*, as we previously mentioned in our chapter on adultery, a man blithely keeps a mistress—then becomes utterly shocked at the thought that his wife may have once had a lover. In *Uncensored Detective* the true story of a murderer is related: "returning unexpectedly to Los Angeles, he said, he had watched his wife and found her cheating. Finally he could stand it no longer, he added, and he slipped into the kitchen one day and stabbed her." At the time he was apprehended for his wife's murder, this man, we are told, was in Glendale, California, "living with his married paramour."

So it goes: with our magazines, comic books, novels, films, plays, and radio scripts literally crammed with stories of girls and women who are miserable, harried, sick, fearful, guilt-ridden, and suicidal because of their fornicative or adulterous sex affairs—and rarely mentioning anything but unadulterated pleasure on the part of the males with whom these girls have had these same affairs.

In the light of this massive evidence it can hardly be denied that a most typical attitude toward the American woman, as expressed by hundreds of our most popular writers, is that she is a relatively "pure" creature, whose main interest in males is love and marriage rather than sex, and who suffers immensely when she gives in to her naked sex desires.

This is one side of the picture, and one which will doubtless not be startlingly new to many readers. The other side, which is almost a complete reversal of the view of woman's sexuality drawn by the double-standard upholders, may come as more of a shock. For this side maintains that women are not merely as frankly and unashamedly sexual as men—but possibly considerably more so. And the surprising fact seems to be not that this notion of woman's wantonness exists today—since some iconoclastic writers of all ages seem to have had it —but that it is exceptionally widespread in virtually all forms of modern mass media.

In the movies, for instance, the musical film, *On the Town*, portrays three relatively romantic, sexually passive sailors—and two red-hot,

216

overeager girls who virtually rape two of them. In the dramatic film, *East Side, West Side,* the hero, who is trying to give up his playboy ways, is re-seduced to them by a girl who fairly seethes with high, and very frankly aimed, sexuality. In *The Facts of Love* Peter first says that he calls his girl *Pepper* "because she's hot stuff." Then he runs into another girl who, under the pretext of having him meet some of her friends on her yacht, lures him there and lets him know that they are alone. This second girl, Fay, puts a hot record on the gramophone and says to Peter while she is madly making love to him: "Music brings out the primitive, savage side of our nature. . . . If music be the food of love, play on!"

Not to be outdone, the modern stage also presents us with various examples of sexually inflammatory women. In *Gentlemen Prefer Blondes* Lorelei Lee's girl friend frankly tells her that "you enjoy giving money to anything that wears trousers," when Lorelei has over-tipped a porter; and Lorelei, who spends a good part of her time on the stage running after good-looking men, willingly agrees. In *Texas Li'l Darlin'* a girl who is trying to win Our Hero away from Our Heroine passionately attacks him while he is sitting on a park bench. "Sway me!" she screams, as she does everything but have intercourse with him right then and there (to the audience's uncontrollable delight).

On the radio, girls who run after men for distinctly sexual reasons are stock characters on several shows, including, for example, *Our Miss Brooks,* who keeps making passes in a most aggressive manner at her very passive boy friend, Boynton.

In the novels we have the never overly sexed hero of *The Egyptian,* who is continually being violently assaulted by voluptuous women to whom he remains unbelievably indifferent. Thus, when he meets up with a group of lovely Cretan women, we hear that they "hung garlands about my neck and looked into my eyes and leaned upon me until their naked breasts pressed against my arm. They took me with them in among the laurel bushes to eat and drink. Thus it was I saw their wantonness, and they were not shy of me. I drank heavily and feigned intoxication so that they had no joy of me but grew weary and smote me, calling me swine and barbarian."

In another novel, *The Man with the Golden Arm,* we are given as realistic a picture as we may ever hope to have of a woman taking a normally highly-sexed male and literally wilting him under her superior sex ardor. The manner in which Vi outcopulates first her aging husband and then her young lover, Sparrow, is told in such lusty and realistic detail that the reader wonders what man could possibly keep up with the sexual prowess of any normal, healthy, uninhibited woman.

As for the magazine stories, here again we find notable examples of woman's terrific sexual ardor and powers. In one tale in *Private Detective* a man goes to a female acquaintance because he is in trouble and needs her help—and she immediately jumps to conclusions and wraps herself around him. In another story in the same issue the hero comes upon a ravishing young thing lying in the arms of a man, "eyes closed, tongue darting in and out like an inquisitive snake." As soon as she sees him she remarks on his cuteness; and two minutes later, when he has slugged her obstreperous, jealous lover, our hero tells us that "suddenly, Rea rushed at me. Strong arms clamped around my neck, forced my face down. Soft, open lips met mine.... I liked the feel of this jet-propelled armful. She pulsed with high-voltage frequency. ... Gently, I grabbed her biceps, squeezed hard and pushed outward. Her body loosened reluctantly. 'Please, please,' she purred, her eyes masked."

Probably the best illustration of the unashamed acceptance of rampant sexuality in women may be found in an *Esquire* story entitled "A Corpse for Christmas." The private-eye hero gets quite involved, on a single page of this story, with three different girls. First he takes Gene up to her "one-room jackknife apartment" and pours himself a drink while she goes into the bathroom to change her clothes. "I was pouring, when she came out. I stopped pouring. It was a long silk robe with a braided belt. That's all. Her feet were bare and her make-up was off and she wasn't smiling. I looked at her, I looked away, looked back. I put the bottle down and the glass. I said, 'Look, sister ...' 'Yes?' ... 'Look, I'm high. I'm loaded right up to here.' 'So am I.' 'I'm going to kiss you sister.' 'You're going to kiss me, are you?' She took my face in her hands, and opened her mouth on mine, bending backward as I held her.... Cold grey was Christmas dawn as I marched home."

When he reaches his home, our hero tells us, a second lovely creature awaits him. "I was met by Gay, slightly nude, tiptoeing out. 'Sh!' she said ... 'I've been waiting for you.' 'Waiting for me? Didn't you hear me ring?' 'Sure. But someone ringing wouldn't be you. You live here.' 'How about some clothes?' 'Clothes?' 'You don't have any on.' 'I said I was waiting for you.' I went to the bedroom and got a bathrobe and tossed it to her. 'Listen,' she said, 'you're insulting.' "

After getting a few hours' sleep this casual detective gets up and visits (on the same page) a third girl—the one he is in love with. We read: "Stella was wan in lounging pajamas, eager, but too tired to do much about it. A tired Stella was something to see, at least you had an opportunity to observe. Lounging pajamas or no, her figure was more exciting than parade music on a bright afternoon. It caught at you and made you tingle. And the glint of her halfclosed eyes did

218

nothing to assuage the tingle. I kept a serving table between us.

" 'Good morning, Miss Talbot.'

" 'Now you come?'

" 'What's wrong with now?'

" 'You finally make up your mind?'

" 'No, I——'

" 'You wanna kiss me?'

" 'No.'

" 'Right now, I don't care. Right now, I'm probably not up to it. But you will, fella, I promise you. Sooner or later.'

" 'Later. This morning, it's business.'

" 'Business? You and me?' She brightened, smiling. 'Maybe *I'm* not up to it, but maybe *you* are. . . .' She reached a hand across.

" 'No. Real business. Money, you know?'

" 'Oh, money.' She settled back. . . .

"I scribbled a contract and she signed it.

" 'That fancy supper invitation still stand for tonight?'

" 'But of course, my sweet.'

" 'I'm going to rest all day. Look out for me tonight, brother. I'm really going to pitch.' "

Just to make it unanimous, the jokesters, too, have no hesitation in portraying the weaker sex as the stronger sexed. Thus Peter Arno, in his *Sizzling Platter*, depicts the manager of a New York baseball team saying to an eager woman in one of the boxes, who is obviously interested in a gorgeous hunk of his team: "We do sell them sometimes, lady, but only to other teams." And in *Cartoon Humor* a stage director is shown telling a charmingly disarrayed beauty as she prepares to go before the footlights to remember that whistling back is not permitted.

Wet Hen gives us this advice: "How to give a girl a surprise: Place arms around waist. Draw her strongly toward you and hold her tight. Start to kiss her. When she says: 'Stop!' release her. Note the amazement on her face."

Finally, *Ram-Buller* has a good-looking young man asking what is home without a mother, and the sweet young thing replying that she is tonight.

It must be admitted that in some of those cases where the woman is publicly displayed as having more than mild interest in seducing the male of the species she is made out to be the villainess of the piece or as an extraordinary kind of girl. There seems to be an increasing tendency, however, to portray her, as in the examples quoted above from *On the Town* and *Our Miss Brooks*, as a very wholesome, indubitably heroine type of girl who merely has sound, healthy sex drives and is not bashful about putting them to good use.

It should also be pointed out that portrayals of lust-sick heroines are conspicuously scarce in magazines with an almost exclusively female clientele, and conspicuously prevalent in the men's magazines. It would appear that the depicting of unabashed sexuality in women is not only titillating to relatively sex-starved males in our culture, but actually provides a masculine-idealized image of womankind which sharply contrasts with the feminine idealization of the female sex.

Ironically enough, then, while the double standard of morality which officially holds sway in our country actually seems to work where woman are concerned and to make them largely ashamed of their biological sex urge, it also tends to make men desire sexually unashamed and uninhibited women. The female and the male ideals of women's sexuality thus tend to grow farther apart and to breed a most unhealthy and conflicting situation between the sexes.

To make matters still worse, many males, dichotomizing their own feelings toward women's sexuality, desire pure wives and wanton mistresses; and many females want, simultaneously, to be revered as chaste matrons and to be desired as passionate bedmates. The chances of these men and these women being truly satisfied in their marital and/or extramarital sex affairs is, as one might well imagine, pitifully slim.

To sum up: In the light of the evidence surveyed in this chapter, it can hardly be denied that the concept of American women's sexuality, as exemplified in popular writings and productions, is that the average woman in our society is low-sexed—and high-sexed; that she dare—and dasn't—not conform to male sex behavior; that she is likely to be ostracized—and immensely popular—if she is sexually unconventional; that, in regard to following strict sex codes, she is damned if she won't and damned if she will.

Attitudes Toward the Sexuality of Women in the 1960's

In the early 1950's, as has just been seen, it was discovered that there were fairly many expressed and implied attitudes toward the sexuality of women and that these were proponderantly liberal and permissive. In the 1960's, the same trend is found, except that there are many more references to women's sexuality to be discovered in American mass media and almost all of these are distinctly prosexual. Particularly the fiction best-sellers and the men's magazines take the position that females are highly sexed creatures who like nothing more, in many instances, than to jump into bed with a man.

The only pronouncedly conservative attitude toward women's sexuality that was uncovered in the material of today was the semi-ranting of D. H. Lawrence, who always did have a problem in connection with highly sexed females and who wrote his novel, *Lady*

220

Chatterley's Lover, in the 1920's, even though it did not become an American best-seller until the present time. Said Lawrence (in the person of Mellors):

"To my experience the mass of women are like this: most of them want a man, but don't want the sex, but they put up with it, as part of the bargain. The more old-fashioned sort just lie there like nothing and let you go ahead. They don't mind afterwards; then they like you. But the actual thing itself is nothing to them, a bit distasteful."

Almost all the rest of modern fiction writers, however, seem violently to disagree with Lawrence. Robert Penn Warren, in particular, has his book, *The Cave*, chock-full of lustful females. On page 16, he has Sallie Mapes, who already is carrying on quite an affair with Jebb Holloway, lusting mightily after Monty Harrick, so that he can see her "suck her lower lip in, staring right at him, and bite it." Sallie, says Jasper Herrick a couple of pages later, "flings it around like a drunk man with a scatter gun. She would do it bare-ass on cockleburrs. No other place handy, she would tell the bacon to move over in a hot skillet for butt space, and not care if you took the turkey wing to fan the fire up."

On page 86 of *The Cave*, Jack Harrick, who has gotten Mac Sumpter's beloved, Mary Tillyard, pregnant, explains: "I'm not denying but one thing. I'm not even denying she hadn't ever been pricked. I'm not denying she was a virgin. But I never made her a virgin and it's not my fault. But virgin or not, I tell you, she has natural talents. I tell you she has talents that would make a circus pony look like a plowbroke mule and the band playing 'Dixie.' What I mean is, when a girl's got talent like that, somebody's bound to be in the line of fire when she finds out she has got something to live for. I'm not denying I was standing there when the tree cracked and nobody yelled 'Timber.' I'm just denying that I throwed her down, like you seem to imply. Hell, I had to hold her up. What I mean is, when her knees buckled under her that first time, I plain had to hold her up ... I wasn't even holding her tight. I was holding her loose, and I wasn't doing nothing worse than counting her vertibray a little and breathing in her hair, and she of a sudden said, oh, God, and gave a moan-like, and it looked like a strut done busted in her.' "

Several other females in Warren's novel, including Jo-Lea Bingham and Rachel Goldstein, are almost as eager to crawl into the sack with the men they care for as is Mary Tillyard. Similarly, in Robert Ruark's *Poor No More*, we find Julie du Fresne (p. 220), Maybelle Grimes (p. 224), and Libby Forney (p. 395), among others, practically raping the not so innocent Craig Price. Says Libby to her brother, when he discovers the affair she is having with Craig (who is at that time married to Maybelle): "There ain't no such thing as a nice girl! There are just girls! Just girls, made for men to love and hold close and take to bed! Just girls! Girls that go to the toilet and have the curse once a month and fall in love with men that they want to. . . . You know what I mean. You use the word all the time. You want me to say it? I'll say it. F . . ."

In John Hersey's *The War Lover*, there are several more examples of women who lust mightily after men—especially the heroine, Daphne, who, when her lover asks her if she is hungry (for food), acts in this wise: "She gave me that melted eye look and said, 'For you.' "

Other examples of wild-eyed women seducing and almost attacking the males to whom they are attracted may be found in such novels as Faulkner's *The Mansion*, Gallico's *Too Many Ghosts*, Drury's *Advise and Consent*, West's *The Devil's Advocate*, Costain's *The Darkness and the Dawn*, and Michener's *Hawaii*. In the last named novel we are told about Nancy Janders, sister of Wild Whip Hoxworth's wife, who induced Whip to sneak away to her hotel "where they fell into wild tormenting embraces. All the longing of three years rushed back up on poor Nancy Janders, and she abandoned restraint. She would lie in bed completely undressed, waiting for Whip to bound up the hotel stairs, and as soon as he burst into the room and locked the door, she would spring upon him and kiss him madly, throwing him onto the bed with laughter that welled up from her entire being. Sometimes she kept him imprisoned for a whole day, and it became obvious to her sister Iliki what was going on."

If possible, contemporary American novels are eclipsed in their portraits of sexually wild-eyed women by the pictures of female lasciviousness persistently displayed in the men's magazines. In a story in *The Gent*, a virgin is raped by an intruder and forced to have intercourse on the gritty floor of a barn-like storeroom; but she starts enjoying the proceedings so immensely that she forgets her attachment to her boy friend and "with a great tearing sob, she flung her arms around the intruder, her hands on his back and shoulders straining to press him even closer."

Twenty-One informs us, in an article on uninhibited women, that a 44-year-old Greenwich, Conn. spinster was haled into court for " 'entertaining' a constant parade of teenage boys in her home." But "she showed no remorse, no regret, or any intention whatsoever to change her way of life."

In a *Hi-Life* story a girl picks up a man, gets him somewhat drunk, induces him to take her home, and eagerly swirls off her dress to take him to bed. In a *Men's Digest* tale, a woman who has hijacked a man's truck in order to escape from the police stops long enough to force

222

him at gun point to have intercourse with her: "She held the cocked gun in her right hand, and she reached out with the other hand, pulling the blouse down to her waist, revealing two rising, full mounds of stored-up passion, hard at the tips. 'Come here,' she said. Her voice was rough. I didn't have to come to her. She was already there."

High-powered descriptions of women's sexuality are to be found in almost every issue of *True, Off Beat Detective Stories, Monsieur, Climax, Man's Magazine, Revels, Rapture, Harem, Confidential Tattler, Scamp,* and other men's magazines. In other kinds of mass media pictures of sexually avid females are also common. In the film, *Wild River,* the young widow, Carol, pleads with the hero Chuck to stay with her all night. In a *Fantasy Science Fiction* tale, "a score of young women whose figures and costumes suggested a handsomely modernized Mussulman heaven . . . were lounging around Goshawk's easel, hoping he might try to seduce them."

In a story in *Mike Shayne Mystery Magazine,* a lovely young girl begs a man to go to bed with her. In the film, *The Fugitive Kind,* Val Xavier is trying to escape from the easy women who'd always pawed him as if he were a stallion at stud. Vance Packard, in the best-selling nonfiction book, *The Hidden Persuaders,* tells us that "A Nielsen check of TV fans watching wrestling matches revealed that ladies outnumbered men two to one. The promotors of the matches, shrewdly calculating the triggers that produced the most squeals from feminine fans, stepped up the sadism (men writhing in torture), the all-powerful male symbolism (chest beating and muscle flexing), and fashion interest (more and more elegant costumes for the performers)."

In the anecdotal field, jokes and cartoons about women's enormous sex drives are commonplace. Some examples:

From *Comedy*: "Jane: Did you get that good-looking extremely shy boy to put his hands on you last night? Lucy: I most certainly did, but it was in self-defense!"

From *Ace*: "One farmer's daughter succumbed to the villain so that he wouldn't foreclose the mortgage he held on the family homestead. She liked it so much she went hunting for the guy who held the second mortgage."

From *Monsieur*: Marcia tells Maybelle that she has found a perfect method of getting her husband to buy her clothes—namely, by not letting him touch her until the coat or dress she wants is hanging in the closet. Maybelle says she will try the same method. "Marcia: What happened? Maybelle: There was a hat I'd seen on the Rue de la Paix and my husband found it too expensive: Marcia: So? Maybelle: So I did as you suggested. Marcia: Did it work? Maybelle: Work! Listen, dear, it worked but not the way I expected. I didn't get the hat and now *I* have to buy my husband a new tie every few days."

From *Snappy*: "Mary: Put your arms around me and teach me to drive, dear. Isn't this wonderful! Larry: Yes, darling, but don't you think we ought to get in the car?"

From *Ace*: "After the newlyweds had been complaining of fatigue their doctor told them to limit themselves by having intercourse only on days of the week with an 'r' in them. They got through the weekend all right, but on Monday evening the young bride was feeling neglected. Finally, she cuddled up to her drowsy husband and nudged him into semiwakefulness. 'Huh?' he asked groggily. 'What day is it?' 'Mondray,' she cooed."

From reviewing this evidence in contemporary American mass media it may still be said, as was noted a decade ago in the first edition of this book, that men may like their women both high-sexed and low-sexed, unchaste and pure—but the demand for frigidity and purity seems to be fast approaching the vanishing point. On the contrary, as I have pointed out in several recent papers in professional journals and in the book, *The Art and Science of Love*, today's women are tending to become increasingly disturbed because they are sexually inadequate, rather than because they are "over-sexed." And they are worrying so much about *not* getting easy arousal and terrific orgasms that they are, perversely enough, focusing on negative thoughts when they do have intercourse and are destroying in many instances their own potential responsiveness.

The picture of the "average" sexually over-eager female who is so prominent in today's literature may therefore have the perverse effect of diminishing rather than of enhancing the sexuality of many women. In some ways it is just as unrealistic as the oldtime portrait of the practically undesirous and sexless "good" woman. The quicker it is replaced by a more realistic, middle-of-the-road picture of the usual American girl, the better it may be for the premarital and marital sexual compatibility of many couples.

CHAPTER 26

Sex Rites and Superstitions

Theoretically this is an age of science. Modern men and women tend to abjure pagan rites and superstitions and to regulate their lives on the basis of scientifically acquired knowledge and logical reasoning rooted in objective evidence. Theoretically.

In sexual areas there can be little question that the factual knowledge acquired during the past fifty years, at least part of which has seeped down into the consciousness of millions of Americans, has made for a lessening of sexual superstition and irrational thinking and for an augmenting of more rationally based sex behavior. Thus relatively few American men seem to believe, as do millions of their more primitive brothers, that if they in any way come in contact with a woman during her menstrual period they will inevitably suffer serious harm. And relatively few American women believe that if they do a special dance or perform unique planting ceremonies in the spring they will soon conceive.

Yet it would appear that the very same sex superstitions and rites which nakedly manifest themselves in primitive societies often tend to survive in a more toned-down or "civilized" form in modern life. Thus, while the average male today is not afraid to touch his wife during her menstrual period, he frequently will not have sexual intercourse with her during this time. He—and she—will rationalize their objections to menstrual coitus by talking about its "unaesthetic" or "unhygienic" aspects, but at bottom their attitudes toward it seem to be largely a survival of old anti-menstrual taboos.

Again, millions of women today who would never dream of doing a dance or incantation to abet their pregnancies will fervently pray to Yahweh, or the Virgin Mary, or St. So-and-So, or some other god for fertility aid. Obviously, therefore, sex superstitions and rites are much closer to our present-day nature than we frequently care to acknowledge.

More specific proof of the present-day existence of sex rites is fairly easily found in our public prints. Our magazines, for example, carry ads like this one from *Hit Parade*: "HONEYMOON LOVE DROPS. Secret Aroma Helps with the One You Love. Unforgettable as a lover's first kiss! . . . Free personal directions REVEAL HOW to use if you wish to experience joyous love. The one you love can be yours . . . can love with great emotion . . . can be awakened to a more exciting you . . . if you KNOW HOW to use these love drops."

In *Eyeful* we find an ad displaying a ring with a naked siren mounted on its surface. "BE A WINNER!" screams the copy, followed by a cut of two intermingled hearts. It continues: "My valuable brochure *Luck Power vs. Mind Power* explains how and is free to anyone who will wear this replica of the oldest Talismanic ring known. Ancient worshipers of Fortune, the Goddess of Luck, wore her emblem always for success and good fortune in all undertakings. . . . Wear it and follow my advice."

Even more to the point, we have this ad from *Personal Romances*: "DO YOU WANT MONEY—LOVE—LUCK! Adam and Eve Root is one of the most famous of alleged LUCK ROOTS. It is believed by many that a person carrying a pair of these roots will be very LUCKY and SUCCESSFUL . . . BEWARE OF CHEAP IMITA-

TIONS! While we make no supernatural claims, we ABSOLUTELY GUARANTEE THESE ROOTS TO BE REAL GENUINE SPECIMENS OF THE VERY HIGHEST QUALITY. Satisfaction GUARANTEED or Money Refunded."

B. A. Botkin, reviewing some of the sex and love charms which are still frequently used in our Southern states, tells us that they include "nails, teeth, hair, saliva, perspiration, dandruff, scabs of sores even, and garments worn next to the person . . . even to dirt from a person's track . . . One eye-winker or the peeling of one freckle being enough to save or ruin a love affair."

To show how widespread the use of these sex charms and rites is, Botkin, in *A Treasury of Southern Folklore*, states that "in the use of love charms (which have European parallels) the whites do not lag behind the Negroes. Thus, whereas the large drugstore sale of sassafras, lodestone, brimstone, asafoetida, resin, and bluestone to the colored trade attests the vitality of Negro conjuring, drugstores in the Ozarks as well as among the Negroes of New Orleans display love powders prominently. And in the Ozarks they are taken so seriously that 'the victim of a love charm or philtre is not held morally responsible for his actions, and many a deserted wife is comforted by the reflection that her man did not leave of his own free will, but was conjured off.'"

Morris Weeks, Jr., writing in *Better Health* magazine, reminds us that aphrodisiacal rites are still quite prevalent and that, according to many word-of-mouth present-day beliefs, "eating oysters, clams, fish, raw eggs, milk, cream, raw vegetables, pomegranates, and ground-up animal organs surely leads to sexual prowess."

M. Ritter, in a *Blue Book* article, "The Male American," points out that the averge male "has some quaint ideas about the superiority of brunettes over blondes as love partners." He also reminds us that, as a result of the popularity of a fairly new—or at least newly revived—American sex rite, some 95 per cent of married men in our country "now either wears a wedding ring or was forced to participate in a double-ring ceremony."

Another common form of sex superstition today is that fostered by hundreds of American newspapers and magazines which have horoscope or obviously unscientific handwriting-analysis columns which purport, very quickly and neatly, to tell their readers all about their chances for sexual, amative, and marital success. Thus, in a handwriting column in the New York *Sunday Mirror*, we read: "Is Ezio Pinza as romantic as the part he so wonderfully plays in *South Pacific*? I've been asked this question many times and, according to his handwriting, the answer is definitely 'Yes.' As you can see, Ezio Pinza has a rapid, forward-slanted script and uses a vigorous pen pressure. Such people are ruled by their hearts. When they fall in love, they fall hard."

Again, in a "Today's Horoscope" column in the Detroit *News*, we find this type of thoroughly unscientific nonsense: "To find what the stars have in store for tomorrow, select your birthday star and read the corresponding paragraph ... Gemini (May 22–June 22)–You may combine marriage and business plans advantageously today.... Virgo (Aug. 24-Sept. 22)–Definitely a day for romance. Attending a dance might bring you a great deal of pleasure."

Newspapers also carry advertisements for spiritualists, palmists, and other caterers to those who would seek sex and marital advice along totally unscientific, superstitious roads. Thus the Amarillo *Sunday News-Globe* carries ads like these: "BLIND Reader. 4 Questions $1.00 by mail"... "PROF. DE SHONE. House 10 A.M. to 7 P.M. Noted reader and adviser. Gives advice in all affairs and solves all problems of life. Private readings daily."

Magazines also abet the astrological and other superstitious dissemination of sex lore. *Love Novels* magazine claims that for only fifteen cents in stamps or currency it will give its readers a handwriting analysis that "tells whether or not you can be happy with the one you love and how you can make a success of marriage." Princess Alexandra Kropotkin, in a column in a national magazine, features the astrologer, Carroll Righter, whom she quotes as follows: "When parents want a planned baby, the plan should begin with an astrological family tree. This means we need the horoscopes of six people–the mother, the father, the two maternal grandparents, and the two paternal grandparents. By constructing a chart from all these, we calculate the best time of year for the child to be born. We determine under which sign of the zodiac it will be best for the child to be born."

The one thing about which relatively little evidence could be gathered in the course of this study was the contemporary existence of sex rites of an orgiastic nature. Doubtless such rites exist in various parts of this country, but the public attitudes toward them seem to be negative, so that they are rarely described or referred to in mass media. However, three references to sex rites were found in our survey.

1. B. A. Botkin, in his *A Treasury of Southern Folklore*, mentions voodooism in the South and tells us that the Queen of Voodoo "reigns as long as she continues to live. She comes to power not by inheritance, but by election or its barbarous equivalent. Chosen for such qualities as would give her a natural supremacy, personal attractions among the rest, and ruling over superstitious fears and desires of every fierce and ignoble sort, she wields no trivial influence."

2. James Aswell, in the Bangor *Sunday Commercial*, states that in present-day New Orleans "black magic and devil-worship continue to

flourish just beneath the surface of apparently modern and sophisticated life.... For several years, nothing is heard of midnight meetings in hidden places, of sacrificial fowls and the dread 'gris-gris' curse—voodoo seems dead, lost in the native past—and then, all of a sudden, the sinister cult will show itself very much alive, thrusting up to horrify the religious and absorb the police."

3.   Hartnett T. Kane, in *Queen New Orleans*, gives quite a lot of material on the famed New Orleans Mardi Gras, about which he writes: "There is French joie de vivre, the endless capacity for a good time, the willingness to let others have theirs.... Forget your inhibitions; dance on the street if you feel like it, sing and hold hands with strangers."

Aside from the foregoing references to sex superstitions and rites, little could be found on these topics in the mass of material read and seen for this study. The general impression to be gained from analyzing this material are:

1.   That sex rites and superstitions are less prevalent today than they have been in the past.

2.   That the official and public attitude to them is that sex superstitions are rather ridiculous and that orgiastic rites are wicked.

3.   That, in spite of these attitudes, many sex superstitions unofficially persist and some, like astrological ones, are widely accepted in a muted way.

4.   That orgiastic rites of an extreme kind are relatively rare, but that milder manifestations of them, such as Mardi Gras affairs, drunken revelries, strip poker games, et cetera, are more common and more sexually oriented than the American public likes to think about consciously.

5.   That sex superstitions and rites, to the extent that they still exist in America, are largely a product of sex ignorance and inhibition, and that their decline is directly proportional to increases in sex education and more liberal sex views.

Attitudes Toward Sex Rites and Superstitions in the 1960's

In the original study of sex attitudes that was made of material of the early 1950's it was found that few references on sex rites and superstitions were published in American mass media and that these were all conservative. In the current follow-up study that has been made, even fewer references of this nature have been found—in fact, almost none—and they again, predictably, are all on the conservative side.

The one main connection between sexual superstitions today and those of a decade ago is the continued running of exactly the same advertisement for "HONEYMOON LOVE DROPS. SECRET

AROMA HELPS WIN THE ONE YOU LOVE." that was widely published in the early 1950's. Apparently, enough superstitious people are left in this world to keep purchasing these same love drops, even though the claim of the advertiser that they are "unforgettable as a lover's first kiss!" has hardly been scientifically substantiated during the last ten years.

Again, in present-day newspapers and magazines, there are still a number of astrological columnists who purport to tell the readers how to influence their love lives by studying the positions of the stars; and there are magazines, such as one called *Fate*, which are chock-full of spiritualistic and other superstitious articles and advertisements which frequently claim that readers and purchasers may be sexually and maritally helped if they follow the mumbo-jumbo of the writer or seller. In today's America, moreover, there seem to be a new rash of ads regarding the power of hypnosis in amative affairs. For example:

"X-RAY EYES. How to Analyze—and influence People—AT SIGHT. Entire course $3. (Adults) Satisfaction or refund. 'PSYCHIC DOMINANCE' 'HOW TO RULE OTHERS WITH YOUR THOUGHTS.' Full course—with stirring exercises. Illustrated (Adults)."

Other than this kind of nonsense, little in the way of out and out sex rites and superstitions could be noted in the mass media that were investigated in the 1960's. Perhaps the fact that these media, as pointed out in the various addenda that have been written to the original chapters of this book, are now considerably more liberal and permissive in their sex attitudes and, consequently, more sexually revealing— perhaps these facts of increasing sex education are helping to dispel some of the old unmitigated superstitiousness that previously prevailed. Certainly, as knowledge of sex accumulates and is made more available to the general public, obscurantism, supernaturalism, and irrationalism in this area might well be expected to decrease. This may be what is now occurring in the field, though the evidence is not yet by any means conclusive.

CHAPTER 27

Sex Education

The most general attitude toward sex education that one currently sees displayed in the public press is that such education is desirable, all right—but that it is, except on a haphazard, hit-or-miss basis, still virtually non-existent in contemporary America.

The nonfictional articles on sex which are so popular in today's magazines are especially replete with variations on this theme. Thus a *Your Psychology* writer complains about "wedding night shock, based upon prior ignorance of the exact functioning of marital relations." Paul Popenoe, in *Your Marriage* magazine, notes that "unfortunately, few men (or women) at the present time have had satisfactory education" for sexual potency in marriage. *Today's Woman* publishes a long, detailed article on the harm resulting from giving girls and women inadequate information concerning menstruation. Judson T. and Mary G. Landis are quoted in *Your Marriage* to this effect: "Only in the field of sex behavior is education seriously neglected. Here the teaching is almost entirely negative; it consists chiefly in impressing the child with taboos. Even the taboos are not standardized."

Not to be outdone by the magazines, writers of nonfictional books closely follow suit. Harry A. Overstreet, for example, in *The Mature Mind*, bitterly complains that "parents . . . blush, stammer, put off the day when they must explain to those children 'the facts of life,' as though sexual factors were somehow divorced from all others that have to do with the how of things."

Evidently, then, a good proportion of American publicists favors far better sex education than normally seems to be given in contemporary America. At the same time, the front-line resistance to these enlightened views on sex education seems to be unusually stiff, since obliging parents, schools, or other agencies which will give individuals the kind of sex education which the authorities keep demanding appear to be exceptionally few and far between.

By way of illustration take the case of Maxine, which the *Ladies' Home Journal* uses for its "Profile of Youth" representation of a typical small-town American girl. A *Ladies' Home Journal* staff writer reported the following on Maxine's sex education: "Because her mother never discussed sex with her at all, Maxine admits now that 'I sure was lucky not to get in Dutch before I found out from the girls in school and a book in the library just how things were.' Every night when she leaves for a date her parents tell her to 'behave yourself,' but they've never explained what they mean—'It probably embarrasses them,' Maxine says."

As a result of this type of embarrassment on the part of parents, effective sex education in America is normally at a minimum, and sex ignorance remains rife. In the latest study of the extent of sex education among teen-agers, done by a teen-age polling organization and reported in *True Story*, the fact is noted that "the great majority of them—four out of every five, approximately—say that whatever information they have about sex was acquired through conversation with friends. Those who got their information from parents, books, or courses at school form a much smaller group, less than two out of every five. Some said they received knowledge from more than one source. But only one in five was able to answer that he or she had learned nothing from the most undesirable source of all—some better-informed but not necessarily well-informed acquaintance."

In consequence of this lack of adequate sex education among young people in our country, we have innumerable instances of unwanted pregnancies, forced marriages, gruesome wedding nights, needless divorces, terrible sex fears, et cetera, constantly occurring among large segments of our populace. Dr. Lena Levine, for example, in an article in *Today's Woman*, tells us that thousands of American women each year submit to abortions when they are not actually pregnant, simply because they are too sexually ignorant to discover for a fact whether they are pregnant or not.

It should not be thought for a moment that there is *no* organized active opposition to sex education in America, since there obviously is. Certain ultra-conservative elements in the Catholic Church, for one thing, are still adamantly opposed to virtually all types of sex education. Father Martin J. Scott, quoted in *American Freedom and Catholic Power*, states that "our predecessors got along without all the sex instruction that is now ruining so many under the pretext of educating them. The purest and healthiest nations of the world have been those least acquainted with sex knowledge." And in an article in *Notre Dame* it is made clear that, in order to prepare oneself adequately for marriage, it is *not* "necessary to study in detail and at great length with books, charts, and pictures everything that is to be known about the physiological and anatomical aspects of marriage." These anti-sex-education views, however, are not necessarily typical of Catholics in general, and many Church officials ostensibly espouse the cause of sex education—though usually of a distinctly restricted and deodorized type.

A more subtle form of resisting sex education that appears to be quite prevalent in modern America is that expressed in the attitude that children should, of course, be taught all about sex—but only under decorous, proper, and well-hemmed-in conditions. Thus a story in *Esquire* cruelly satirizes the notion that sex education could possibly be given in the public schools. A quotation in *Your Psychology* firmly cautions against telling the child too much or too soon about sex facts. A caption in *Home Sweet Zoo* makes it clear that even when sex education is given in the home it must be handed down from father to son and from mother to daughter, and never, heaven forbid, in heterosexual converse between parent and child. These public attitudes make it clear that sex education is viewed by a large part of the populace as something which, while it really must be given, you know, is still not quite nice and must therefore be as hedged and hemmed in as possible.

Perhaps the best proof of all that American families and other agencies have, in fact if not in theory, unusually puritanical, do-nothing attitudes toward sex education may be found in the numerous advertisements for sex books which stud most of the popular newspapers and magazines. "THIS BOOK WILL OPEN YOUR EYES!" screams one of these ads. "The GREATEST PICTURE STORY EVER UNFOLDED," cries another. "SEE the organs of sex and how they function. See how SEX affects the BLOOD STREAM, the MUSCULAR and the INTESTINAL SYSTEM. SEE the exact structure of the complicated sex nerves which VIBRATE VIRILITY!!" "LATEST SEX FACTS," proclaims a third ad. "Every YOUNG MAN should have a copy of this book," says still another. "Learn about POTENCY AND IMPOTENCY, SEXUAL POWER ... CONSERVATION OF SEX ENERGY ... LOVE AND SEX IN MARRIAGE!! Carries a PUNCH in every line." And a fifth one opens: "IF HUSBANDS ONLY KNEW——!"

Precisely what, it may be inquired, *are* the "latest sex facts," the "intimate discoveries now revealed," the "latest improvements and methods" which are so frankly depicted in these books and which are so indispensable to getting and keeping you, you, and you happily married? These life- and love-saving facts include—to list a few items from the "partial list of enlightening contents" of one of these advertised books—such hard-to-come-by knowledge as:

> intercourse methods
> vital parts of sex organs
> sex act itself
> five senses important in sex
> sex differences in man's and woman's bodies
> attaining pregnancy
> female sex organ—how virgin differs
> plus many more unusual pictures

Patently, if these are typical, as indeed they are, of the proudly proclaimed contents of modern American sex books, sex education in America is in a sorry way. If Americans know *so* little about sex as to make the sale of literally scores of these "highly informative" volumes most profitable year after year, the amount of satisfactory sex education being given by our families, schools, and other agencies must obviously be microscopic.

The current condition regarding sex education seems to be analogous to Mark Twain's famous remark about the weather: that everybody talks about it but no one ever does anything about it. Aside from a few die-hard sectarian groups which, while not exactly opposing sex education per se, do object to certain modes of disseminating it, organized opposition to sex education in America seems to be in-

232

consequential. But unorganized opposition or a generalized passing-of-the-buck attitude toward sex teaching appears to be most prevalent among most of our parents and educational institutions. The result is widespread abysmal sex ignorance. Everybody, in a word, seems to want sex education—provided the other guy is the one to give it.

It may be appropriately noted at this point in our investigation that the current want-much and do-nothing attitudes of Americans on sex education are the logical *result* of the generally conflicting sex beliefs that we have been finding throughout our study. That is to say, while millions of us apparently are intellectually convinced of the necessity of giving our children adequate sex education, we are emotionally unable to bring ourselves to do so, or unable to do a satisfactory, objective job of presentation when we do force ourselves to educate our offspring sexually. This dichotomy between our intellectual comprehension of the need for adequate sex education and our emotional inability to foster or give it is a grim mirroring, no doubt, of our completely conflicting attitudes regarding all types of sex behavior which we have been turning up in chapter after chapter of this book. Only men and women who maturely and unequivocally face the facts of human sexuality can properly impart these facts to the generations who succeed them; but maturely and unequivocally facing sex behavior is precisely what we are *not*, in this day and age, doing. Exactly the reverse, as the findings of this study consistently show.

This means, in effect, that our *general* conflicting sex attitudes make it impossible for our *specific* attitudes and actions regarding sex education to be anything but conflicting and ineffectual. Sex confusion, in other words, cannot help breeding still more sex confusion—which later confusion, of course, serves to augment the former, thus making the vicious circle almost perfect. And the end, as yet, is nowhere in sight.

Attitudes Toward Sex Education in the 1960's

It was originally found that there were fairly few attitudes toward sex education in American mass media and that these were somewhat evenly divided on the liberal and conservative sides. In the follow-up study that has been made of sex attitudes in the 1960's, it has been found that many more references to sex education are being made today than a decade ago and that the majority of these are liberal and permissive.

The only negative reference to sex education that was found in the follow-up study was an article in *Cavalier* magazine which blasts Dr. Joyce Brothers for her TV program on the National Broadcasting Company and remarks that "she has a go-ahead from the network to titillate idle housewives by wallowing in such juicy (and usually taboo) subjects as adultery, oddball sex, infidelity, bed habits, toilet training and premarital chastity." The objection here, however, is not to TV sex education in itself, but to the particular kind parceled out by Dr. Brothers.

Other than this, contemporary references to sex education are invariably favorable. In a *Personal Romances* story, a doctor is incensed because of the heroine's faulty sex education and forcefully says that "I'm going to have a talk with your parents now and tell them a few of the facts of life." In an article in *Sexology* magazine, Professor Curtis E. Avery has an article on *The Problem of Children's 'Sex Play*,' which is one of a series of articles in this magazine dealing with sex education and guidance for parents and children.

In Dr. Benjamin Spock's latest edition of his best-selling book, *Baby and Child Care*, he gives quite liberal advice on the teaching of sex education to children: "Where do babies come from? This question is also pretty sure to come up in the period around three. It's easier and better to begin with the truth, rather than tell him a fairy story and have to change it later. Try to answer the question as simply as he asks it."

Even in contemporary jokes, there are some expressions of favorable attitudes to sex education. Thus, in *Snappy* there is a cartoon of a girl and a fellow by a parked car, with the fellow reading a sex book and the girl saying: "I've got to be home by eleven—you should have read the instructions before you called me!"

Advertisements for sex books and manuals in the 1960's are considerably bolder and more widespread than ever before in American history. Whereas such ads were formerly found mainly in sensational periodicals, especially the men's magazines, they are now to be read in some of the most respectable and sexually conservative publications, including *Screen Parade*, *Popular TV*, *The New York Times*, *Intimate Romances*, *Personal Romances*, and *My Love Secret*.

And the copy! Here are some luscious samples:

From *Man's Danger*: "TARGET FOR TONIGHT. No woman is safe (*or really wants to be*) when a man's mind is in the bedroom. See the tempting, puffed-up featherbed to be despoiled! Hear the irrepressible squeals of pleasure! Those to whom bedtime has come to mean 'bed and bored' will find 'bed and better'...."

From *My Love Secret*: "OVID WAS HER MASTER. HE GUIDED HER FROM THE FIRST FLIRTATION TO THE ULTIMATE CONQUEST. From him she learned the ancient mysteries of love, its unsuspected pleasures. Under his tutelage, her dormant womanhood awakened and she became irresistible. Men broke down the doors in surrender to her will. Ovid's ART OF LOVE is now available to adventurous women who are not afraid to try the unusual. Banned when first published and still hard to get in the full-blooded version, the book tells all in clear, unashamed language."

From *Screen Parade*: "LOVE IS NOT FOR ANGELS! Your 'sexcess' depends on when, where, how, how much, with whom—and a lot more. It calls for the right line and the sure touch. And what you don't know can hurt you! EVERY DETAIL PICTURE-CLEAR. Lay questions, doubts and fears to rest. Get straightened out and 'cued up' with the best-selling FROM FREUD TO KINSEY, now in its ninth large printing."

Of course, as pointed out in the early part of this chapter, advertisements such as these, which can now be found by the score in our current periodicals, prove not only that sex education is a good and acceptable thing—but also that it is not very widely taught in families, schools, and other "respectable" channels—otherwise there would be little sale for the sex manuals that are continually advertised. So we still have the paradoxical condition where it is deemed highly desirable, in public print, for the reader to know all about sex—and yet where, quite obviously, he frequently or usually knows little of what it is highly desirable for him to know.

Serious contradictions still exist, then, in regard to our attitudes and practices toward sex education. But the current trend, quite consistently shown throughout our follow-up study in the 1960's, seems to be that we are becoming more liberal and permissive and less puritanical in regard to sex enlightenment. The millennium, in this respect, is hardly at hand; but the march toward real progress continues, continues, continues. . . .

CHAPTER 28

Statistical Considerations

Modern science apparently cannot escape statistics: this book included. Where we have thus far presented the facts of our study through illustrative quotations and have used a kind of case history or anecdotal approach to the subject of sex attitudes in the 1950's and 1960's, we shall now make some attempt at quantifying and comparing some of our data. While the figures we are about to present are not very formidable, and while they have—as, indeed, have all attempts to quantify human attitudes—distinct limitations, it is to be hoped that they will help objectify and round out some of the facts that we have been presenting in this volume.

Our main method of gathering the statistics we are about to present was as follows: In reading the publications or listening to the productions analyzed in this study, each observed reference to sexual behavior was examined to determine (a) whether it expressed an attitude that was liberal, permissive, or accepting; or (b) whether it expressed a sex attitude that was conservative, restrictive, or rejecting. In the original study that was made of attitudes in the early 1950's,

TABLE I

NUMBER AND KINDS OF SEX ATTITUDES EXPRESSED IN AMERICAN
MASS MEDIA, CLASSIFIED ACCORDING TO TYPE OF SEX ACTIVITY

Type of Sex Activity	Number of Liberal Attitudes	Number of Conservative Attitudes
Extramarital coitus[a]		
1950	182	187
1960	266	163
Non-coital sex relations[b]		
1950	125	30
1960	65	11
Sex relations leading to pregnancy[c]		
1950	8	34
1960	75	33
Sex organs, desires, and expressions[d]		
1950	138	68
1960	740	60
Sex "perversions" and crimes[e]		
1950	5	20
1960	79	68
Sex control, censorship[f]		
1950	51	136
1960	116	51
Totals		
1950	509	475
1960	1341	386

[a] Includes fornication, adultery, sexual promiscuity, prostitution and venereal disease.
[b] Includes kissing, petting, and masturbation.
[c] Includes illegitimacy, birth control, abortion, and pregnancy.
[d] Includes nudity, sex organs, scatology, "obscenity," lasciviousness, and sexual intercourse.
[e] Includes sex crimes, incest, sex "perversions."
[f] Includes censorship, puritanism, romanticism and sex, sexuality of women, sex rites and superstitions, and sex education.

1,095 concrete references to sexual feelings and behavior were found, of which 551 expressed liberal and 544 conservative attitudes. Since, however, some of the media investigated in the original study, including plays, radio, television shows, and scientific journals, were not employed in the follow-up study of attitudes in the 1960's, it was decided to use for the statistical presentation in this revised edition only 984 of the original attitudinal references, which were derived from exactly the same kind of mass media as those found in the follow-up study. In this way, comparisons between the two studies are possible.

Table I indicates the sex references found in both studies, classified

TABLE II

NUMBER AND KINDS OF SEX ATTITUDES EXPRESSED IN AMERICAN MASS MEDIA, CLASSIFIED ACCORDING TO TYPE OF MEDIUM

Type of Mass Medium	Number of Liberal Attitudes	Number of Conservative Attitudes
Best-selling fictional books		
1950 (N-27)	27	57
1960 (N-20)	247	81
General magazines		
1950 (N-61)	44	71
1960 (N-56)	60	82
Humor magazines		
1950 (N-19)	277	65
1960 (N-12)	123	20
Men's magazines		
1950 (N-28)	37	19
1960 (N-47)	774	80
Women's magazines		
1950 (N-49)	32	99
1960 (N-32)	72	67
Miscellaneous periodicals and productions[a]		
1950 (N-85)	92	164
1960 (N-62)	72	67
Totals		
1950 (N-269)	509	475
1960 (N-226)	1348	397

Includes newspapers, motion pictures, religiously oriented magazines, and best-selling nonfictional books.

in accordance with the type of sexual behavior to which these references apply. Some highly interesting information can be noted from examining this table. First of all, it can be seen that although the total number of sex attitudes in the early 1950's was almost evenly divided between liberal and conservative sides of the fence, the balance, by the time the 1960's arrived, had swung far over to the liberal side. This was true in every single aspect of sex behavior examined in this study; and in most of the cases when the observed differences were tested by Chi-square analysis they were found to be significant. Only in the cases of extramarital coitus and non-coital sex relations was it found that even though significant trends toward liberalization of mass media attitudes took place, these trends were not statistically significant. In all other areas, and in sex behavior as a whole, the trends toward liberalization were highly significant.

Whereas, in the 1950's, almost 40 per cent of the observed sex attitudes were found to relate to extramarital coitus, in the 1960's attitudes toward sex organs, desires, and expressions had taken the center of the stage and constituted over 50 per cent of the observed references to human sexuality. This trend itself indicates even more liberalization of views than the rest of the information in the table would at first indicate: since the discussion of extramarital relations is practically old hat in American literature, while only recently have more down to earth matters become the frequent subjects of novelists, story writers, and other publicists. If the women's magazines and the general periodicals debate the advisability of premarital or adulterous behavior, that is hardly news; but if, as increasingly is the case, they mention nudity, sex organs, and sexual intercourse, that is certainly an indication of radically new permissiveness.

Speaking of different types of magazines, it was thought advisable to compare the references listed in Table I for the early 1950's and the 1960's when they were categorized in accordance with the kind of mass medium in which they were noted. These comparisons may be found in Table II. From the data in this table it may be seen that for every type of medium used in the two decades that were studied there was a tendency for sex attitudes to be distinctly more liberal in the later than in the earlier period. When tested for statistical significance by Chi-square analysis, it may be noted that in all categories of media except the humor magazines and the women's magazines, this tendency toward greater liberalization in the 1960's over the 1950's is highly significant.

It may also be seen that there are some rip-roaring reversals of direction in some instances. Thus, in the 1950's sex attitudes were preponderantly conservative in the fiction best-sellers, the general magazines, and the miscellaneous media; while in the 1960's attitudes in these three classifications of media, especially the first two, had changed to preponderantly liberal. While references in the men's magazines remained on the liberal side, they became considerably more so than they had been in the earlier decade.

To return to Table I for a moment, it can be seen that there, too, highly interesting reversals of attitudes between the 1950's and 1960's are shown in several of the main categories of sexual behavior employed during this study. Thus, whereas in the 1950's mass media attitudes toward sex relations leading to pregnancy, sex "perversions" and crimes, and sex control and censorship were much more often than not on the conservative side, by the time the 1960's had arrived attitudes in these three categories, especially the first and the third, were significantly reversed.

Not only the proportions of liberal over conservative responses have changed between the 1950's and the 1960's, but the absolute number of liberal references has significantly increased in almost all categories of sex behavior during the decade. Thus, even though 226 different publications and productions were investigated in the 1960's as against a larger number, 269, in the 1950's, more than two and a half times as many sex references are turned up in the latter period. Increases in the number of liberal allusions is to be noted in all categories except that of non-coital sex relations, where there is a decrease. This single decrease may well be caused by the fact that mass media today are so much more frank about intercourse, sex organs, nudity, etc. that they can well dispense with many of the references to kissing and petting that previously were used to titillate their readers.

As indicated in Table II, absolute numbers of liberal attitudes toward sexual behavior have increased in all categories of mass media examined except humor magazines and miscellaneous publications and productions. In both these instances, however, only about half the number of publications and productions were examined in the 1960's as had been examined in the 1950's; and this decrease in the number of outlets investigated may well have accounted for the fewer liberal attitudes discovered. In the case of the women's magazines, where only a slight increase in liberalized attitudes was found, this increase may again have been considerably greater if as many of these kinds of periodicals had been analyzed in the later as had been in the earlier decade.

In spite of the fact that most categories of investigated mass media became more liberal and permissive in their sex attitudes in the 1960's than they had been in the 1950's, distinct inter-media differences remained. Even in the 1950's women's magazines (and especially those that cater to teenage girls) remain considerably more conservative in their sex outlook than do other kinds of media; and humor and men's magazines remain far more prosexual in their numerous references than do other kinds of mass media. If the present trend continues, however, the fiction best-sellers may well catch up with the humor and men's magazines in the proportion of prosexual attidues they include.

To return again to a consideration of the data in Table I, differences in the acceptance of certain kinds of sex behavior are again still prevalent to some degree in the 1960's, even though they were more prevalent in the 1950's. That is to say, in the earlier decade there was a much greater acceptance of non-coital sex relations and sex organs, desires, and expressions than there was of extramarital coitus, sex relations leading to pregnancy, sex "perversions" and crimes, and sex control and censorship. In the later decade, most nonacceptable modes of sex behavior have become significantly more approved; but there is still relatively less acceptance of extramarital relations and sex "perversions" and crimes than there is of the other categories of behavior.

The information in Table I also shows that in the 1960's, as well as in the 1950's, many more references to extramarital relations and to sex organs, desires, and expressions are to be found in American mass media than references to most other categories of sex behavior, especially to non-coital sex relations, relations leading to pregnancy, and sex "perversions" and crimes.

CHAPTER 29

The Whys and Wherefores of the Facts Discovered

Some of the facts brought forth in the course of the present study were to be expected and their explanations obvious. Some are surprising and their explanations subtle or unknown. We shall now try to answer the main questions raised by these facts.

1. *Why are so many references, both liberal and conservative, to extramarital relations and to sex organs, desires, and expressions found?*

Probably because millions of Americans, in fact the great majority of them, actually do engage in fornication or adultery sometime during their lives; and because, when they do not do so, they still have distinct desires thus to engage and are concerned with the propriety of their desires. Also, American attitudes toward extramarital as well as marital relations seem to be changing in a more liberal direction; but because the older and more conservative attitudes are by no means yet eradicated, considerable controversy still

240

exists and tends to make the issue a lively one.

There is a tendency for mass media to portray the masculine viewpoint as a liberal one and the feminine view as conservative. Thus, male characters in both men's and women's magazine stories, novels, and motion pictures more often express favorable attitudes toward adultery and fornication than female characters. These mass media presently reflect a dichotomously trended male-female viewpoint in regard to extramarital affairs and, to a lesser degree, sex enjoyment in marriage.

2. *Why are most attitudes regarding kissing and petting liberal rather than conservative?*

Probably because kissing and petting are relatively mild forms of sex behavior and are virtually ubiquitous in our society. On the other hand, while kissing and petting are frequently mentioned in mass media, masturbation is one of the least mentioned sex acts. This tends to indicate that modern Americans are far more ashamed of masturbating than they are of engaging in kissing and petting and that, in spite of our sex books condoning masturbation (while still often emphasizing the dangers of petting, fornication, and adultery), the nineteenth-century attitude toward autoerotism lingers on in our mores.

3. *Why are attitudes toward abortion, birth control, illegitimacy, and pregnancy relatively few?*

Probably because these are not "romantic" sex topics and therefore not as likely to be included in fictional presentations as are more "respectable" subjects. While attitudes toward pregnancy and abortion seem to be loosening up recently in our society, they have not yet sufficiently done so for fiction writers to accept them too enthusiastically and use them for romantic effects.

4. *Why are so many attitudes toward nudity and sex organs extant and why are they so preponderantly liberal?*

Because nudity and references to sex organs apparently represent, in our communities, toned-down modes of sex activity which may be favorably espoused, while more direct modes of sex behavior are often greeted with more mixed or unfavorable reactions. Thus, viewing a nude woman or thinking about her hips and breasts is a step removed from *having* sex relations with her and is apt to arouse less guilt in a prim person.

5. *Why are relatively few attitudes toward incest, sex crimes, and sex "perversions" found, and why do they tend to be relatively conservative?*

Probably because these acts are still considered so heinous that they can directly be mentioned with only relative infrequency—especially in "respectable" outlets such as the women's magazines and general magazines. In this respect, our mass media doubtless mirror the contemporary attitudes of the majority of Americans who violently oppose most manifestations of sex crimes or "perversions."

6. *Why are so many attitudes, and especially liberal attitudes, found in relation to women's sexuality?*

Probably because, owing to the large amount of sexuality appearing in contemporary literature, readers have become somewhat jaded and can more easily be titillated by, say, a heroine's lustiness and unconventionality than by similar behavior on the part of a hero. Just as sadistic and other extreme types of sex activity are now being used to arouse sex-glutted novel and story readers, so, for purposes of sensationalism, promiscuous women are to some extent replacing promiscuous men as the protagonists of popular fiction.

7. *Why are sex attitudes in the 1960's so much more predominantly liberal than those in the 1950's?*

Largely because of the much greater freedom now apparent in fictional best-sellers and in the men's magazines. Particularly in relation to attitudes toward sex organs, desires, and expressions these two outlets have become amazingly more permissive in the last decade; though in regard to almost all other forms of sex behavior they have also become more pro-sexual. Whereas the women's magazines have remained similar in sexual tone to those of the 1950's, and other kinds of media have changed only moderately, the men's magazines and the best-selling novels are now radically different from their forebears and seem to be becoming still more openly sexual every year.

8. *Why are some kinds of mass media, such as best-selling novels and men's magazines, considerably more liberal than other kinds of media?*

Probably for several reasons. First of all, some outlets, such as the men's magazines, are patently read by male rather than female readers; and there is no question that a double standard of sexual morality still exists in the United States, with males generally more prosexually oriented than females.

Secondly, there would seem to be a considerable educational and intellectual difference in the readers of various types of publications. The best men's magazines, such as *Esquire* and *Playboy*, and the most literate novels, such as those of William Faulkner, Robert Penn Warren, D. H. Lawrence, and Vladimir Nabokov, are almost certainly perused by a reading public that is distinctly more educated and intelligent than readers who generally dip into the motion picture and TV magazines and the true-confession type of periodicals. In consequence, publications which cater to the more educated and more intelligent reader seem to be, on the whole, vastly more liberal and prosexual than those which cater to duller teenage readers.

Thirdly, several types of mass media, such as motion pictures and general magazines, are more widely read or witnessed than other types of media such a humor or men's magazines. Various groups of readers of these most popular media—for example, Catholics and hardshelled Baptists—tend to complain to editors and producers when sexually permissive ideas are presented; and, being economically dependent on their vast audiences, these media feel (rightly or wrongly) that they cannot afford to antagonize even minority groups. Consequently, they tend to stay much more sexually "pure" than do publications or productions with a more select type of audience.

Fourthly, some modern publications, such as the men's magazines, seem to be particularly designed to provide sexual release for the members of the public who are strongly denied titillation and education in the more "respectable" type of outlets. Just as various types of prostitutes will tend to flourish when "good" women are strict about denying their sexual favors to males, so will various highly sexualized publications develop when publications such as the *Saturday Evening Post*, the *Ladies' Home Journal*, and the *Reader's Digest* remain rather prim about their sex attitudes.

Fifth, as Ivor Williams has recently shown in a perceptive article in *Playboy* ("The Pious Pornographers," reprinted in Ray Russell's *The Permanent Playboy*), although today's women's magazines are still conservative about their formal presentations, they actually contain considerable lascivious portrayals and allusions in their stories, articles, and advertisements, which make some of the more honest (and hence less salacious) material in the men's magazines seem a little cloistered by comparison.

9. *Why is there still relatively less acceptance of extramarital relations and sex deviations and crimes than there is of other forms of sex behavior?*

As far as extramarital relations are concerned, the antisexualists are still fighting a strong, if losing, battle. The very heart of the Judeo-Christian sex ethic is that men and women shall remain virginal until marriage and that they shall be completely faithful after marriage. In regard to premarital chastity, this ethic seems clearly on the way out, and in many segments of the populace is more and more becoming a dead letter. Premarital coitus or petting to orgasm are now being experienced by the great majority of American males and females. The churches and other social institutions, however, are still battling this tendency and their influence is strong in popular literature, especially in general and women's magazines.

Adultery is less practiced and condoned today than are premarital sex relations—partly because it is more likely to be disruptive of marriage and family ties. Although there is probably a trend toward increasing adultery (including adulterous petting) on the part of many men and, especially, women today, this trend is not half so pronounced as the trend toward increasing premarital affairs. Again, the churches and other social institutions are waging a heavy war against adulterous relations and still wield a considerable amount of influence in this connection.

Sex deviations (when properly defined) and crimes are certainly not healthy or happy in their own right; and even though negative attitudes toward deviants and sex offenders have been ameliorated in recent years, it is not to be expected that they will ever become enthusiastically approving. Moreover, many puritans who today cannot effectively rant against premarital intercourse, petting, kissing, nudity, and other forms of sex behavior seem to be making the most of the fields where their efforts are still effective—namely, in the fields of deviation and sex crime.

10. *What are some of the main factors that influence contemporary sexpressions as they appear in our mass media?*

1. The factor of human psychobiological *needs* and *desires*: which, sexually speaking, cannot easily be downed and which, when sexually unsatisfied, encourage the presentation of considerable liberal sex attitudes and salacious sex materials that, officially and traditionally, are supposed to be taboo in our society.

2. The factors of social change in general, and change in sex codes and ideas in particular, which encourage confusion, doubt, and ambivalence concerning a good many of our current sex views.

3. The factors of sexual discomfort and inconvenience, even when basic sex needs are partly satisfied, which motivate millions of Americans to act differently than they think and unconsciously to think differently than they consciously permit themselves to think they think.

4. The factors of individualism, democracy, and secularism, which discourage men and women from uniformly following traditional, authoritarian, religiously based sex tenets.

5. The factors of fear, guilt, and inhibition, which influence readers and auditors to resist and discourage the publication of many direct sexual representations and which encourage, instead, their indirect (and often salacious) presentation.

6. The factor of modern romanticism, which bolsters traditional sex mores on the one hand, but leaves loopholes, under certain circumstances, for more liberal codes and modes on the other hand.

7. The factor of differing masculine-feminine standards in our society, which encourage one kind of sex attitudes and usages for males and quite a different, often conflicting, kind for female readers and auditors.

8. The factor of unconscious feelings, urges, desires, and beliefs, which encourage men and women, sexually and generally, to think one way and to act another and even think they think one way, while actually thinking another.

9. The factor of exceptionally strict, puritanical, and traditional sex views which linger on in such a strait-laced fashion as to necessitate some semi-automatic counterbalancing tendencies on the part of many people who try most rigorously to hold to the letter of these traditional views.

10. The factor of certain strong pressure groups, particularly church groups, which stoutly defend conservative sex mores and attempt to bar and censor liberal or salacious sex references in public media.

11. The factor of capitalist enterprise, which views sex as another commodity which may be profitably sold for public consumption and which therefore encourages highly salacious presentations in those media which are hospitable to them.

12. The factors of sexual displacement and erogeneity, which make it possible for highly genitalized sex acts (like intercourse and incest) to be symbolized by quasi- or non-genital modes of sex behavior (like kissing or gazing at nudity) and which thereby allow for a good deal of public presentation of toned-down sexuality that, in more direct modes of presentation, would otherwise be banned.

13. The factor of the prevalence of modern humor, which also enables much sex material of a liberal or salacious nature to be publicly displayed that, if presented in more serious guise, would not be allowed.

14. The factors of modern technology, scientific discovery, literacy, and universal education, which are making it increasingly difficult for traditional-conservative views of any type, including sexual views, to flourish unchallenged, unopposed, and unalloyed.

15. The factor of cultural lag, which permits many highly illogical, inconsistent, and immature sex views to linger on decades and centuries beyond their original usefulness and logical applicability to human affairs.

CHAPTER 30

The Behavioral Implications of the Facts Discovered

Now that we have seen what the facts of sexpression in America are, and why they are, the question arises: What are the behavioral implications of these facts? Or, in other words, what do these facts mean in terms of the thoughts, feelings, and actions of the average American man and woman?

The most important implications would seem to be the following:

1. *The average American—in fact, virtually every living American—is completely muddled-, mixed-, and messed-up in his sex views, feelings, and acts. Much of the time he is quite consciously confused and knows that he does not know sex "right" from "wrong." Or else he keeps changing his mind about what is sexually proper and improper. Or he engages in sex acts which he feels he should not perform but which he would feel even more uncomfortable about not performing. When—occasionally—this average American does manage to get consciously straight in his sex views, he still remains unconsciously caught and tangled in beliefs that are frequently as consistent with his conscious thoughts as Isadora Duncan was with Anthony Comstock. The result, in terms of the modern American's external and internal sex harmony, is a degree of peacefulness remarkably like that now existing between the United States and the Soviet Union. (This goes, incidentally, for the consciously libertarian sexualist, who normally —in our culture—has underlying puritanical attitudes and feelings, as well as for the consciously straitlaced antisexualist, who underlyingly has distinctly libertine impulsions.)*

(a) In consequence, the typical American male or female has no monolithic sex attitude, but only very pluralistic attitudes. And, while his or her attitudes on politics, religion, economics, or what you will may tend to be fairly consistent and self-harmonious, his or her sex beliefs normally tend to be self-contradictory and, in many ways, self-defeating.

(b) Officially, legally, and traditionally most of the sex views of our society are negativistic and disapproving, and (consciously) the majority of Americans appear to adhere to these traditional antisexual viewpoints. Unofficially, extralegally, and actually, however, the sex attitudes of millions of Americans (and particularly of male Americans) are at least partially positive, approving, and prosexual.

2. *Whenever official and legal American sex views tend to become too rigid, negative, and puritanical, an unofficial and extralegal reaction*

against these views appears to arise and to take one or more of the following forms:

(a) The views on the banned mode of sex behavior itself may become (unofficially or semi-officially) more liberalized. For example, ultra-strict views on fornication may give way to more liberal views.

(b) The views on the banned form of sex behavior may remain fairly constant, but views on related, substitutive, or sexually toned-down forms of behavior may become more liberalized. Thus attitudes toward fornication may remain conservative, but attitudes toward kissing and petting may become more liberal.

(c) The views on the banned sex act may remain consciously constant, but unconsciously they may become more liberalized. Thus people may continue to *say* that adultery is wrong but may remain relatively guiltless when they actually commit adultery.

(d) The views on the interdicted mode of sex behavior may remain the same as far as one's personal behavior is concerned but may become more liberalized when the behavior of others is at issue. Thus a girl may think it wrong for her to lose her own virginity but may think it perfectly all right for her girl friends to lose theirs.

(e) The views on the "bad" sex activity may remain steadfast, but the actions concerning it may be decidedly more liberal. Thus people may think it quite wrong to be "obscene" in public—and may then continually recount the most "obscene" kinds of jokes.

(f) The official interdictions against certain types of sex activity may be unofficially channelized into certain restricted areas and may be liberalized or ignored in other areas. Thus bans against telling "dirty" stories or jokes may be upheld when one is in mixed company, but relaxed in men's smokers or women's dressing rooms.

(g) Specific outlets may arise where more liberalized sex attitudes and acts are unofficially tolerated, even though they are officially taboo. Thus burlesque and night-club shows may be permitted to display nudity openly, and "lovers' lanes" may spring up where heavy petting is unofficially tolerated.

(h) Where liberal expressions of sex viewpoints are not permitted, substitutional salacious uses of sex material may arise instead. Thus those who dare not *say* that masturbation or adultery is a good mode of sex behavior may continually write about them in a lascivious way or greatly enjoy reading or hearing salacious references to them.

(i) Sex activity that is banned and condemned may easily become "naughty" as well as "wicked"—and its naughtiness may give it a spice that makes both its discussion and its participation more enjoyable, and perhaps more frequent, than would otherwise be true.

(j) When specific sex acts (like masturbation or fornication) are

247

banned, non-sexual or semi-sexual acts (like defecation or urination) may take on a super-sexualized meaning and may serve as sexual outlets.

(k) When direct, normal sex acts—e.g., masturbation or heterosexual intercourse—are banned or discouraged, indirect, abnormal acts —e.g., exhibitionism or sexually assaulting young children—may tend to rise in their stead.

(1) Violent, anti-sexual protests on the part of some individuals may provoke and serve as a mask for bizarre, pro-sexual acts by them. Thus people who are most vituperative and crusading against sexual "vice" may pruriently be indulging their sexual sadism.

(m) When extreme forms of anti-sexuality become rampant—such as asceticism or inquisitional persecution of sexual nonconformists— the energy and drives behind the anti-sexual crusading tend to take on a highly sexualized character and to serve as an (unconscious) sexual outlet. Thus the anti-sexual fervor of certain religious sectarians seems to result in orgasm-like releases.

3. When specific modes of sex behavior are officially banned, they often tend, by the very virtue of their banning, to become particularly pleasurable and inviting to many of our citizens.

(a) Prohibited sex acts may become unusually exciting in themselves. Thus kissing seems to be a fairly mild form of sexual entertainment where it is freely permitted—so mild, in fact, that many peoples of the world do not engage in it at all—but to become unduly sexually arousing and enjoyable when it is discouraged.

(b) Proscribed kinds of sex behavior may take on aspects of novelty and adventure which otherwise they would scarcely hold. Thus American men and women frequently seem to desire adulterous relations not because their mates are no longer sexually satisfying to them, but because there is an element of danger, thrill, and novelty in illicit adultery which adds to its pleasures.

(c) Tabooed sex behavior frequently enhances the pleasure of substitutive modes of sex activity which ordinarily would not be too exciting for their own sake. Thus enjoining fornication often puts a premium on kissing and petting, which are normally found to be far less satisfying when fornication is freely permitted.

4. When certain modes of sex behavior are interdicted, people often resort, instead, to various types of neurotic symptomatic behavior.

(a) Prohibitions of sex acts may lead to repression of sex desires —with consequent frigidity, impotence, fear of marriage, unconscious hatred of one's spouse, et cetera.

(b) Prohibiting certain modes of sex conduct may lead to guilt about very normal sex desires, to an intensification of normal desires, and then to an intensification of guilt about the intensified desires. The result may be neurotic symptomatology of many different kinds.

(c) The bottling up of certain modes of sexual expression may force normal persons to turn to compulsive modes of behavior and to do precisely those sex acts which they are most (consciously) ashamed of doing. They may compulsively, and joylessly, perform normal illicit sex acts (e.g., fornication or masturbation), deviational sex acts (e.g., homosexuality or intercourse with animals), or offensive or criminal sex acts (e.g., exhibitionism or forcible rape).

(d) Discouragement of sex pleasures, and designation of them as "disgusting" and "revolting," may lead to neurotic loss of feeling and enjoyment in normal sex acts—including loss of pleasure in marital intercourse.

(e) Discouraging or toning down sex education may lead many men and women to become irrationally and neurotically fearful of normal sex acts like masturbation, nocturnal emissions, menstruation, et cetera.

(f) Interdicting various sex acts may lead to neurotic overemphasis on and preoccupation with these acts and may result in compulsive promiscuity, prurient obsessions on "obscenity," backhanded preoccupations with scatology, continual lascivious thoughts, et cetera.

(g) Damming up sex urges may lead to all kinds of unconscious personality distortions and impulsions. Thus preventing a man from having adulterous relations may cause him to hate a wife whom he otherwise loves, and may even eventually induce him to harm or kill her. Forcing women to live in accordance with a double standard of sex morality may cause them to become obsessively jealous, or to become compulsively enamored of aggressive, masculine life goals.

(h) The essence of good mental hygiene is to enable people to face squarely their desires and behavior and to understand their conscious and unconscious impulses. But banning sex acts normally involves concomitantly banning the discussion of many of these acts, and thus banning the individual's facing his underlying sex feelings and urges. Hence, good mental hygiene procedure and even effective psychotherapy are not given a chance, and sexually impelled or aggravated neurosis tends to run rampant in our society.

(i) Banning a sex act frequently makes it, at the same time, more desirable (because of the scarcity, novelty, and danger thereby attached to it) and less desirable (because of the guilt, anxiety, and fear thereby attached to it). This concomitant heightening and lessening of its desirability inevitably leads to serious conflict on the part of many individuals who have psychobiological impulses to perform a banned sex act. And since conflict is one of the main sources of neurosis, an unhealthy mental situation thus arises for many of our countrymen and countrywomen.

(j) Once a sex act that is still psychobiologically urgent is banned, it is bound to cause mental anguish and conflict: for if we frankly enjoy the act, on the one hand, we will still feel guilty about it underneath; and if we strictly abjure the act, on the other hand, we will feel distinctly deprived and will have (conscious or unconscious) cravings for it. In either eventuality, we will tend to build up (largely unconscious) feelings of doubt, anxiety, and depression—which may easily encourage neurotic outbursts and symptomatology.

(k) The banning of certain sex outlets—e.g., homosexuality—which would be, under normal circumstances, merely peculiar and idiosyncratic modes of behavior, serves to make the users of these outlets neurotic—and to make neurotics use these outlets. In this sense, sex "perversion" does not render society sick, but society makes sick people out of "perverts"—and induces disturbed individuals to use "perversions" as neurotic symptoms.

5. Debarring certain modes of sex behavior often results in individual and social hypocrisy, evasion, and downright lying.

(a) Sex behavior may be wholly excoriated when it is frankly enjoyed, and hypocritically accepted when it is mildly disguised. Thus prostitution is roundly condemned when it directly involves a man paying a woman for sexual favors, but is quite acceptable when the same man indirectly spends money on the same woman or supports her in legal marriage only to gain sex favors from her.

(b) Sex behavior may be tolerated when its genital aspects are disguised, but condemned when they are obvious. Thus a woman may publicly display most of her breasts, but she dare not show the tiniest bit of her labia. And, among certain elements of the American populace, heavy petting up to and including mutual orgasm is not considered to be engaging in sex relations, while the slightest interpenetration of the male and female genitalia, even without orgasm, is definitely so considered.

(c) Those who are no longer capable of various types of sex behavior may tend hypocritically to assume smug, holier-than-thou attitudes and to look down upon those who are still desirious of engaging in banned sex acts—and do. Thus judges who might have been sex hellions in their youth may hand out stiff sentences for minor sex infractions by the current younger generation.

(d) A double standard of sex behavior tends to grow up, under which certain acts are tolerated for one group but not for another. Thus a man who openly has a mistress roundly condemns his wife for taking a lover. Or a wealthy girl is envied her sexcapades, while a salesgirl is excoriated for hers.

(e) In actual practice, banning sex acts in our country has often resulted in (i) an increased desire for them and (ii) little lessening of

250

participation in them. This means that millions of Americans consciously *think* one way (e.g., that adultery is "bad") and then *desire* and/or *act* quite another way (e.g., actively commit or desire to commit adultery). Such Americans frequently (consciously or unconsciously) look upon themselves as arrant hypocrites.

(f) Since direct approval of many banned sex acts is impossible in our society, and since the desire for these acts remains high (and often is, ironically, aggravated by the ban), many quasi-serious or humorous allusions to these acts are publicly presented—and this indirect form of presentation constitutes another mode of social hypocrisy. Thus bald-faced "obscenity" is rarely employed in America—but humorous stories, the very essence of whose wit lies in their "obscene" core, are ubiquitous.

(g) Rigorous puritanical sex codes, as we have seen, frequently encourage prurience and lead to the most hypocritical forms of sex behavior. Thus, in order to collect "obscene" material legitimately, men and women may become "vice" crusaders.

6. *Interdicting various types of sex conduct normally leads to considerable individual and group antagonism between those who conform to the interdictions and those who do not.*

(a) In contemporary American society there seems to be a good deal of antagonism between the sexes, part of which stems from the fact that our double standard of morality allows much greater sex freedom to males than to females. Thus girls resent boys' trying to seduce them—and then insisting on marrying virgins.

(b) Within individual couples there presently appears to exist much antagonism and much inhibition of potential love as a result of differing sex goals. Thus girls try to get boys to marry them before having intercourse, and boys try to get girls to have intercourse with them before marriage. Frequently masculine and feminine sex goals are so diverse that, primarily on that count, boy-girl romances never get started or break up quickly after they do start.

(c) Individuals and groups who are forced to conform to prohibitory sex codes frequently become antagonistic to other individuals and groups who manage to evade these codes to some extent. Thus married individuals may tend to resent the comparative sexual freedom of single individuals and violently to condemn the latter.

7. *The contrabanding of various sex acts often leads to illogical and self-contradictory individual and social sex philosophies.*

(a) Some aspects of sex behavior may be discouraged which, were they not banned, would help uphold the bans on other aspects of sex behavior. Thus masturbation, which normally acts as something of a substitute for and inhibitor of fornication, is illogically interdicted along with fornication itself. And birth control, which would prevent

251

abortions and illegitimate pregnancies, is excoriated along with th
latter aspects of sex behavior.

(b) Some sex acts (e.g., illegitimate pregnancy) are unofficiall
prosecuted although not legally banned, while other sex acts (e.g
fornication) are legally banned (in some states of our union) but ur
officially highly tolerated.

(c) Some intrinsically harmless sex acts (e.g., masturbation an
homosexual relations between adults) are placed in the same con
demned category as other intrinsically harmful acts (e.g., assaultiv
rape).

(d) Publicly anathematizing a given mode of sex conduct may
ironically, give additional status and esteem to some of those wh
frankly partake of this mode of conduct. Thus men become enviou
of other men who are notorious fornicators or whoremongers; an
even women may prefer promiscuous men for their bedmates. Agair
being able to employ "obscenity" or scatological language in a fran
and open manner may become a mark of sophistication or hard
boiledness and be thereby duly (and even unduly) esteemed.

(e) Emotionalized, illogical sex attitudes grow up because of ban
ning certain activities; and these emotionalized attitudes often lea
to inadequate, emotionalized types of sex education, which, in turn
maintain the original emotionalized, illogical sex attitudes, thus effec
tuating a continuing vicious circle.

(f) Men and women, because of sex bans, often crave the sexually
impossible. Thus current sex contradictions cause men to want wive
who are "pure"—and wanton; and cause women to want husbands wh
are good economic supporters—and unpredictable, exciting lovers.

(g) Sex prohibitions encourage obscurantism and sex superstitions
which are most idiotic and illogical. Thus lack of adequate sex edu
cation encourages people to believe in astrological influences on thei
love lives, or to hold to sex rites—e.g., taboos on intercourse during
menstruation—which have long been scientifically invalidated.

8. *Forbidding various modes of sex conduct frequently results no*
in the disappearance or even lessening of that conduct, but in its con-
tinued performance—with concomitant self-punishment, guilt, anxiety
pain, and anguish on the part of those who practice it.

(a) Even when people "get away with" banned sex conduct and go
"scot-free" for violating the bans, they are usually (consciously or unconsciously) guilty over their behavior and suffer direct pangs of
conscience or indirect unpleasant psychophysical effects.

(b) Sometimes the banning of a sex act directly or indirectly *causes*
dire consequences for its perpetrators. Thus banning fornication
logically leads to banning birth control and venereal disease control—
and these latter bans provide distinct penalties (e.g., illegitimate preg-

nancy, abortion, and syphilis) for many fornicators.

(c) When society bans a sex act for which many of its members still feel strong psychobiological urges, these members have the choice of (i) consciously favoring the sex act, and feeling unconsciously guilty and shameful about it, or (ii) consciously disfavoring the act, and feeling unconsciously compelled to resort to it nevertheless. In either eventuality, the banned act is usually, in one degree or another, actually *performed*—and then regretted. Thus birth control, in contemporary America, is utilized by the great majority of us; but the negative propaganda that is subtly or frankly dispersed in connection with it forces us unconsciously to feel guilty though we consciously accept it, or consciously to feel guilty when we reject it in theory but are nevertheless driven to its practice. In either event, we perform it with pain, trouble, and qualms.

The foregoing behavioral sequelae of our contemporary sex prohibitions, and of the utterly conflicting and confused attitudes which we have acquired in relation to them, are, it will be noted, virtually all dismal and unfortunate. Are there, then, no advantages to prohibiting or discouraging certain modes of sex behavior?

Doubtless there are, since obviously our civilization seems to be better off for banning sex acts like assaultive rape than it would be if it encouraged this practice. It may also be argued—and, indeed, often, and at great length, has been—that societal prohibitions against sex activities like fornication, adultery, promiscuity, and prostitution have a distinctly salutary effect on civilized life.

Perhaps so. But the findings of this study offer no supportive evidence in this connection. What they do show—and that fairly conclusively—is that in contemporary America most of our official and legal sex bans are *not* very effective, *are* being continually and widely flouted in both theory and practice, and *are* accepted by our citizenry in an incredibly conflicting and confused manner. Under *these* conditions, the behavioral results, when viewed in terms of thoughts, feelings, and actions of the everyday common garden-variety American male and female, are truly dreadful and depressing. To say otherwise would be completely to contradict the main findings of this study.

253

CHAPTER 31

What May Be Done About the Facts Discovered?

The facts of this study seem clearly to point to one main moral; namely, that human sexuality cannot easily be downed and that even—perhaps especially—in a society like our own, which is officially and legally sexually repressive and inhibited, human psychobiological sex drives remain sufficiently high and undownable, causing endless individual and societal conflicts, confusions, and contradictions.

Otherwise stated: whatever the intrinsic demands of human sexuality may or may not be, it seems clear, in this day and age, that when we attempt to push sex down here it tends to rise up there, and that all our attempts to outlaw, penalize, and denigrate various modes of sex behavior have resulted mainly in liberalizing reactions against conservative proscriptions; in pluralistic instead of monolithic sex views; in sex acts which directly contradict sex theories; in unconscious sex urges which effectively sabotage conscious motivations; in people's finding heightened interest and pleasure in many banned sex acts; in the growth and abetting of multitudinous forms of sexual and general neuroses; in the prevalence of widespread sexual hypocrisy; in the promotion of formidable amounts of sex antagonism; in the formation of numerous illogical and idiotic sex philosophies and rules; and in the production of enormous degrees of sexual and general pain, dissatisfaction, anxiety, and woe for literally millions of Americans.

The question, therefore, obviously arises: What should be done to alleviate or correct our current sexual embarrassments, inconsistencies, inequities, and chaos?

Since this purports to be a scientific study, moralistic *shoulds* and *musts* are probably out of place in it. The writer, partly because of his findings in the course of this research, and partly because of his own emotional prejudices and biases, has as pronounced views on these *shoulds* and *musts* as has anyone. Scientifically, however, these views may not be entirely relevant and should perhaps appear in a different context rather than in the present volume. (Since writing the first edition of this book, many of my personal sex views have appeared in *The American Sexual Tragedy* and *Sex Without Guilt*.)

Sticking, however, to the objective findings of this study, and avoiding (for the nonce) moralistic *shoulds* and *musts*, it may still be legitimately noted what Americans *may* do to resolve, to some extent, their contemporary disordered, deranged, and disheveled attitudes and acts relating to different modes of sex behavior.

In general, it would appear that we have the choice of: (1) learning to tolerate our present contradictory, liberal-conservative sex views in a more democratically accepting manner; (2) continuing to change our sex attitudes so that they become more consistently liberal; or (3) returning to a distinctly conservative, rigorously monolithic state of sexual philosophy and activity, and ruthlessly uprooting all the sexual laxity, liberality, and lasciviousness which we have allowed to creep into our present-day mores.

The first alternative—that of our learning to tolerate both liberal and conservative sex viewpoints and allowing them to exist side by side in our society—is probably impractical for several reasons: (1) It leads, as we have been seeing throughout this book, to conscious and unconscious confusion, guilt, and grief on the part of both liberals and conservatives. (2) It cannot be tolerated by sexual arch-conservatives—such as the religious pressure groups—since it at least allows *some* individuals and groups to preach and to practice sexual liberalism. (3) Consequently, it will lead to a continual—and perhaps total—warfare, which will result, in all probability, in the victory of alternative 2 or alternative 3—consistent sexual liberalism *or* conservatism eventually becoming the order of the day.

The ultimate choice, then, seems to be between our going forward to be as consistently liberal in our sex views and acts as the limitations of human nature will allow—or in our going back to consistent, ultra-conservative sex attitudes and activities. Both these alternatives comprehend human risks and dangers, and involve the development of patterns of thinking, feeling, and living which are radically different from those most of us follow today. One of them, it may fairly safely be predicted, will ultimately prevail among those elements of humanity who somehow manage to survive our present troubled times.

Which do you suppose it will be?